Spelling K—8

Spelling K—8

PLANNING AND TEACHING

DIANE SNOWBALL

& FAYE BOLTON

STENHOUSE PUBLISHERS
YORK, MAINE

Stenhouse Publishers, P.O. Box 360, York, Maine 03909
www.stenhouse.com

Credits
Pages 125–126: *The Frog Who Would Be King* by Kate Walker. Copyright © 1994 Kate Walker.
Martin Education, a division of Horwitz Arahane in association with Ashton Scholastic.
Available in the United States through Mondo. Reprinted by permission.

Library of Congress Cataloging-in-Publication Data

Snowball, Diane.
   Spelling K–8 : planning and teaching / Diane Snowball and Faye Bolton.
     p. cm.
   Includes bibliographical references and index.
   ISBN 1-57110-074-1 (alk. paper)
   1. English language—Orthography and spelling—Study and teaching (Elementary)
I. Bolton, Faye. II. Title.
LB1574.S6 1999
372.63′2044—dc21
                                                                     98-43714
                                                                    CIP

Cover and interior design by Cathy Hawkes, Cat and Mouse
Typeset by Technologies 'N Typography
Manufactured in the United States of America on acid-free paper
04 03 02 01 00 99 9 8 7 6 5 4 3 2

Contents

Contents

List of Terms

Acronym   A word formed from the initial letters in a phrase, such as *scuba* (from *self-*contained *u*nderwater *b*reathing *a*pparatus).

Alphabetic principle   An assumption underlying alphabetic writing systems that speech sounds are represented by letters.

Analogy   In spelling, using a known word to help in the spelling of other words.

Base word   A word to which prefixes and suffixes may be added to create words related in meaning.

Blend   The joining of sounds represented by two or three letters with minimal change in those sounds—for example, *spl* in *spl*it.

Blended word   A word formed from portions of two words—for example, *smog* = *sm*oke + f*og*. The meaning of a blended word is also a combination of the meaning of the two words it came from.

Comparative form   Form of an adjective or adverb to compare two items.

Compound word

1. A word having as its meaning the meaning of the two or more smaller words within it—for example, the compound word *roommate* relates to the meanings of *room* and *mate*.

2. A word consisting of two or more free morphemes (the smallest units of meaning) with a meaning that is unrelated to the meanings of the morphemes—for example, *butterfly*.

Consonant

1. A speech sound made by partial or complete blockage of the breath.

2. A letter of the alphabet representing any of these sounds.

Contraction   The shortening of a spoken or written expression by the omission of one or more sounds or letters. There are two types of contractions: one is formed from two words in which the omitted letters are represented by an apostrophe (*we're*); the other is the shortened form of one word in which the omitted letters are not represented by an apostrophe (*Dr.*).

Derivative   An English word or portion of a word derived from other languages such as Greek, Latin, or Old French.

Digraph   Two or more letters that represent one speech sound—for example, the vowel digraphs *eigh* and *ai* and the consonant digraphs *th* and *ch*. See also *Spelling pattern*.

Diphthong   A vowel sound created by combining two vowel sounds, such as in *buy*.

Eponym   A word derived from the name of a person, a place, or an institution—for example, *pasteurization,* after Louis Pasteur.

Generalization   In spelling, a general conclusion about how written English works.

High-frequency words   Words used often in reading and writing.

Homographs   Words that sound different, but are spelled the same and have different meanings—for example, *minute* (time) and *minu/te* (small).

Homonyms   Words that sound the same and are spelled the same, but have different meanings—for example, *table* (furniture) and *table* (math).

Homophones   Words that sound the same, but are spelled differently and have different meanings—for example, *hear* and *here*.

Interactive writing   A writing partnership in which the teacher and the students plan and compose texts together, and the teacher shares the pen with the students. It provides opportunities for the teacher to demonstrate and the children to practice strategies good writers and spellers use.

Letter name   A consistent label given to each letter of the alphabet.

Meaning strategy   Using the structural relationships between words when attempting to spell unknown words—for example, using the generalization that past tense is often indicated by the suffix *ed* when attempting to spell an unknown word in the past tense.

Modeled writing   Demonstrating writing in front of students or introducing previously written print. (All print is a form of modeled writing.)

Onset   The consonant or consonants preceding the vowel in a syllable—for example, /l/ in *look*. See also *Rime*.

Phoneme   The smallest sound unit of spoken language. For example, the word *telephone* has seven phonemes: /t/-/e/-/l/-/e/-/f/-/o/-/n/.

Phonemic awareness   Awareness of the separate sounds in words.

Phonic strategy   Using the sound-letter relationships in words when attempting to spell unknown words—for example, using the generalization that the /w/ sound is usually represented by the letter *w* when attempting to spell an unknown word with the /w/ sound.

Phonics   Letter-sound correspondences in a language.

Phonological awareness   The ability to hear and manipulate sound units in the language, such as syllables, onsets and rimes, and individual sounds in words (phonemes).

Phonology   The study of speech sounds and their functions in language.

Prefix   An affix attached before a base word that changes the meaning of the base word.

Rime   The first vowel and any following consonants or vowels of a syllable—for example, /ook/ in *look*. See also *Onset*.

Schwa   In English, the midcentral vowel in an unstressed syllable. For example, /a/ in above, and /u/ in industry.

Shared writing   A writing partnership in which the students and the teacher together compose a piece of writing, then the teacher writes the piece. Unlike interactive writing, the pen is not shared between the students and the teacher, even though the students may suggest how the words should be spelled.

Spelling pattern   A group of letters representing a sound, including groups of letters, such as *ould* and *ear,* and digraphs. See also *Digraph*.

Stress   The emphasis or degree of loudness placed on a syllable.

Suffix   An affix attached to the end of a base word that changes the meaning or grammatical function of the word.

Superlative form   Form of an adjective or adverb used to compare more than two items.

Syllable   The smallest unit of sequential speech sounds consisting of either a vowel sound or a vowel sound with one or more consonant sounds.

Visual strategy   Using the visual relationships between words when attempting to spell unfamiliar words—for example, knowing that the spelling pattern *eigh* represents the /ay/ sound in *eight* when attempting to spell the word *weigh*.

Vowel

1. A voiced speech sound made without stoppage or friction of the air flow as it passes through the vocal tract.

2. A letter of the alphabet representing any of these sounds: the letters a, e, i, o, u.

Word family   A group of words related in meaning. Words in a word family might be derived from the same base word and have different prefixes and/or suffixes added to it. For example, the word *replays* is derived from the base word *play;* the prefix *re* and the suffix *s* have been added to form a new word related in meaning to the base word, *play*. Compound words may also be part of a word family. For example, the words *playground* and *playpen* are related in meaning to the word *play*. Other word families may be based on derivatives. For example, the words *photographer* and *telephoto* are related in meaning to the derivative *photo*.

/ /   Used to indicate a sound.

Acknowledgments

We wish to acknowledge the hundreds of teachers who have asked us questions about spelling and its relationship to other areas of literacy, and who have invited us into their classrooms to try out ideas and to demonstrate our teaching practices. We didn't think we would write another book about spelling, but the teachers' probing questions, and their requests to provide more and more details, have inspired us to write more here than we've written in our previous two books. Their questions guided us to search for teaching practices that were both manageable for teachers and worthwhile for children, and current research has also helped us reshape our ideas.

We also want to thank the thousands of children we have worked with in the United States and Australia. They have taught us how to be better teachers and have confirmed our beliefs about their ability to think and learn when their work is respected and they have an authentic reason for learning.

Thanks also to Margaret Moustafa, currently at California State University at Los Angeles, who helped clarify the meaning of onsets and rimes.

The ongoing discussions that we have with each other always help both of us to focus and improve our teaching and learning, and Greg Snowball has supported us in innumerable ways during the eighteen years that we have worked and written together.

Finally, thanks to Stenhouse Publishers. Philippa Stratton and Tom Seavey are always a joy to work with, and their advice is spot on.

Introduction

Teachers and school administrators are searching for ways to improve how children are learning about spelling. Although spelling is only one aspect of writing, it is one that receives a lot of attention from parents and the media. Even schools where many successful practices are in place may not take a consistent approach to the teaching of spelling across a grade level or throughout a school. Many teachers include the learning of words in their spelling program, but there may not be agreement in a school about whether children should regularly have words to learn, who should choose them, how children should learn the words, and how their learning should be assessed.

As well as the learning of words there are many other aspects of spelling that children should have the opportunity to learn about. Competent spellers use many strategies in tackling unfamiliar words, and growth in the range of these strategies should be part of children's writing strengths and needs. Even when such strategies are taught in a school, however, there is not always a consistent approach applied.

All of this inconsistency is not helpful to the children, because what this means is that each year they need to adjust to a new way of dealing with spelling. Children who do not find it easy to learn have a particularly hard time, and parents are apt to wonder if the school has any sort of plan at all for this part of the curriculum.

In this book we provide a possible school plan for the teaching of spelling for the purpose of writing and we suggest a constructivist approach that can be used for teaching all aspects of spelling. Our suggestions are based on what is understood about children's development in spelling, principles of English orthography, and the ways people acquire understanding and an ability to apply what is learned. Our ideas are the result of many years of teaching experience in both Australia and North America, with various kinds of school populations. From this experience we have been able to find out what is successful and exciting for children and teachers alike, and what meets the needs of both teachers and parents. Everything suggested in this book has been tried successfully in classrooms by both of us and by teachers with whom we have shared our ideas.

It is not our intention here to describe in detail children's stages of development in spelling or how to develop a total literacy curriculum. We have written extensively about these topics in other books, particularly *Ideas for Spelling; Teaching Spelling: A Practical Resource;* and *Bookshop Teacher's Resource Book,* Stages 1, 2, and 3. Teachers have often asked us for more explicit information about how we teach spelling; this is our aim in this book. We have tried to provide sufficient detail for all teachers to feel comfortable about trying new ideas that they think will improve students' learning about spelling. Some teachers will not need all of the information, and some will want to try just a few suggestions first. We hope that our suggestions will push teachers beyond where they are now in their teaching of spelling, particularly in the ways they ask children to reflect on and articulate their learning. The index is intended to allow teachers to select the areas that they would like to learn about and try first, or the areas that they are unsure about and would like to try some new or extended ideas.

Although the focus of this book is to provide practical ideas for the teaching of spelling, the purpose of learning about spelling is to enhance ability in writing. We presume that spelling instruction is taking place in classrooms where there are ample opportunities for children to read and write. Children learn a great deal about spelling through reading, and writing provides the authentic purpose for learning about spelling. We believe it is also helpful to focus on specific aspects of spelling, especially if the children are encouraged to reflect continually on how spelling helps them as writers and readers.

The book is divided into four major sections. In Part One, Chapter 2 outlines our beliefs about the fundamental principles and practices underlying a successful spelling program and provides a general description of the process used to enable children to learn about spelling. Chapter 3 provides a basic school plan for children's spelling development and an explanation of the factors that influence this in different school settings.

We have separated the teaching of spelling into two major strands: the exploration of phonetic, visual, and morphemic features of words; and the proofreading and learning of words. Although these aspects of spelling are described separately, the learning that occurs in each influences the learning that occurs in the other.

The chapters in Part Two of this book deal with specific spelling explorations as suggested in the overall plan. We describe how they can be taught and evaluated, and what to communicate to parents.

Part Three, Chapters 16 to 18, deals with proofreading and learning words. Finally, Chapter 19 in Part Four provides some suggested spelling plans during a one-week or two-week period for specific grade levels, showing how the two spelling strands work together.

Our intention is to help individual teachers and school systems to deal with their concerns about spelling, to build school and community knowledge about spelling, and to help children become competent spellers. At the same time, the process we suggest is a model of the way all aspects of writing may be taught. We focus on ways that children can learn through an approach that encourages:

- inquiry,
- thinking,
- the forming and testing of hypotheses,
- the development of responsibility,
- the ability to reflect on and articulate what has been learned, and
- the ability to transfer knowledge and understanding from one situation to another.

We describe this approach in each of the chapters in Part Two for two reasons. First, we want to be sure that readers who select just parts of the book will understand the process no matter which part they choose. Second, we want to show that teachers can adopt a consistent approach throughout a school to teach all aspects of spelling.

Many of the examples of classroom practice are described with a whole class because we have high expectations of all children and like to give children many opportunities to learn from each other and to listen to each other's explanations during shared explorations. The same ideas can easily be applied to a small group or an individual, but the sharing of ideas will not be as rich and varied. You will learn most about what your students know and need to know by looking at their writing. This will be your best guide about what to focus on with the class, with groups, and with individuals.

We think that learning about spelling is exciting and enjoyable, and we hope that you and the children you teach will feel the same way.

References

Bolton, F., and D. Snowball. 1993. *Ideas for Spelling*. Portsmouth, NH: Heinemann.

———. 1993. *Teaching Spelling: A Practical Resource*. Portsmouth, NH: Heinemann.

———. 1995. *Bookshop Teacher's Resource Book: Stage 1*. Greenvale, NY: Mondo.

———. 1996. *Bookshop Teacher's Resource Book: Stage 2*. Greenvale, NY: Mondo.

———. 1996. *Bookshop Teacher's Resource Book: Stage 3*. Greenvale, NY: Mondo.

Principles and Practices

A worthwhile spelling program guides children to recognize and develop the strategies and habits of competent spellers. It best occurs in an environment where both the teacher and the students recognize the students' spelling strengths and needs, where there are specific plans to work on the needs, and where there is a real-life purpose for learning about spelling. The overall goals should be for children to:

- understand that the primary purpose for learning about spelling is so that others can read their writing;
- know that their writing is valued regardless of the stage of development of their spelling;
- develop an interest in words and spelling and want to do their best;
- learn how to apply spelling strategies that will help them to write or learn any word;
- learn specific words that they use frequently and so become able to correctly spell these words automatically; and
- know how to use a variety of resources to help with spelling.

It's interesting to ask children why they think it is worthwhile to become a better speller. If their responses include "to pass the spelling test" or "to get a good report" or "to go to the next grade," but do not include "so that other people can read my writing," then for some reason they are getting a distorted message or misinterpreting teachers' intentions. Similarly, children can misinterpret statements such as "Spelling doesn't matter; just get your ideas down" and think that there is no need to be doing their best in spelling. To help children with spelling and to avoid such misinterpretations there are some essential principles and practices that need to be in place. These include the following.

Frequent Purposeful Writing

Children must be given many opportunities to write for various purposes and audiences and in different genres. This gives them the chance to try out unknown words, figuring out ways to spell them and how to use various resources for finding words and checking spelling, and to practice new spelling strategies that they have learned. If the type of writing is limited then the range of learning is also limited. For example, the common practice of having beginning writers write on one page in a journal every day limits the amount and kind of writing that they do and therefore the range of words they will try or practice. Beginning writers who mostly write in a journal tend to write only about personal experiences, and often the same experiences are repeated many times. Constant journal writing frequently causes children to think that writing begins with the thought "What will I write about today?" rather than "What kind of writing will I do today?" or "Who will I write something for?" When these children can't think of anything to write about in their journal, they may manage to write only one sentence, or even suffer from writer's block. But when children are encouraged to do a variety of kinds of writing—letters or postcards, stories, nonfiction pieces about things they know about or want to research, instructions, signs or messages—they learn much more about all aspects of writing, including spelling. To enable this to happen, different kinds of writing paper and tools need to be available so that children may choose material to suit the purpose of their writing, and supportive environments, including class mailboxes or access to e-mail, need to be established.

Opportunities for Children to Read Each Other's Writing

When children have an audience for their writing, they have a reason for learning about spelling and for doing the best they can. Although writers may read their own writing to others, it is a different experience for children to try to read what others have written. Readers are still encouraged to make constructive comments about the content, but they are also likely to query the writer if the handwriting is illegible or if they find it hard to figure out a word because of the spelling. This gives writers the sense that learning about spelling is useful and that proofreading and editing have value.

Teachers should allow time for children to read each other's writing in all curriculum areas, even if the writing will not be published. One way to encourage this is to provide a basket labeled "unedited writing" where children could place their pieces of writing; another way is to have children exchange such things as science notebooks or literature response journals. This gives the children's writing a genuine audience other than the writers themselves or the teacher.

Children also need to frequently select writing to publish, so that they have a purpose for learning how to proofread, take responsibility for correcting whatever they can, and come to understand the function of an editor or peer proofreader, who will assist with the writing before it is published. The classroom library should have many examples of children's published work. Beginning writers' work may be published with both their version of the print and the editor's version. This allows children's writing to be used as reading material for other children, while also making clear that their own attempts are highly valued.

Many Opportunities to See and Read Print

Through seeing print in the environment and being involved in shared and independent reading, children can notice and recall what words look like. If the reading material includes nonfiction as well as fiction and does not have limited vocabulary, the opportunities are much richer. Many children will form their own hypotheses about words, such as that all words have a vowel, that some words are spelled with the same patterns as other words, that there are various ways to represent each sound, and that there are generalizations to be made about how prefixes or suffixes are added to words. You can guide children to form these sorts of hypotheses by pointing out examples in material that the children are reading. Because children see the same words in most material they read, many will start to spell these high-frequency words correctly in their writing. You can help children notice and learn these words. When exploring any aspect of spelling it's important to use material that the children can read so that spelling lists can be built from words they know the meaning of.

Beginning readers and writers also need to be involved in many kinds of reading experiences, such as being read to, joining in shared reading, and reading independently, in order to learn about the conventions of books and print. They need to know what a word is, to understand one-to-one correspondence between spoken and written words, and to know what a letter is before they can learn about the relationship between letters and sounds. Adams (1990) claims that children need many hours of experience with written texts before being taught phonics in any formal way, and Weaver (1998) points out that it is essential for children who have not been read to at home to be given extensive, intensive experiences with print of all kinds at school. When children are read to, they understand the many purposes of written language and hear the way language works. Shared reading allows you to demonstrate concepts about print and later show children how to use analogy to go from a familiar word to an unfamiliar word (such as from *and* to *land* or from *day* to *lay*) and how to use word structure to figure out longer words (such as *playing* being made up of *play* + *ing* or *misunderstanding* being made up of *mis* + *under* + *stand* + *ing*); you can also explain how this strategy helps with writing as well as reading.

The only way that writers could possibly know how to spell all of the words they know is because of the amount of reading they do. Reading enables writers to recall what words look like and helps them select from two or more possible spellings that they have tried. Growth in children's spelling is greatly influenced by the amount and range of reading they do. Daily sustained, independent reading is absolutely essential for literacy development, including development in spelling.

Assessing Children's Writing to Inform Teaching

Children's writing provides the best indication of class, group, and individual needs. Although you may have a school plan or a set of standards to guide you, it is essential to analyze your students' writing to observe what each of them knows about spelling and the particular types of mistakes they may be making. The unfamiliar words that children attempt reveal much about the strategies being used or not for spelling. It's helpful to look for patterns that emerge in the type of errors students make so you can focus your teaching on what will help the most children with the greatest number of words. For example,

- If the misspellings or approximations are words such as *lrn* (learn), *mite* (mighty), *icsidide* (excited), or *tud* (turned), they indicate that children are working at hearing sounds in words and how those sounds are represented. At this stage, it's useful to help children explore the sounds of English and the various ways to represent each sound (see Chapter 7).

- If the misspellings are words such as *wlord* (world), *relly* (really), *coleful* (colorful), *beacuse* (because), *sum* (some), or *snak* (snake), they indicate that children are aware of the letters in words, but may not be sure of all of them or the correct order. These children may also be focusing on the sounds in a word without thinking about what the word looks like. In this case, it's useful to help children explore spelling patterns and develop visual strategies (see Chapter 8).

- If the misspellings are words such as *favrite* (favorite), *learing* (learning), *remberd* (remembered), *useing* (using), or *geting* (getting), they indicate that children are not aware of the concept of base words with prefixes and suffixes and the rules related to this concept. Here you should focus on this aspect of spelling (see Chapter 13).

It's not useful for anyone—you, the child, or the parent—when assessments such as a letter grade or numerical score are given, or when a child is said to be a "good" or "poor" speller, without being more specific. By looking at your students' spelling habits and attitudes, and at their use of phonic, visual, and meaning-based strategies, your teaching could be more purposeful. With the children, build a picture of all of the strategies that competent spellers use, relevant to the children's stages of development. You and the children can then use this as an assessment tool and as a guide for teaching and learning. Appendix A is a spelling checklist that may be used as a guide; the school plan outlined in Chapter 3 provides more detail.

Basing assessment of children's spelling on the results of a spelling test can be misleading and may give children the impression that the test is the main reason for learning about spelling. In one class, where children were mainly choosing their own words to learn and testing each other in pairs, with the teacher recording each child's weekly mark, the children admitted they were only choosing words they already knew so that they would score highly on the test.

Modeling Spelling Strategies

During modeled writing (where you, the teacher, are responsible for the content and the actual writing), shared writing (where you and the children construct the content together but you do the actual writing, perhaps with suggestions from children about spelling and punctuation), or interactive writing (where both you and the children actually write the words) there should be demonstrations of ways to work out how to spell words, how to use various resources to help with spelling, and how to proofread to check spelling. The focus will vary according to the stages of spelling development your students are in and what you are currently helping them to learn about. Demonstrating spelling strategies should be done with all kinds of writing so that the students are simultaneously getting different models for the writing they could do. If modeling of spelling strategies is always done with just one kind of writing, such as a morning message to the class, then children are not provided with models representing the diverse functions and forms of print.

In modeled and shared writing you have many opportunities to demonstrate specific spelling strategies that you have noticed the children need to learn more about; but in interactive writing the children's existing knowledge is used, so that the class or individuals tell you how to spell or attempt a word and you focus the children's attention on what they are currently learning about. The focus for beginning writers includes strategies such as understanding the concept of a word, remembering the spelling of high-frequency words, using onset and rime analogy to figure out how to spell a word, listening for sounds in words, and thinking about what words look like. For more experienced writers the focus shifts to strategies such as working from the base word to build compound words and using generalizations for adding prefixes and suffixes, knowledge of derivatives, and knowledge about homophones and apostrophes. Some of the children's spelling in interactive writing may be approximations, but because the writing is going to be used for reading, the conventional spelling is finally arrived at through your questioning and demonstration. Published pieces are spelled correctly.

Children should also be given insights into the spelling strategies you are using when you write. This varies with different age groups, but includes writing words several ways to see which one looks right, using knowledge of similar words, listening for sounds in words, using a variety of resources to check spelling, and admitting that you do not know how to spell all words but are still striving to learn more about spelling. (For more information about shared and interactive writing, see Snowball et al. 1995, 1996, Dorn et al. 1998, Button et al. 1996, and Pinnell and Fountas 1998.)

Encouraging Risk Taking

No one knows how to spell all words in the language they use to write. Beginning writers may know how to spell only a few words the conventional way or may still be at the stage of using pictures, scribbles, or some signs or a few letters to communicate in written form. (See Chapter 7 for more details about stages of development.) If children when writing are limited to using only the words they know how to spell, all aspects of their writing will be impeded. They need to spell words according to what they know at their different stages of development, because this will help them figure out the ways words work and provide evidence for you about what they know about spelling and what they need help with. By analyzing the ways your students spell words you will get a good indication of whether they have phonemic awareness, are able to use sound-symbol knowledge, or know about common spelling patterns, generalizations about adding suffixes and prefixes, and so on. As they invent spelling of words in their attempts to map speech to print, children's spelling and decoding are enhanced; in fact, the low achievers benefit the most from this experience (Clarke 1988).

Some parents will ask, "When will invented spellings stop?" Even adults still invent ways to spell unfamiliar words, but they know how to spell more words the conventional way than beginning writers do and have a greater range of spelling strategies to use in their inventions. If children are not allowed to attempt words they do not know they may become safe spellers rather than good spellers. One of the misconceptions about invented spelling is that it means that teachers don't care about spelling. This is far from the truth. Children's use of invented spelling facilitates self-expression (Wilde 1996) and signifies a readiness for formal spelling instruction (Moats 1995). Because some beginning writers are too frightened to try unfamiliar words it is helpful to have an area in the classroom with a sign saying "WE ARE ALL AUTHORS," with all sorts of children's writing displayed—including pictures, scribbles, strings of letters, and invented spellings. Beginning writers are also helped by hearing you praise others' attempts at spelling.

It's also important for children to understand the difference between taking a risk to try new words and being sloppy about writing words they know. It is not only in final drafts or at the end of writing a piece that writers pay attention to spelling, grammar, and punctuation. It is easier to do the best possible work in the first place than to have so much to fix up at the end that the task becomes overwhelming.

Linking Spelling to Reading and Writing

If spelling strategies are developed as isolated knowledge they are not useful, so children need to realize that they can learn about spelling by studying what other authors do in published writing and to continually reflect on how the strategies they are learning can help them with their own writing. Although there will always be incidental learning and the "teachable moment" that wasn't planned for, teachers and schools need to plan how they want children to learn about spelling, and what they should learn. This does not mean setting up a rigid plan that does not take into account children's strengths and needs as identified in their writing or the diverse needs of different children; rather, these observations should lead to a deliberate plan of instruction that focuses on a particular aspect of spelling as materials are read and that applies what is learned.

One of the best times to search for spelling words to focus on is after a shared reading experience with the class or a group or after a guided reading experience with a group, and the most suitable time to demonstrate what has been learned is during shared and interactive writing. Shared reading material should be texts that children are able to read along with you, perhaps after two or three readings. (If a Big Book is used because the content relates to a theme the class is studying, but the children cannot read along with you, this is a read-aloud rather than a shared reading experience, and children will find it more difficult to locate specific words or word features.) In guided reading, a group is temporarily formed to work at improving a particular reading strategy, and the material is chosen because the children can read it by themselves after just a little support from you. This is also an appropriate time for children to be able to locate specific words or word features and reflect on ways that their learning can help them as readers and writers.

A Process of Inquiry

Children can attain real understanding about spelling and can apply what they have learned if they are guided in a process of inquiry and discovery. The following steps provide one way to do this:

1. State the purpose and focus of the inquiry, relating it to what you have noticed about the children's writing needs (for example, learning common spelling patterns).

2. Use the class reading materials to find and list examples of words containing the spelling focus (for example, to find examples of words with a particular spelling pattern).

3. Have the children find further examples from material they can read and add examples to the class list.

4. Guide children to notice ways to categorize the examples to see what can be learned from them (for example, to notice that the spelling pattern may be pronounced different ways) and to group the words accordingly. Children can continue to find further examples and place them in appropriate groups.

5. Guide children to form hypotheses based on their examples, to verbalize and write about their understanding, and to reflect on how their new understanding can be applied to their own writing and reading.

6. Demonstrate how to use the new knowledge or strategy during shared

and interactive writing, and observe and confer with children about this during independent writing time.

You will find many examples of this process throughout this book.

It is helpful if teachers throughout the school are consistent in the method used for learning about spelling. Once children have been involved in the process two or three times they will understand how to apply the same process to most aspects of writing they want to learn about. They will probably be familiar with this process from other aspects of the curriculum, so it makes sense for them to learn spelling the same way. Using this method of teaching will also help students develop an inquiring mind and will get them to read more like writers, noticing the things that published writers do, including how they spell words. Fortunately, this process is not costly; all you need are the reading materials you already have, and chart paper.

Each spelling topic, or "focus," may be explored and learned about at an appropriate time for the majority of students in a class to properly understand it. This does not mean that children should be excluded from a class exploration, but the same focus may be returned to at a later date with a small group or individuals. Children who already have a grasp of the focus being explored benefit from the opportunity to articulate what they know and to share their understanding with others. Sufficient time should be spent to properly explore a spelling focus, so that children can develop a deep understanding of it and can apply their new knowledge with confidence. This is far more productive than teachers' dealing with the same issue for a short time, year after year after year, with many children still left in the dark.

Statements provided by adults, such as some found in workbooks, often confuse children rather than help them, particularly if they are not universally true. Class charts may be kept for referral and for either revising or adding to hypotheses. Ideas can also be transferred to class journals about spelling. Children's collections of examples, statements about what they have learned, and personal word learning work can be recorded in individual spelling journals. When children are asked to use their own words to explain what they are learning, their knowledge is much more meaningful and is more likely to be applied.

Using Children's Writing to Demonstrate Strategies

Strategies used by good spellers, ways to proofread, how to select words to learn, and how to learn words can be demonstrated and discussed by using examples of children's writing. Every child can learn something from every other child in the class, and you can develop a community of learners where each child's strengths are valued and children know what the others are working on. The process demonstrated to the class or group can then be applied by each child to his or her personal writing. This process is described in detail in Chapter 18.

Focus on Strategies

There is a place for learning how to spell specific words, but the success of this aspect of spelling depends on whether children understand why they are learning the words. Children need to be involved in the word choice and be taught useful ways to learn words. Competent spellers use many strategies to try unfamiliar words and to learn words. The emphasis needs to be on children's learning these strategies rather than their being given a list of words to be learned by rote. To develop competent readers we teach children to use many different strategies to help them determine whether a word looks right, sounds right, and makes sense. In teaching spelling it is just as important to show children how to use many strategies in determining how to spell a word.

Children will become more powerful spellers if they are taught that knowing how to spell one word can help them spell many other words. This analogy idea broadens as students learn more about written language. They may begin by building lists of words with the same spelling pattern (such as *may, say, stay, play, way, hay, day, lay*), but they can broaden this idea by building lists in the same word family by forming compound words or by adding prefixes and suffixes (such as *spell, spell-check, spelling, spelled, spells, misspell, misspelling, misspelled, misspells*). This way of thinking about words is included in all the spelling explorations in this book; children use the words they are personally learning to build lists of related words.

Every Teacher Teaches Spelling

Writing and reading occur in most curriculum areas, so spelling needs to be dealt with by most teachers. Because there are specific high-frequency words that children may use in each curriculum area or topic being studied, it is just as important for teachers of science, mathematics, social studies, and music to help children learn words and to discuss useful strategies for learning them. Sometimes specific spelling strategies can be useful for the spelling of words in particular subjects (for example, knowing derivatives can aid in the spelling of many science words). Subject specialists have the best opportunities to help children search for such words and learn about them.

Teachers of other subjects should also have the same expectations for written work as English or language arts teachers do. They should note common spelling mistakes being made in their classes and help children learn strategies that will prevent such errors.

Informing Parents

Many parents are interested in how spelling is taught and may not think anything useful is being done in class if they don't see their children learning a weekly list of class words or filling in spelling workbooks. They need to be informed that you are trying to do something much better than those activities, that they have never helped all children to become better spellers, and that the children's writing does not necessarily improve as a result of these activities. Explain that you want children to learn words, but that you would rather teach children to choose relevant words than waste their time on words they already know or would not use in their writing; tell these parents that you will teach the children many useful strategies for learning those words. Explain also that the spelling strategies you are teaching can apply to all of the words the children may wish to use as writers. The best evidence is in the richness of the children's spelling journals and the children's ability to articulate what they are doing. Appendix B provides answers to the most common questions parents ask.

Children are often asked to do spelling homework, and parents tend to have certain expectations about this. If spelling homework is assigned it should be relevant to the children's writing needs and help them develop an interest in language and improve their spelling.

Classroom Environment

The organization of a classroom and the resources available for reading and writing affect children's literacy development, including their learning about spelling. Models of different kinds of writing should be displayed and read. The environmental print should reflect the rich diversity of the forms and functions of language, and should include charts, signs, posters, directions, lists, messages, and labels, many written with or by the children. The class library should include class-made and commercial Big Books, and fiction and nonfiction for read-alouds, shared reading, guided reading, independent reading, buddy reading, and literature group studies. There should be a range of reference materials, including atlases and a variety of dictionaries and thesauruses. Alphabetically organized "word walls" and word lists related to spelling explorations should be accessible for referral and for annotation. Print may be displayed in other languages as well as English, reflecting and valuing the diversity of students' first languages.

Every classroom needs a place where students can gather together to search print for words related to a spelling focus, to collectively develop charts, and to take part in shared and interactive writing. Children also need to be able to gather together around an overhead projector. It is very difficult to develop a supportive community of learners with the focus on shared learning if the children are spaced around the room at desks or tables. They also need places to work in small groups and independently.

Also needed is a storage area with writing and publishing supplies, such as lined and unlined paper of varied sizes, shapes and colors; pens, pencils, and markers; art materials; staplers; rulers; scissors; lettering stencils; various sizes of envelopes; a date stamp; a hole puncher; book-binding materials; cardboard; and pencil sharpeners. In classrooms for beginning writers a word study center could include magnetic, foam, and plastic letters of the alphabet, alphabet blocks and tiles, magnetic boards, erasable boards with markers and erasers, alphabet strips in lower- and uppercase, alphabet and word cards and board games, sentence strips and matching words, and classroom-published books of spelling investigations about letters, sounds, and spelling patterns. In older grades the word study center could have commercial spelling games, such as Scrabble, Boggle, and Word Bingo; class-made card and board games; classroom-published books of spelling investigations about compound words, plurals, homophones, prefixes, suffixes, and derivatives; and crossword puzzles.

Children need demonstrations of ways to use all of these materials and need to be guided toward those that will be most helpful to them at a particular point in time. Center work should be planned according to individual children's needs, rather than making every child engage in every task on a rotating basis. Some children profit most from being able to work with a set of materials for several sessions until they feel successful, rather than being directed to a different activity each day.

Spelling in Perspective

Although this book focuses on children learning about spelling, other aspects of writing also need to be considered. Spelling should be made important but not overemphasized. Society values and expects good spelling, but the teaching of spelling should not be treated in such a way that students' reluctance to make spelling mistakes turns into a fear of writing. There should be a sensible balance between children feeling free to write their ideas and being concerned with correct spelling. Some children feel inhibited as writers because no one is systematically helping them with spelling; others know how to spell but are sloppy or careless. Neither situation is desirable. If spelling is dealt with in a purposeful and enjoyable way, and if schools develop a consistent, planned approach to the teaching of spelling, all children will benefit.

References

Adams, M. J. 1990. *Beginning to Read: Thinking and Learning About Print.* Cambridge, MA: MIT Press.

Bolton, F., et al. 1995, 1996. *Bookshop Teacher's Resource Book: Stages 1, 2, and 3.* Greenvale, NY: Mondo.

Button, K., M. J. Johnson, and P. Furgerson. 1996. "Interactive Writing in a Primary Classroom." *The Reading Teacher* 49, 6: 446–454.

Clarke, L. K. 1988. "Invented Versus Traditional Spelling in First Graders' Writings: Effects on Learning to Spell and Read." *Research in the Teaching of English* 22, 3: 281–309.

Dorn, L. J., C. French, and T. Jones. 1998. *Apprenticeship in Literacy: Transitions Across Reading and Writing.* York, ME: Stenhouse.

Moats, L. C. 1995. *Spelling: Development, Disability, and Instruction.* Baltimore, MD: York Press.

Pinnell, G. S., and I. C. Fountas. 1998. *Word Matters.* Portsmouth, NH: Heinemann.

Weaver, C., ed. 1998. *Reconsidering a Balanced Approach to Reading.* Urbana, IL: National Council of Teachers of English.

Wilde, S. 1996. "A Speller's Bill of Rights." *Primary Voices K–6* 4, 4: 7–10.

Planning a School
Spelling Program

lthough the outline we give at the end of this chapter for a school spelling program suggests a range of spelling focuses for a class to explore together, actual decisions about what children should learn about must be influenced by observing children's writing and evaluating their particular spelling strengths and needs.

Children's development in spelling is influenced by such factors as the amount of time spent on literacy learning in kindergarten, the amount of time devoted to reading and writing, the time at which ESL children are in transition to English, and the ways in which spelling has previously been taught. All of these factors should be taken into account when developing a plan and necessary adjustments made at both school and grade levels. When a plan such as the one suggested here is first implemented, a further consideration is whether or not particular spelling focuses have been previously dealt with thoroughly; this will be evident from observation and analysis of children's writing. Once the plan is adopted, yearly adjustments can then be made.

On the outline for each suggested probable year level, the proportion of time devoted to particular types of spelling explorations is indicated by column width. For example, in grades 3–5, time spent on the phonic strategy is only half that devoted to each of the other explorations.

Across the years K–8, emphasis changes, reflecting children's varying stages of spelling development and spelling needs. (For more information on children's spelling development, see Bolton and Snowball 1993 and Gentry and Gillett 1993). In general, teaching related to phonic and visual strategies is more promi-

17

nent in the earlier years because it is evident from invented spelling that these are the strategies the children are trying to figure out.

Our outline reflects the fact that as children gain experience in reading and writing they develop a wider repertoire of strategies to use for spelling. It also reflects the notion that children can be guided in this development by the types of spelling explorations teachers engage them in.

Although we have provided suggestions of what could be studied, it is not necessary to spend time on anything the children already understand. For example, if children demonstrate an understanding of the letters that represent the /b/ sound in their writing and can form and apply generalizations about the letters that represent the /b/ sound, it would be inappropriate to explore that sound; more time should be spent in relation to children's actual needs.

At each year level a certain proportion of time is devoted to high-frequency words. Since the 100 most frequently used words make up about 50 percent of our written language, it is helpful for beginning writers to learn how to spell these words. Once these words are learned, students can learn how to spell other words that are relevant to their personal writing in all curriculum areas, including words used frequently in the current topics they are studying. Some of these may be words the class has chosen to learn; others are individually chosen.

Although we suggest certain class spelling explorations for approximate year levels, we do not intend to exclude groups or individual children from being engaged in different spelling explorations relevant to their own writing needs. For example, if a group of grade 2 children were experienced readers and writers, they may have the necessary grammatical understanding required to undertake an exploration of homophones, even though homophone exploration is listed as a later study. Likewise, if an exploration is introduced that some children are unable to understand (for example, a sound exploration), it may be best to concentrate on an earlier exploration first (for example, activities that develop phonemic awareness), returning to the more advanced exploration at a later time.

Although a particular exploration is listed within a range of specific years, this does not mean it should be excluded from others. For example, derivatives are suggested as explorations to be undertaken in grades 5 to 8. However, it may be that children in earlier grade levels will explore a particular derivative, such as *tele,* because it relates to a topic they are investigating and is a commonly used derivative.

We assume that all of the spelling focuses suggested will be taught using an inquiry process (outlined in Chapter 2) so that children can truly understand and apply what they are learning. Children should help gather examples related to the focus, form hypotheses and generalizations, and reflect on how the learning will assist them with their writing. They should also be aware that all their spelling studies are related to their own writing needs, rather than just to meet a curriculum requirement.

Apart from the spelling focuses suggested, children should be taught strategies and habits to help them learn unknown words. These include the "look, say, name, cover, write, check" technique for learning words (see Chapter 17), the use of memory aids, and the use of dictionaries, word books, and other appropriate resources to determine or check spelling. Children also need to develop the habit of proofreading as early as possible and work at becoming more proficient at this as they become more knowledgeable about spelling. Computers may be used as a tool in proofreading, but if children notice that they are consistently misspelling particular words identified by the spell checker, it is wise for them to select these words to learn.

Our suggested plan is based on the assumption that spelling is taught in classrooms where much reading and writing is taking place, and where students' writing is frequently read by peers. This allows children to see that there are real purposes for learning about spelling.

There should be a consistent approach taken to spelling throughout a school, and there should also be consistent standards, so that children become familiar with the inquiry approach to learning about spelling and use it when working independently. A schoolwide plan also ensures that children will engage in a variety of spelling explorations suited to their particular stage of spelling development. In addition, children always need to be encouraged, at each grade level, to try unfamiliar words, and always to do their best.

In general, children must be involved in a range of literacy experiences across the entire curriculum to ensure they become competent and successful users of language. These experiences include demonstrations, shared and guided practice supported by the teacher, and independent use of newly acquired knowledge by the child. They include read-alouds as well as shared, guided, and independent reading; and shared, interactive, guided, and independent writing.

In each of these literacy experiences are opportunities for learning about spelling. Table 3.1 outlines ways to link spelling with reading and writing, using reading materials familiar to children. Note, however, that a given spelling investigation is likely to relate to only one or two of these literacy experiences.

When planning your daily literacy experiences, it is important to plan more reading and writing than spelling. Obviously, you will devote more time to spelling on some days than on others; but on average, across the entire curriculum, no more than ten to fifteen minutes need to be set aside daily specifically for spelling.

References

Bolton, F., and D. Snowball. 1993. *Ideas for Spelling.* Portsmouth, NH: Heinemann.

Gentry, J. R., and J. W. Gillett. 1993. *Teaching Kids to Spell.* Portsmouth, NH: Heinemann.

TABLE 3.1	Relationships Between Reading, Writing, and Spelling
Literacy Experience	*Relation to Spelling*
Read-aloud	Children may listen for words related to a spelling focus. For example, children may listen for words that rhyme or words that are plurals.
Shared reading	Children may listen and look for words related to a spelling focus. For example, children may listen for words with a specific sound, or may find words with a particular spelling pattern or suffix.
Guided reading	Children may return to the text to find examples of words relating to a class spelling exploration, or teachers may focus on the specific spelling needs of the particular group. For example, beginning readers may be asked to locate a high-frequency word and learn it, and more experienced writers may be asked to find examples of homophones from a particular set.
Independent reading	Children may notice examples of words related to the class exploration or particular words they are personally interested in.
Independent writing	Children use all the strategies they have learned in other reading and writing experiences. Teachers assess children's spelling strengths and needs and plan suitable spelling work for the other literacy experiences.
Shared writing	Spelling strategies can be demonstrated by the teacher and suggested by the children.
Interactive writing	Spelling strategies can be demonstrated by the teacher and attempted by the children.
Guided writing	Teacher writes with groups of children with common spelling needs.

Note: The class or individuals may choose to learn words, including high-frequency words, from any of these reading or writing experiences. The teacher demonstrates and children practice proofreading skills—using resources such as the word wall, class lists, dictionaries, word books, and other references—and using tools such as "Try It Out" or "Have a Go."

KINDERGARTEN — Children Are Engaged in Daily, Sustained Reading and Writing Experiences.

Letter Knowledge	Phonological Awareness	High-Frequency Words	Visual Strategy	Meaning/Word Structure Strategy
Recognizing twenty-six upper- and lowercase letters by name in all positions in a word. Realizing that a letter may be pronounced in different ways (for example, the letter *c* in *cat, circle, ocean*).	Immersing children in experiences that develop phonological awareness.	Creating awareness of high-frequency words. Learning some high-frequency words. Building on one-syllable high-frequency word knowledge using onset and rime structure.	Building words where rime has same spelling pattern, such as *w-ent, s-ent, b-ent, t-ent.* Encouraging children to notice what words look like.	Building word families, such as *play/plays; hat/hats.*

PROBABLY GRADE 1 — Children Are Engaged in Daily, Sustained Reading and Writing Experiences.

Letter Knowledge	Phonological Awareness	Phonic Strategy	High-Frequency Words	Visual Strategy	Meaning/Word Structure Strategy
Learning letter names if necessary.	Providing experiences for some children if necessary.	Exploring sounds and grouping according to letters representing the sound: /b/, /d/, /k/, /p/, /g/, /t/, /w/, /f/, /h/, /v/, /z/, /y/, /j/, /l/, /r/, /sh/, /zh/, /ch/, /m/, /n/, /th/ (the), /th/ (with), /ng/, /ks/, /gz/, /sk/, /s/	Choosing high-frequency words to learn and using various strategies for learning them. Using onsets and rimes in these words to build lists of other words.	Building words where rime has same spelling pattern. Changing other letters to form new words (*hat-hot-hit-sit-set*). Strengthening visual strategies using the "look, say, name, cover, write, check" technique.	Building word families, such as *play, plays, playing, played.*

PROBABLY GRADES 2–3	Children Are Engaged in Daily, Sustained Reading and Writing Experiences.		
Phonic Strategy	*High-Frequency Words*	*Visual Strategy*	*Meaning/Word Structure Strategy*
Exploring sounds and grouping according to letters representing the sound: /ay/, /ee/, /igh/, /oh/, /oo/ (food), /yoo/, /a/, /e/, /i/, /o/, /u/, /oo/ (good), /ou/ (now), /er/, /ar/, /ah/ (bath), /or/, /aw/, /air/, /ear/ (hear), /oy/, schwa and rounded schwa sounds. Forming generalizations, such as the most common ways to represent a sound or how position in word affects pronunciation.	Selecting class high-frequency words to learn from across the curriculum plus individual words of own choice.	Exploring common spelling patterns and grouping words according to their pronunciation: *th, sh, wh, ph, ch, ea, a-e, o-e, i-e, ee, ow, ai, oo, ou, ar, or, ay, ie, igh, -y, oa, ew, e-e, oi, u-e.* Forming generalizations, where appropriate, about common ways to pronounce a spelling pattern, such as *ou* is usually pronounced as in the word *round.*	Contractions. Some compound words. Prefixes *re, un.* Building word families, such as *play, plays, playing, played, replay, replays, replayed, player, players, playtime, playschool, playground, playmate, plaything.*

PROBABLY GRADES 3–5	Children Are Engaged in Daily, Sustained Reading and Writing Experiences.		
Phonic Strategy	*High-Frequency Words*	*Visual Strategy*	*Meaning/Word Structure Strategy*
Revising some sound explorations with more extensive vocabulary, and according to children's writing needs. Homophones, especially *there, they're, their; too, to, two; which, witch*.	Selecting and learning class high-frequency words from all curriculum areas plus individual words of choice.	Exploring spelling patterns: *oe, ir, ur, ough, aw, er, ui, au, augh, oy, ey, ue, ei, iew, uy, are, ear, ere, eir, our*.	Common plurals, such as adding *s*, adding *es*, and changing *y* to *i* before adding *es* to words that end in consonant plus *y*. Exploring how to add other common prefixes: *dis, il, im, ir, in, mis, anti, under*. Exploring suffixes *ed* and *ing* and other ways to form past tense: *write/wrote, take/took, teach/taught, mean/meant, catch/caught*. Building word families: *run, running, ran, runner, runs, rerun, reran, rerunning; satisfy, satisfying, satisfies, satisfied, dissatisfied*. More compound words.

PROBABLY GRADES 4–6		Children Are Engaged in Daily, Sustained Reading and Writing Experiences.	
Phonic Strategy	*High-Frequency Words*	*Visual Strategy*	*Meaning/Word Structure Strategy*
Revising some sound explorations with more extensive vocabulary according to children's writing needs.	Selecting and learning high-frequency words from all curriculum areas plus individual words of choice.	Exploring spelling patterns: *eau, eigh, aigh, eo, ua, uar*. Some revision of previous spelling patterns with more extensive vocabulary, according to children's writing needs.	Other common plurals: words ending in *f, lf, ff, fe*. Other forms of plurals, such as *tooth/teeth, man/men*. Other common prefixes: *ex, sub, extra, super, uni, tri, bi, quadri, trans, inter, semi, pre*. Exploring *er* and *est* for comparatives and superlatives. Less common plurals: *larva/larvae, gateau/gateaux, radius/radii, phenomenon/phenomena, memorandum/memoranda*. Blended words such as *smog* (*smoke + fog*). Shortened words, such as *vet*. Common suffixes: *ly, ist, er, or, ment, proof, th, ive, ship, tion, sion, ion, able, ible, ful, less, ness*. Building word families, such as *playful, playfulness, playfully; love, loves, loving, loved, lovable, unlovable, lovingly, lovely, lovelier, loveliest*.

PROBABLY GRADES 5–8	Children Are Engaged in Daily, Sustained Reading and Writing Experiences.	
High-Frequency Words	*Visual Strategy*	*Meaning/Word Structure Strategy*
Selecting and learning high-frequency words from all curriculum areas plus individual words of choice.	Revising some spelling patterns with more extensive vocabulary, according to children's writing needs.	Less common prefixes: *auto, non, circum, be, en, co, contra, counter, dia, macro, micro, post, pro, octa, multi, fore, vice.*
		Less common suffixes: *ation, age, ary, oid, ate, ic, ure, ance, ence, ant, ent.*
		Derivations: *aqua, aero, auto, chloro, centum, cyclos, deca, demos, electro, grapha, photo, mono, hemi, octo, logy, video, bio, audio, geo, hydro, mille, pedi, phono, tele, scribe, scope, thermo.*
		Acronyms such as *scuba, Qantas, flak.*
		Eponyms (words named after person or place) such as *fuchsia, pasteurization.*
		Words from other languages.
		Possessive apostrophe.
		Building word families, such as *direct, directs, directing, directed, direction, directions, directive, directives, director, directors, directly, indirect, indirectly, misdirect, misdirects, misdirected, misdirecting, misdirection, misdirections.*

Part Two

CHAPTER

4

Letters

hildren beginning school vary greatly in their knowledge of letters and letter names. Some children will know that words consist of letters, some will be able to name and identify the twenty-six letters of the alphabet, some may refer to a letter by its name and others by a possible sound associated with that letter. Some children may recognize letters but not use them accurately when writing, while others may have very little understanding of the alphabetic system in the English language and the way in which speech may be written down. Involving young children in instruction that helps them learn about letters helps them learn about the alphabetic system. Such instruction should occur alongside the regular reading and writing activities in the classroom.

Letter explorations are introduced to assist children in:

- understanding the concept of letters;
- learning letter names and knowing that the names of letters are constant;
- learning the names of the twenty-six letters in alphabetical order;
- identifying upper- and lowercase letters;
- distinguishing between letters based on their similarities and differences;
- understanding that letter names are different from sounds;
- knowing that letters occur in initial, final, and medial positions in words;
- learning that most letters in English represent more than one sound, and that this sound is influenced by the surrounding letters and the letter's position in the word;

27

- understanding the usefulness of alphabetical order in organizing and locating information; and
- hearing the terms *consonant* and *vowel.*

✿ *Evaluating Children's Understanding and Needs*

Before introducing letter explorations it is important to find out what your students already know about letters. This can be done by performing some of these activities:

1. *Check children's understanding of the concept of letters.* Have them do the following:
   - Count the number of letters in words.
   - Group words of the same number of letters.
   - Cut words on cards into letters and count the number of letters.
   - Cut words on cards into letters, mix them up, and assemble the original word plus others.

2. *Check children's knowledge of letter names.* Have them do the following:
   - Name the letters of the alphabet in sequence, starting with the letter *a.*
   - Name the letters of the alphabet in sequence, starting from different letters, for example, *o.*
   - Name and point to letters when saying letter names in alphabetical order.
   - Identify letters pointed to randomly.
   - Identify letters in their names.
   - Write their initials.
   - Match upper- and lowercase letters.

3. *Observe children when writing* to gain a sense of what they know about letters.
   - Do they use alphabet strips to assist them in identifying letters when writing?
   - Do they write random strings of letters?
   - Do they use letters to represent sounds they hear in words?
   - Do they use the letter-name strategy when writing?
   - Are they aware that most letters occur in all positions in words?
   - Can they form generalizations related to a letter's position and the sounds it represents when looking at class lists?

4. *Observe children when reading* to gain a sense of what they know about letters.
   - Do they comment on letters in words?
   - Do they relate the letters they see in books to letters in their own names or the environment?

Teaching Letter Names

Teaching letter names is an important purpose of letter explorations. It is usually better if children know the names of most letters of the alphabet before exploring the idea that a letter may represent more than one sound, although this knowledge may develop simultaneously. Teaching the letter names of both lower- and uppercase letters provides children with a consistent label for each letter.

The exploration of letters provided in this chapter complements the exploration of sounds provided in Chapter 7. In this chapter, the focus is on exploring letters so that children can recognize and name each letter and discover the positions in which letters occur in words and the sounds they represent. In Chapter 7 the focus is reversed: the focus there is on the sounds heard in words and the possible letter(s) or spelling patterns that represent the sounds.

Trying to teach children about letters before they are involved in frequent and extensive shared reading and writing experiences is very difficult. If children do not understand what a word is and what a letter is within a word, the upper- and lowercase letters merely become fifty-two abstract shapes. Children's understanding of words and letters can only develop through numerous reading and writing experiences during which teaching about letters occurs.

Letter explorations can begin early in the kindergarten year and may need to continue into grade 1, depending on your children's literacy experiences. Letter explorations will assist children who use a variety of symbols, such as numerals, musical notes, and letters (see Figures 4.1 and 4.2), when writing and children who use random or repeated strings of letters (see Figure 4.3). A further indication of children's readiness to engage in letter explorations is their recognizing letters during reading, noting that certain letters appear at the beginning of their names, in signs, and so on.

Before introducing letter explorations, find out which lower- and uppercase letters children in your class know the names of, so that you can know whom to assist more in letter-name activities in small groups and individually. You may want to use Marie Clay's (1993) *Observation Survey of Early Literacy Achievement* for this assessment. In the Letter Identification section of Clay's *Observation Survey* children are asked to identify lower- and uppercase letters by name, sound, or first letter of a word.

Be aware if using commercial programs when studying letters that many of them incorrectly use the terms *letter* and *sound,* which confuses children. In addition, many incorrectly indicate that a letter represents one sound, stating, for example, that "*c* says /k/." This also confuses children, particularly if they know the letter *c* can represent other sounds, such as the /s/ sound in *cent*.

Activities to Teach Letter Names

The following activities can be introduced on a regular basis throughout the year and used repeatedly and frequently, although you may also want to explore one

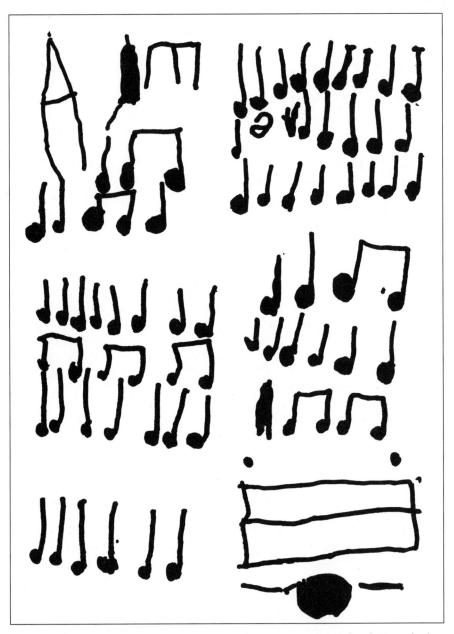

FIGURE 4.1 Andrew's piece.   Andrew is learning music at school. Note the letter *A* for *Andrew*.

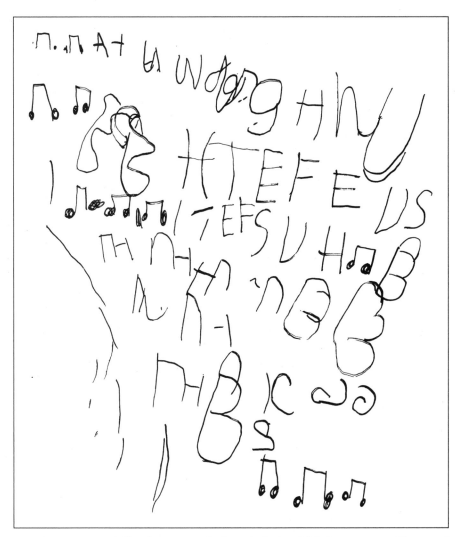

FIGURE 4.2 Anjali's piece. Musical symbols, Punjabi characters, and letters of the alphabet are placed randomly on the page.

or two letters in depth each week. Many experiences that involve children in learning about all of the letters are better than introducing just one letter at a time.

Many of the suggestions involve using children's names. When done on a regular basis, using children's names is one of the most powerful means of teaching children about letters.

- Set up a spelling center containing foam, wooden, cardboard, or magnetic letters. Make alphabet blocks and tiles, and provide children with alphabet strips of both lower- and uppercase letters. Place jigsaw puzzles based on upper- and lowercase letters at the center, alongside commercial alphabet card games, and show children how to play with these materials.

FIGURE 4.3 Qiao's piece. Here are random strings of letters, some repeated, not yet representing sounds.

- Read alphabet books to children on a daily basis. A list of alphabet books you may like to read is given at the end of this chapter. Place the books in the classroom library for children to browse through and read. Publish class alphabet books based on children's names, plants, animals, food, and so on, and place them in the classroom library for children to read and for you to use in read-aloud and shared reading.

- Place commercial and classroom-published picture dictionaries and word books in the classroom library for children to browse through and read.

- Begin an alphabet word wall at children's eye level. Allow a section for each letter of the alphabet. Display each child's name on a card under the appropriate letter. Play alphabet games, such as finding all the names on the word wall that begin with or contain a particular letter.

- Write children's names on a set of cards and select one each time you want a child to do a task. Chant the letters in each name, with the children joining in as you point to each letter. Use children's names for activities, such as counting the letters in the name, looking for letters that appear more than once, asking particular children to find a named letter, and comparing two or more names to see if any of the letters are the same.

- Have children sort their names according to length. This activity helps children distinguish between letters and words. Rather than writing names on cards of the same length, write longer names on longer strips to help children develop the idea of words and letters. This can be made even clearer if each letter is written on a box, for example:

- Make two sets of name cards; one set the children will cut into letters and match with an identical, intact card. Help children name the letters as they match them.

- Look for similarities, differences, and interesting features in children's names. For example, have children with double letters (Ro*bb*ie), two of the same letters (Da*v*i*d*) or the same last letter (Mar*y* and Harr*y*) form groups. Have children name the letters that caused them to be grouped.

- Ask children to form groups according to the first letter in their names, either their first names or their family names. Have them say their names, then have them name the first letter in their names. Vary this game by asking a group of children whose names begin with different letters to be leaders—for example, Lucy, Celeste, Sam, and Don. Have leaders name the letters their names begin with. Explain to the children that each leader, for example Lucy, will take turns asking a child, "Do you know a word that begins with the same letter as *Lucy?*" Tell children who have a correct answer to say the word, name the "same letter" and join that team. The biggest team at the end of the session wins.

- Ask children to sign in each day. At first, if necessary, supply a list of their names to copy. As they become more literate, use alphabetical lists with the first letter only of each name written, and have children find their initial and write their name beside it. This can be extended to include the initials of their last names.

- Encourage children to write their names or initials on all of their work. Throughout the day have the children tell you or their friends the names of the letters written.

- Have children form small groups to make words. Provide each child in the group with the same set of approximately ten letters. To enable you to model the task, select larger examples of the same ten letters that the children have, and place these in sentence pockets. Help children use the large set of letters to make words (for example, a two- or three-letter word) or to substitute (*ran/man*) and manipulate (*and/Dan*) letters to form new words. Have the children name the letters as they make the words. Write the words the children make on separate cards. Display these for children to refer to, and provide time for children to play with their letters. Help children identify the similarities and differences in letters in the words they make.

- Introduce games to children that focus on letters, and encourage children to invent their own. For example, they could play Hopscotch using alphabet tiles, I Spy with a word that begins with a certain letter, and card games such as Bingo, in which children match letters written on two sets of cards. Be sure children name the letters as they play these games.

- Talk about and demonstrate how knowing how to read and write one word can help you read and write other words. Make a word using magnetic letters—for example, *sing,* then make the word *ring,* explaining that the first letter changed from an *s* to an *r* and noting how the sound at the beginning of the words changed accordingly. Demonstrate this procedure substituting letters in the beginning, medial, and final positions in words. Have children name the letters that are changed.

- During modeled, shared, and interactive writing sessions, use a large alphabet strip of lower- and uppercase letters to identify letters for sounds heard in words. Have children say the names of the letters with you. For example, if you want to write the word *jump* in a sentence, ask the children something similar to the following: "What sound can you hear at the beginning of *jump?* Yes, the /j/ sound. Which letter represents the /j/ sound? Yes, the letter *j.*"; or "Which letter represents the /j/ sound? Yes, the letter *g* does represent the /j/ sound in *giraffe.* But *g* is not a letter in *jump.* Which other letter could it be? Yes, the letter *j.* Let's find the letter *j* on our alphabet strip." Then, beginning at the letter *a,* say the names of letters up to and including the letter *j.* Discuss with children whether the word begins with a lower- or an uppercase *j.* Write the letter *j.* Continue for each letter in the word *jump* and other words being written.

  Occasionally during writing sessions, begin naming the letters at a point partway through the alphabet. For example, when trying to identify the letter *u* you may decide to start at the letter *m* or *s* instead of *a.* By modeling the use of different starting points the children will realize they can do this themselves when they write. Of course, children who know the letters can write them without going through the alphabet.

- When writing in front of the children, be sure to name each letter as you write each word, even if you have used other strategies such as listening for the sounds in a word or stretching out the sounds to help you spell it.

Children Whose First Language Is Not English

If there are nonnative English speakers in your classroom, try to find out what they know about their native languages so that you can be aware of any similarities and differences that may cause confusion for them as they learn the names of letters in the English alphabet. For example, children may know the names of letters in Spanish and will need to know that there are some differences in English letter names, such as that in Spanish the letter *e* is called *i* and the letter *i* is called *e*.

Some children who live in communities where they are apt to see a lot of environmental print in characters other than English (Chinese, for example) may begin their invented spelling using signs similar to these characters. These children need to know that their writing is as valued as the writing of those who are using identifiably English-language letters. Through being immersed in reading and writing experiences with English words, these children will gradually come to use and recognize all the English-language letters.

Selecting Letters for Letter Explorations

When selecting letters to explore, a practical place to begin is with the letters in children's names. Consider these, then refer to the following alphabetical list of letters with common words for each. You will notice that most letters represent a variety of sounds. Although listed in alphabetical order, letters need not be introduced in this sequence. Rather, the needs of the children in your classroom should dictate the sequence.

Remember, too, that when exploring a specific letter children need not be introduced to all the sounds that the letter represents. For example, when exploring the letter *i* children may not learn that the letter *i* can represent the /a/ sound in *meringue*, because the word *meringue* may not yet be part of their vocabulary. Nor is it expected that children memorize the letters and their associated sounds.

a	sat, any, angel, naive, last, was, alone, rascal (schwa)
b	because, comb
c	can, mice, magician, cello
d	date, soldier
e	get, entree, pretty, evil, fete, like, secret (schwa)
f	from, of
g	gone, germ
h	happy, honor
i	it, kind, ski, medicine (schwa), meringue, Australia
j	jump, Jose
k	kite, know
l	like, talk, tortilla
m	most, mnemonics
n	nothing, hymn
o	often, over, women, to, love, one, second (schwa)
p	plug, pneumonia
q	quack, quay
r	ring
s	said, pigs, sugar, leisure, isle
t	toast, listen, station, creature
u	cut, bury, busy, unit, language, cushion, lieutenant, industry (schwa)
v	very

w   <u>w</u>ent, <u>wr</u>ong, la<u>w</u>n
x   bo<u>x</u>, <u>x</u>ylophone
y   <u>y</u>acht, happ<u>y</u>, s<u>y</u>rup, t<u>y</u>pe, mart<u>y</u>r
z   <u>z</u>ebra, a<u>z</u>ure

Be aware that some words listed may be pronounced differently in your country or region, and may not need to be listed because the sound the letter represents in that word occurs in another listed word. Even within your own classroom you may find that children vary in the pronunciation of words, and that each pronunciation is acceptable. You need to develop lists according to the way your own students pronounce words. There may also be other ways that letters represent sounds, especially in their names.

🌀 Discovering the Generalizations About Letters

Tell the children that you have noticed that some of them write letters as they write and name letters as they read, so you are going to explore letters together and find out how knowing about letters, their positions in words, and the sounds they represent can help with their spelling and reading.

Letter explorations should be done using the reading and writing that is occurring in the classroom so that children will be looking for letters in words they already know and can say, and can thus hear the sounds the letters represent. The activities described below link letter explorations to shared reading and interactive writing.

Letter Explorations During Shared Reading

Observe children's writing and note what they know about writing letters to create words and identifying letters to represent sounds. Then, identify a letter to explore and search familiar materials used for shared reading (Big Books, charts of songs, rhymes, poems, and so on) that will give children practice in looking for the letter. Note whether the letter occurs in the initial, medial, or final positions in words and the variety of sounds it represents.

For example, if you decide to explore the letter *o*, suitable titles would include the familiar songs or rhymes "If You're Happy and You Know It" or "Hot Cross Buns." As your exploration of the letter *o* progresses you may need to collect other familiar reading materials, such as the song "Polly Put the Kettle On."

In the early stages of a letter exploration several books or charts should be introduced that contain the focus letter in a variety of positions in words and representing a variety of sounds. In this way children will learn to recognize the letter in all positions rather than only at the beginning of a word, and they will not develop misconceptions about a letter representing only one sound.

When you want children to search for a particular letter, point to your eyes. Tell the children you will read, for example, the rhyme "Hot Cross Buns" together. While the rhyme is being read they are to look for words containing the letter *o,* and whenever they see the letter *o* they are to give a clap.

Be sure to give clear instructions. It is essential that children understand that they are *looking* for the letter, not listening for it. You may want to make a pair of king-size glasses for a child to wear when the class is looking for letters.

It will help if you demonstrate the task of *looking* by reading the title, such as "Hot Cross Buns," then rereading each word. Read "Hot" and, pointing to your eyes, say something like, "I am looking for the letter *o.* I can see the letter *o* in the middle of the word *Hot.*" Have a child point to the *o* and give a clap. Repeat this procedure with the words *cross* and *buns.* You may need to remind the children to look for the letter *o* in all positions in words, not just in the beginning.

Here are the two examples just mentioned, with the *o* words underlined:

If You're Happy and You Know It	*Hot Cross Buns*
If you're happy and you know it,	Hot cross buns! Hot cross buns!
Clap your hands	One a penny, two a penny,
If you're happy and you know it,	Hot cross buns!
Clap your hands.	If your daughters do not like them
If you're happy and you know it,	Give them to your sons
And you really want to show it,	One a penny, two a penny,
If you're happy and you know it,	Hot cross buns!
Clap your hands.	

To help children focus on the letter being explored, list the letter *o* words (underlined in the previous charts) as the children identify them. As the exploration progresses, list other words children know or find with the letter *o*—for example, the children's names *Antonio* and *Dione*—and each time have children identify the position of the letter in the word, underline the letter *o* or use a marker to highlight the letter, and identify the sound it represents. For example, for the two rhymes above, the lists would look like this:

The letter o

you're	One
you	two
know	do
your	not
to	sons
show	Antonio
Hot	Dione
Cross	

The children may also find and copy words containing the letter *o* onto strips of paper, which may then be attached to the class list.

Once sufficient words have been listed have the children suggest and discuss ways of grouping the *o* words. If necessary, show them how to group the words according to the position of the letter *o* or the sounds it represents depending on the children's previous experiences in exploring letters. Where more than one example of the letter being explored occurs within a word (for example, the letter *o* in *Antonio*), you may need to show the children how the word may be part of two groups. Similarly, if a letter occurs twice in a word and represents different sounds, it may be necessary to explain to the children why the word should be listed twice.

Here are the letter *o* words grouped according to the position of the *o*:

One	Hot	two
	Cross	to
	not	do
	sons	Antonio
	you're	
	you	
	know	
	your	
	show	
	Antonio	
	Dione	

When appropriate, also help students group the words listed during the letter exploration according to the sound the letter represents. When doing this, it is better to exclude words in which the letter is part of a spelling pattern. For example, where the letter *o* occurs in words containing the spelling patterns *our, ou,* and so on, it would be better to keep these words from the sound grouping activity, because the sound represented by the letter *o* in these spelling patterns is greatly influenced by the surrounding letters and is not easily distinguishable.

Here is our list of *o* words grouped according to the sound represented by the letter *o*:

/o/	/oh/	/w/	/u/	/oo/
Hot	know	One	sons	to
Cross	show			do
not	Antonio			
	Dione			

Throughout the letter exploration, rewrite words from class lists onto individual cards and help children identify the position of the letter in each word, underline or highlight the letter, and (if appropriate) identify the sound the letter represents. These cards may then be used for grouping activities as described above.

Encourage the children to think of other criteria for grouping the words—for example, whether or not they are high-frequency words, whether or not they contain a letter studied previously, and so on. This may be done as a class or as a small-group activity.

At regular intervals, ask the children to tell the class what they have learned about the letter *o*. Direct their attention to the position of the letter in words, the variety of sounds the letter *o* represents, and the sound most frequently represented by the letter *o*. Write these generalizations on a class chart. Write the date on the chart and have the children write their initials next to their generalization.

Here is an example of the type of statements children may make after being involved in several letter explorations:

> There are more words with the letter *o* in the middle than at the beginning and at the end.   R. G.
> The letter *o* represents the /oo/ sound at the end of words.   H. S.
> The letter *o* represents the /o/ sound in the middle of words.   L. V.
> The letter *o* represents the /o/ sound more than the /w/ sound.   R. G.
> The letter *o* always represents the /w/ sound at the beginning of words.   M. O.

Initially, some generalizations may be inaccurate—for example, M. O.'s statement above, "The letter *o* always represents the /w/ sound at the beginning of words." This is, however, the child's (or maybe several children's) understanding, from the words encountered up to this point in the exploration. When this happens, be sure to list other words from the children's reading and writing that will cause them to rethink the inaccurate generalization (in the case of *o*, try *on*, *off*, and *over*). Help children review and revise their generalizations in light of additional words. Have children cross out an inaccurate generalization and help them rewrite a new one. Talk with them about how this is evidence of their learning, and that they are doing what good spellers do: reviewing and refining their generalizations. Discuss how forming generalizations helps them as spellers and as readers.

Ask children what they have learned that could help them with their spelling in the future. Encourage them to look for words containing the letter being explored during shared reading, read-alouds, buddy reading, and independent reading. As the children identify new words, add them to the class list.

Because knowing about high-frequency words is of great benefit to writers and readers, allow time for children to review the word lists to identify high-frequency words that could be added to the alphabet word wall (see Chapter 17).

Children will also become better spellers if you regularly demonstrate and comment on how knowing how to spell one word on the class list can help them spell many other words. For example, show children that knowing how to spell *hot* can help them spell *not, spot, shot, cot, dot, slot,* and so on. When selecting words to demonstrate these analogies, select words the children will use often when writing or reading. Be sure they understand the principle that thinking about the spelling of a known word will help them spell an unknown word.

Throughout the letter exploration, talk with children about the use of upper- and lowercase letters, and demonstrate the similarities and differences in the size and shape of the lower- and uppercase version of the letter being studied and the way each is formed.

Display the class letter charts (for example, the *o* charts) or make the class lists into a class spelling journal or letter book (for example, an *Our Letter o*

Book). You could have separate pages depicting the letter in the initial, medial, and final positions, or separate pages for each sound the letter represents. You may choose to leave some pages blank for children to add more words as they discover them in their reading and writing. On completion of the study, place the book near the writing center for children to browse through and refer to when proofreading their writing. You may also want to store the cards containing the words with the letter that was studied in an envelope and place this where children have easy access to it.

Letter Explorations During Interactive Writing

Identify a letter for a letter exploration: one that occurs frequently in children's names and high-frequency words—for example, the letter *t*. Talk with the children about why you have selected the particular letter to investigate. If the children understand why a particular letter is being explored they are more likely to relate what is being taught to their personal writing and reading needs.

Have children whose names contain the letter *t* come to the front of the room. Write their names on a class list, and have them identify and underline the letter *t* in their names. If any names begin with the letter *T,* talk with children about the use of the upper- and lowercase forms of the letter *t*, and the similarities and differences in their shapes. It may also be beneficial at this point to show the children how both letters are formed, again discussing the similarities and differences.

You may decide to invite some children to show the class writing they have done containing the letter *t.* In this case, say some of the *t* words with the children and have them look for and identify the position of the letter *t* in each word.

At the beginning of the interactive writing session, explain to the children that you are going to write a piece together. Guide them in choosing a purpose and a topic for the writing. For example, the children, with your assistance, may decide to recount an experience the class has had, or compose a narrative based on a familiar story they know, or write a poem. Help them organize their thoughts and write them down. Tell the children they will all help write the piece by listening for the sounds in words, using the large alphabet strip to find the letters that represent the sounds, and writing any letters and words they know.

Explain that you need them to help you identify the letters for all of the sounds in the words, but you particularly want them to think about the letter *t* during the writing session—its position in words and the sounds the letter *t* represents.

Write the piece with children, stretching out the pronunciation of the words, listening for the sounds in all positions in the words, and identifying the letter or letters that represent the sounds. Encourage and assist the children in writing letters and known words, and help them use the alphabet strip when appropriate. In short, provide the support necessary to ensure the success of the children's attempts.

The first language of children whose first language is not English may not

Tuesday 16th September.

We had an illustrator
Come to our school today.
His name was Terry Denton.
He drew this fish.

FIGURE 4.4 An interactive writing piece done with kindergartners, used to introduce an exploration of the letter *t*.

be alphabetic, and they may require more assistance in learning the names of the letters of the alphabet and in identifying the sounds they represent. They may also require a greater degree of support during interactive writing sessions.

When the piece is complete, reread it to be sure it makes sense and sounds right. Figure 4.4 is an example of an interactive writing piece done with kindergarten children after illustrator Terry Denton's visit to their school. When complete, the piece was used to introduce an exploration of the letter *t*.

Once the children are satisfied that the piece makes sense and sounds right, reread it with the children to look for words with the focus letter—in this case, the letter *t*. List the words as they are identified. For Figure 4.4, the list would look like this:

Tuesday
September
illustrator
to
today
Terry
Denton
this

When grouping words on the class list containing the letter *t* the children could complete an activity similar to the one shown in Figure 4.5. In this exam-

three   tomato   Tessa   they

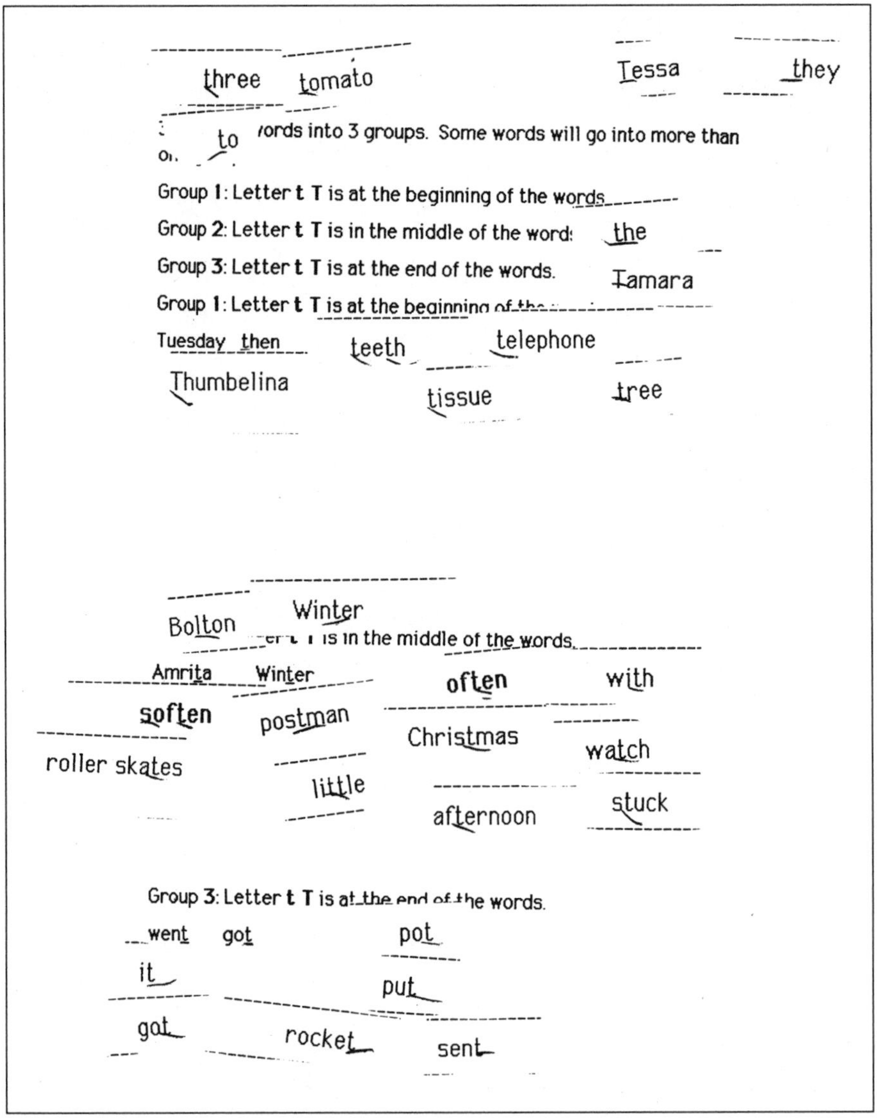

: to   ords into 3 groups. Some words will go into more than
o.

Group 1: Letter t T is at the beginning of the words
Group 2: Letter t T is in the middle of the words   the
Group 3: Letter t T is at the end of the words.   Tamara
Group 1: Letter t T is at the beginning of the

Tuesday then   teeth   telephone
    Thumbelina   tissue   tree

                Winter
Bolton   ert t is in the middle of the words.
    Amrita   Winter   often   with
    soften   postman
                    Christmas   watch
roller skates
            little
                afternoon   stuck

Group 3: Letter t T is at the end of the words.
    went   got   pot
    it   put
    got   rocket   sent

FIGURE 4.5 Words grouped according to the position of the letter *t*. A kindergarten child pasted *t* words at the top, middle, and bottom of the page.

ple, the class list was typed and made available to children, who then cut out individual words and pasted the *t* words into groups according to the position of the letter *t* in the words.

Throughout the interactive writing session, repeat the term *letter name*. If you find children are confusing the meaning of *letter name* and *sound*, it may be because you are wrongly using these words interchangeably. Remember, a *letter* is any one of the twenty-six letters in the alphabet, but a *sound* is a phoneme that we hear. We *look* for letters and *listen* for sounds.

When writing sentences with the children, you may choose to leave a blank space for one of the words, preferably a high-frequency word containing the letter under study for the children to attempt during the day. For example, in exploring the letter *t*, the word *to* could be omitted in a transcript of the piece in Figure 4.4. Then, during the day the children may be encouraged to attempt to spell the missing word, placing their initials beside their attempts. In the case of the Figure 4.4 piece, the transcript would look like this, with two of the children's attempts included:

16th September

We had an illustrator come ——————— our school. His name was Terry
Denton. He drew this fish.

   t   Enri

   do   GH

To ensure that all children feel sufficiently confident in attempting the omitted word, it may be necessary to provide the less experienced writers with a high degree of support by helping them identify the sounds in the words and use an alphabet strip to identify the letters that represent the sounds. However, it is not necessary to support them to the extent that they spell the word conventionally. After being assisted in this way on several occasions, less experienced writers usually become more confident and more willing to attempt unknown words when writing independently. This approach is particularly important for children who are so concerned with spelling words conventionally that they are reluctant to try different strategies to spell unknown words.

At some point later in the day return to the chart and praise all the children's attempts, discussing with them the strategies they used when attempting the word. Then write in the missing word, saying something like, "This is how it is written in a book."

Reread the entire piece with the children and display the completed language experience charts where they can be read frequently for shared reading, or by individuals or pairs who are able to "read the room." After a week or two make them into a book to place in the classroom library.

Sentences written during these sessions could also be written on two identical sentence strips and used for matching and sequencing activities.

Continue adding to the class letter lists. Opportunities to add words will occur during shared, guided, and independent reading sessions, and other interactive, shared, modeled, and independent writing sessions. When grouping the words, help children form generalizations about the position of the letter in words and the sounds it represents. Display the class lists or bind them into a class book for children to browse through.

Scheduling Letter Explorations

When planning to teach letter names, time needs to be allotted for activities that involve children in thinking about all of the letters as well as time for specific letter explorations.

Sometimes, experiences that focus on all letters may occupy an entire spelling session. At other times they may be introduced alongside letter explorations, phonological and phonemic awareness activities, or activities related to high-frequency words, onsets and rimes, or word families.

Once children are familiar with the routine associated with spelling explorations, it generally is possible to explore approximately two letters a week, or three letters over two weeks. This, however, would vary, depending on:

- the children's experience with spelling investigations;
- the children's grade level and their knowledge of letters;
- whether the listed words were grouped once or twice, according to position only, or position and sound;
- the variety of sounds a letter represents (for example, if a letter represents two sounds only, the investigation may be less extensive than if a letter represents more sounds).

An important factor to consider when scheduling is that letter explorations are likely to be the first spelling exploration many children engage in. Because the children may not be familiar with the inquiry process, the first few letter explorations may continue for a period of one week on a daily basis. Once they are familiar with the process, the letter explorations may well be of shorter duration, allowing for two a week or three over two weeks.

Earlier in the school year, with children who are unfamiliar with spelling investigations, spelling sessions may be twenty to twenty-five minutes' duration. However, once the investigation is under way, a few minutes a day may be sufficient.

Another variable is other spelling focuses. Rather than continuing a letter exploration on consecutive days, a class's attention may be diverted from the letter exploration to a study of onsets and rimes or high-frequency words.

Schedules should be flexible, allowing you to take into account a variety of factors. As well as your students' needs, you must consider your own needs. If you are not totally familiar with the approach to the teaching and learning of spelling outlined in this book, you may find that your initial sessions take longer than expected. If you would like further guidance in scheduling spelling sessions, see Chapter 19.

Writing Letters Correctly

It is important to observe children as they write to determine who is ready for some assistance with letter formation. However, learning about correct letter formation does not necessarily happen at the same time as learning to recognize and name a letter. For example, if children are struggling to have control over a pencil or if they are still in the scribble stage of writing, learning letter formation is not appropriate. These children may require assistance with pencil grip or posture and placement of paper, or you may still want to encourage them simply to make marks on paper and perceive themselves as writers.

Help with handwriting is more effective when it is done with individuals or small groups.

As children write and attempt to form letters, note the letters they need assistance with. In the beginning years of school it is important to teach children writing habits that will result in fluent and legible handwriting, so that they do not have to labor when forming letters and are free to concentrate on what they are writing.

When teaching children to form letters, start by grouping letters that have similar starting points and formation. Point out the similarities of the grouped letters. It may also be helpful to revise the name of each letter introduced when teaching children how to write the letters.

A possible grouping of letters and sequence for script is as follows:

l i I t F H L T E (letters with straight vertical and horizontal lines)

o a c d g s q O C G Q f S (letters based on a circle, starting at the top right side of the circle)

b p B D P R (letters that begin with a downward line, then a circular part)

h m n r u j U J (letters that begin with a downward line, then a curved part)

K A M N V W X Y Z v w x y z k (letters with straight lines that include diagonals)

Notice that the upper- and lowercase of a given letter may be formed quite differently and therefore the two versions of the same letter are not taught at the same time in handwriting.

Children must learn where to start letters and how to form them so that they are doing this correctly when they learn to join letters in cursive writing.

Practice sheets can be developed for each lower- and uppercase letter. Children can select the one they need to practice their handwriting at any particular time.

Other practice sheets, where the letters are both isolated and in words, are also helpful. If onsets and rimes are used in these words understandings about spelling can be developed at the same time. For example, letters with straight vertical and horizontal lines could appear together on a practice sheet:

ill   till   Hill   Fill
it   lit   Fit

Or, to practice the circular letters *a* and *d,* a practice sheet could contain:

add   bad   dad   had   lad   mad   pad   sad   daddy

Make sure that children understand that the most important reason for developing legible handwriting is so that people can read their writing.

☞ *Homework Ideas*

Children may be given homework tasks related to the letter exploration they are doing. For example:

- Have them cut out words from magazines, catalogues, and newspapers that contain the focus letter in a variety of positions. These could then be added to the class chart.

- Play a card game using approximately twenty cards of matching upper- and lowercase letters. Separate the cards into two packs—one for uppercase and one for lowercase letters. Give each of the two players a pack of cards. Have the two players take turns placing cards face up on a pile in the middle. When two cards with an upper- and lowercase version of the same letter are placed on top of each other, the first player to call "Snap!" wins the pile of cards; the player with the greatest number of cards at the end of the game is the winner.

Alphabet Books

Base, G. 1986. *Animalia*. New York: Harry N. Abrams.

Bender, R. 1996. *The A to Z Beastly Jamboree*. New York: Dutton/Lodestar.

Boynton, S. 1987. *A Is for Angry*. New York: Workman.

Cox, L. 1990. *Crazy Alphabet*. New York: Orchard.

Ehlert, L. 1989. *Eating the Alphabet: Fruits and Vegetables from A to Z*. San Diego: Harcourt, Brace, Jovanovich.

Elliott, D. 1991. *An Alphabet of Rotten Kids!* New York: Philomel.

Garten, J. 1994. *The Alphabet Tale*. New York: Greenwillow.

Hubbard, W. 1990. *C Is for Curious: An ABC of Feelings*. San Francisco: Chronicle.

Martin, B., Jr. 1989. *Chicka Chicka Boom Boom*. New York: Simon & Schuster.

McNab, N. 1989. *A–Z of Australian Wildlife*. Victoria, Australia: Lamont.

Preiss, L. P. 1990. *The Pigs' Alphabet*. Boston: David R. Godine.

Sandved, K. B. 1996. *The Butterfly Alphabet*. New York: Scholastic.

Shannon, G. 1996. *Tomorrow's Alphabet*. New York: Greenwillow.

Snow, A. 1991. *The Monster Book of ABC Sounds*. New York: Dial.

Sullivan, C. 1991. *Alphabet Animals*. New York: Rizzoli International Publications.

Twinem, N. 1994. *Aye-ayes, Bears, and Condors: An ABC of Endangered Animals and Their Babies*. New York: W. H. Freeman.

References

Clay, M. 1993. *Observation Survey of Early Literacy Achievement*. Portsmouth, NH: Heinemann.

Hanna, P. R., R. E. Hodges, J. L. Hanna, and E. H. Rudolph. 1966. *Phoneme-Grapheme Correspondences as Cues to Spelling Development*. Washington, DC: U.S. Office of Education.

Phonological Awareness

P honological awareness is referred to by Weaver (1998) as "an awareness of the sound system of the language, and, more specifically, to units of sound within the language. In order of descending size, these include syllables; the major parts of syllables (onsets and rimes . . .); and phonemes, the sounds that we adults have learned to hear as separate within words" (p. 5).

The term *phonemic awareness* is frequently misused when it is more accurate to use the broader term, phonological awareness. Phonemic awareness is the conscious awareness of phonemes, the smallest sound units of spoken language; thus, it is only one aspect of phonological awareness. Phonemic awareness is the ability to recognize that a spoken word and the syllables within that word consist of a sequence of individual sounds, or *phonemes.* Phonemes roughly correspond to individual *graphemes,* or letters.

For example, the word *telephone* has nine letters but only seven phonemes, /t/, /e/, /l/, /ee/, /f/, /o/ and /n/. Because "phonemic awareness" has become such a commonly used term it is often accepted as meaning the same as "phonological awareness."

There is a great deal of controversy about the relationship between phonemic awareness and learning to read. Some researchers believe that phonemic awareness precedes reading acquisition. Not only do they believe that it is a contributing factor in success in learning to read, but they also believe that phonemic awareness in preschoolers predicts later reading achievement. Other researchers disagree. They argue that phonemic awareness is largely the result of learning to read, even in the initial stages of reading. Regardless of their positions, however, researchers agree that phonemic awareness is important. (If you would like to read further about this controversy, see Adams 1991, Griffith and Olson 1992, Yopp 1992, Moustafa 1997, and Weaver 1998.)

Most of the research on the significance of phonemic awareness relates to reading acquisition, not writing and spelling. From our observation of inexperienced writers, we have concluded that the introduction of activities to heighten phonemic awareness may help prevent some children from experiencing early writing and spelling difficulties. Because developing an understanding of the link between the sounds of speech (phonemes) and the signs of print (letters) is one of the tasks beginning writers and readers face, we believe that beginning writers in particular need to understand that words can be broken into syllables and phonemes and represented by letters in an alphabetic writing system.

We also recognize that as a consequence of most children's learning to spell and read words they also develop phonemic awareness and an understanding of how spoken language maps onto written language. In fact, many children develop phonemic awareness without formal instruction. This may be due to the quality and frequency of experiences they have with spoken language and the amount of exposure and interaction they have with print. However, understanding that words are composed of phonemes may be difficult for some children to grasp, and they will require help in developing phonemic awareness. One reason for these children's difficulty is that phonemes are abstract units of language; they carry no meaning. Children, however, generally think about words in terms of their meanings, not abstract linguistic characteristics. In addition, phonemes are not produced in isolation. Words are not pronounced as a series of discrete phonemes; rather, the attributes of a phoneme combine with those that precede and follow it in a word, and when the word is pronounced the phonemes become blended.

Phonemic awareness is not synonymous with phonics. It is not learning letter-sound correspondences: it is about hearing sounds in language. It is possible that children who lack phonemic awareness will not benefit fully from phonics instruction. However, some research findings suggest that when children have acquired a high degree of phonemic awareness and are taught to segment words into phonemes in conjunction with letter-name and letter-sound instruction, such instruction has immediate beneficial effects on their reading and writing.

❦ *Evaluating Children's Understanding and Needs*

Before introducing activities focusing on phonological awareness, you must find out what your children already know. To do this, observe children writing or have them complete activities similar to the following:

- Recognize rhyme—for example, identify the rhyming words *Humpty* and *Dumpty.*
- Produce rhyming sets when given a word—for example, when given the word *chair,* children suggest such words as *bear, hair, where, scare,* and *share.*
- Blend phonemes to form words—for example, the phonemes /sh/, /o/, /p/ to form *shop.*

- Segment words into syllables—for example, *birth/day* and *di/no/saur;* and segment syllables into onsets and rimes (*hide, h-ide*).
- Isolate phonemes in the beginning, final, and medial positions in words—for example, the /t/, /a/, /b/, and /l/ sounds in *table*.
- Delete phonemes to produce new words—for example, delete /p/ from *park* to produce *ark*.
- Manipulate phonemes to form new words with different meanings—for example, isolating the phoneme /w/ in *went* and substituting the phoneme /s/ to change *went* to *sent*.

Teaching Phonological Awareness

Explicit instruction related to the various levels of phonological awareness should be situated in daily reading and writing activities rather than in isolated drill-type exercises. Activities designed to develop phonological awareness should:

- stimulate children's curiosity about spoken language;
- be fun and capitalize on children's natural propensity to play with language;
- encourage children to explore and experiment with systems of sound separate from the meanings of words; and
- take individual differences into account and relate to each child's level of phonological awareness.

Connecting Phonological Awareness to Reading and Writing

When introducing activities to develop children's phonological awareness try to link them to the various reading and writing activities occurring in your classroom. Be sure to show children how the activities they do will help them when they read and write. For example, if children encounter the word *bent* when reading or writing, demonstrate how being able to hear all the sounds in the word *bent* will help them spell and read the word. If they can write or read *bent*, demonstrate how knowing about the sounds they hear and the letters that represent the sounds in *bent* will help them read and write other words as well, such as the word *sent*.

During Read-Alouds To facilitate children's development of phonological awareness during read-aloud sessions, reread children's favorites with alliteration, rhyme, and other sound features that will assist them in becoming more conscious of the sounds in language. For example, read books such as *Six Sleepy Sheep* (Gordon 1991), which is about six sheep that drop off to sleep one by one. Throughout *Six Sleepy Sheep* numerous examples of alliteration (/s/ and /sh/), phoneme substitution (*sheep/sleep*) and phoneme deletion (*sleepy/sleep*) occur.

Books read during read-alouds may also be used as a stimulus for creating children's own texts that play with language. For example, *Six Sleepy Sheep* could become *Five Funny Fellows,* in which *Five funny fellows fell on five fluffy feathers.*

You may want to select some titles that focus on aspects of phonological awareness for read-alouds from the list at the end of this chapter.

During Shared Reading   During daily shared reading sessions introduce books and charts that play with the sounds in language. Introduce activities that focus on the concept of a word to assist children in becoming aware of words as separate entities in a stream of speech. Explain to the children that knowing where one word begins and ends in speech will help them when writing and reading. For example:

- Use a frame to locate particular words in a Big Book or on a chart and read the sentence with the children, leaving out the framed word. Have children listen, predict, identify, and say the framed word within the sentence.
- Have children count the number of words within spoken and written sentences.
- Write two copies of sentences from Big Books or charts used for shared reading on sentence strips. Cut one copy of each sentence into words. Have children count the number of words and match these words with an identical sentence strip. Reread the matched sentences, then remove words one at a time and help children listen for and identify the removed words within the spoken sentence.
- Prepare cloze exercises using familiar texts by covering predictable words. For instance, the following cloze exercise could be used with "Twinkle, Twinkle, Little Star" (or other rhymes the children know) to focus on a word in a line of print. Cover the words *wonder* and *high* and tell children that there is one word covered in each line. Then, read "Twinkle, Twinkle, Little Star" with the children, have them match each spoken word with a visible or a covered word, and have them identify the missing words.

> Twinkle, twinkle, little star,
> How I _____ what you are,
> Up above the world so _____,
> Like a diamond in the sky.

Have children check that the words they predict make sense. When you are predicting the missing word *high,* show the children how they could use the rhyming word *sky* in the next line to help them.

During Modeled, Shared, and Interactive Writing   During daily modeled, shared, and interactive writing sessions, do the following:

- Model how writing is speech written down.
- Model saying words slowly and stretching out their pronunciation in order to hear the individual sounds within them.

- Demonstrate strategies to use when attempting to spell unfamiliar words. In particular, focus on listening for the sounds in the words (and identifying the letter or letters that represent the sounds).
- Demonstrate the use of spaces between words, and focus children's attention on the point where one word ends and another begins.
- Have children count the number of words in sentences.
- Use a frame to locate particular words and read the sentence with the children, leaving out the framed word. Have children listen, predict, identify, and say the framed word within the sentence.

Independent Writing   As well as writing sessions that involve the modeling of various aspects of writing, children also need daily opportunities to write independently. When they are allowed to write for sustained periods of time, children become more competent in attempting spellings, often by consciously isolating the phonemes they hear in spoken words. When writing their own pieces, the children are also writing for real purposes as well as gaining practice in listening for beginning, middle, and ending sounds in words.

Identifying Children Needing Instruction

Not all children will need help to develop phonological awareness. Observe children's writing to see if they can isolate sentences into words and words into sounds. If they can, they are phonologically and phonemically aware and will not require much instruction to further develop this awareness. However, you may find that some children in kindergarten or grade 1 are continually writing strings of letters and other symbols, such as numbers and musical notes. These are the children who will benefit from involvement in a range of experiences that will help them develop phonological awareness. It may be useful to have these children complete a commercially available phonological awareness test, or to have them complete some of the following activities to determine their level of awareness.

If there are children from language backgrounds other than English in your class, they may have difficulty hearing and producing sounds in English. In addition to introducing phonological awareness activities in English with these children, make use of rhymes and traditional songs they know in their first languages. For example, here is a Cape Veridan (Creole derived from Portuguese) street rhyme:

Rei, capitão (King, captain)
Soldado, ladrão (Soldier, thief)
Menina bonita (Pretty mistress)
do meu coração (of my heart.)

And here is a Native American rhyme:

Hominy, succotash, raccoon, moose.
Succotash, raccoon, moose, nimoose . . .

If you wish, you can adapt any of the activities presented in this chapter for use with other languages.

When developing children's phonological awareness, be selective in the activities you choose. It is not necessary for children to complete all the activities described below. We have included them to suggest the variety of activities you may choose from.

Remember, do not spend so much time on these types of activities that you wind up with insufficient time for reading and writing.

Activities to Develop Phonological Awareness

Although there is general consensus among researchers about the need for children to have phonological awareness, there is little agreement about how it should be taught.

We present a range of activities designed to develop children's phonological awareness for you to try. In general, however, we suggest you make this teaching a form of action research in your classroom. Try to be aware of the effects and benefits that various activities have with your children, and only continue with those you find useful.

Phonological awareness tasks vary in the degree of challenge. Easier tasks include:

- recognizing rhymes and producing rhyming words;
- blending phonemes (for example, /s/, /a/, /t/ to form the word *sat*); and
- segmenting syllables into onsets and rimes (*c-ake, b-ake, sh-ake*).

When children can complete these tasks successfully, introduce the more difficult phonemic awareness tasks:

- segmenting phonemes (*dog:* /d/, /o/, /g/);
- isolating phonemes (the /s/ in *mess*);
- deleting phonemes (changing *meat* to *me*); and
- manipulating phonemes to form different words (*an* to *as*).

The tasks that follow are grouped according to the skill taught and are organized according to degree of difficulty, progressing from simple to more challenging.

Before investigating the sounds of speech, it may be necessary to introduce children to the concept of differentiating sounds by engaging them in sound discrimination activities based on human, animal, musical, or environmental sounds. Introduce activities that involve children in identifying sounds, distinguishing between far or near, loud or soft, and high or low sounds. Once children are able to understand the concept of sound, and distinguish these sounds, you may then introduce activities that focus on phonological awareness.

Rhyming Activities

Explain how words that rhyme sound the same at the end. Demonstrate how some words rhyme and others do not. Read rhyming texts, such as nursery rhymes, number rhymes, street rhymes, finger plays, stories with rhyme, and rhyming poems, to the children daily. Once they know the rhymes, you can use these texts to teach the concept of rhyme. When reading aloud or doing shared reading with texts that rhyme, pause before the second rhyming word and encourage children to predict what the word will be; one that should rhyme and make sense. The children may also locate the rhyming words in a text, although this is not necessary if you are focusing on their *hearing* the rhyme.

Splitting Rhymes   Have children select a rhyme they know for the following activity. Divide the class into two. Explain that one group will say or read the whole rhyme except for the second rhyming word, which the second group will say. For example:

> *Group 1:* Baa baa black sheep,
>   Have you any wool?
>   Yes sir, yes sir.
>   Three bags—
> *Group 2:* full.

Rhyming Substitution   Select a rhyme the children know well for rhyming substitution activities. Have them identify the rhyming words in the verse and help them think of different rhyming words to create new verses. For example:

> Eenie meenie, minie, mo,
> Catch a tiger ~~by the toe~~ in the snow,
> If he hollers let him go,
> Eenie meenie, minie, mo.

Oral Cloze   Create oral cloze activities using rhymes the children have memorized, focusing on rhyming words. For example, in the nursery rhyme "Humpty Dumpty," the word *fall* could be covered. The children would then use the rhyming word, *wall,* to assist them in predicting the covered word.

Games   Play games with the children to teach the idea of rhyme. For example:

- *We sound alike.* Use the children's names to make simple two-line jingles, then ask them to identify the words that rhyme. For example, "Tsei always likes to *play,* she likes to run *away*" and "Paul likes to throw the *ball,* high, high over the *wall.*"
- *Which words rhyme?* Use sets of three words in which two of the three rhyme. Explain to the children that you will say three words and two of them sound alike: they rhyme. Explain that one is different: it does not rhyme. Say the three words—for example, *"Fly, high, big"*—and ask, "Which two words rhyme?" Have several children name the rhyming pair to ensure and reinforce their understanding.
- *I am thinking of a word.* Say to the children, "I am thinking of a word for something we eat. It rhymes with *parrot.*" They then guess what the rhym-

ing word is, and whoever comes up with the correct word becomes the leader.

- *Alike—not alike.* Say various pairs of words, some rhyming and some not (for example, *bump/jump* and *hard/soft*). Have the children clap their hands when they hear the words that rhyme.
- *Finishing the rhyme.* Begin a rhyming couplet and have the children suggest words to finish the couplet. For example, have them complete the couplet "I can see Mary. She is so _____" (scary, hairy, . . .). For this activity, children may suggest nonsense words as long as they rhyme.
- *Rhyming groups.* Say a word, then have the children suggest words that rhyme with it. As the children say the words, list them on a chart. Have children underline the letter or letters that represent the rhyming sections of the words; help them see that the rhyming section occurs at the end of words. Throughout the week, add to the list and say the rhyming words.

Sound Blending Activities

Sound blending tasks require children to put together a series of discrete speech sounds to create a recognizable word. Here it is important to emphasize the connection between the blended word and its meaning in order to ensure that the children understand they are forming real words. Tell them that you have noticed that sometimes they try to sound out a word when they are reading, whether to check a prediction or to help them work out what the word is, and that you are going to help them do this.

Prior to introducing the more challenging task of blending isolated sounds, have the children blend compound words, syllables, and onsets with rimes.

Syllable Blends   Explain and demonstrate the meaning of syllables. Young children understand them when described as beats in a word. Beginning with words of two syllables, show children how syllables are blended to form words (*birth/day, yell/ow*). Instruct them to listen as you say a word, and pause between each syllable. Then ask them to say each word normally. When children can successfully complete this task with two-syllable words, increase the complexity by including words of three syllables (*yes/ter/day*) or four (*rhi/noc/er/os*).

Onset and Rimes   Blending activities should include blending onsets with rimes. An *onset* is the consonant or consonants preceding the vowel in a syllable (the /sh/ in *sh-op*), and a *rime* is a vowel and any following consonants of a syllable (the /op/ in *sh-op*).

Ask the children to listen as you say an onset with a rime, pausing between each; then ask them to say each word normally. Begin with words that have different onsets but the same rime—for example, /w/-/ell/, /b/-/ell/, /s/-/ell/, /d/-/ell/, /t/-/ell/, /sh/-/ell/, /y/-/ell/, and so on. When the children are ready, increase the complexity by introducing a variety of onsets with a variety of rimes—for example, /b/-/ack/, /r/-/ide/, and so on. For further information about onsets and rimes, see Chapter 6.

Games   Engage the children in games to help them understand blending sounds—for example:

- *Say the name.* Call the children to line up, to have lunch, and to move into other activities when they hear their name being said sound by sound (for example, /j/-/a/-/k/). Have them blend the sounds to say the name. The named child then responds to the instruction.
- *Robot talk.* Tell the children that you are a robot and will be saying words sound by sound, and their task is to say the word normally. Choose words that the children are familiar with, and for which the sounds can be easily distinguished. Begin playing this game with words of two phonemes (for example, *am*—/a/, /m/), then introduce words with three phonemes (*apple*—/a/, /p/, /l/) or four (*most*—/m/, /o/, /s/, /t/). Say each word slowly and have the children identify the word you are saying "like a robot." Have children take turns being the robot.
- *What am I thinking of?* Explain to the children that they have to listen carefully to identify what you are thinking of. Provide an initial clue, then articulate each sound of the answer separately. Children then blend the sounds together to identify the object. For example:

  I am thinking of a vehicle.
  I am a /t/-/r/-/u/-/k/.

Singing and Blending   Introduce blending activities sung to repetitive tunes, such as "When You're Happy and You Know It Clap Your Hands" and "The Bear Went over the Mountain."

- Sing the words below to the tune of "When You're Happy and You Know It Clap Your Hands." Tell the children that you will say a word slowly, sound by sound—for example, /b/-/ee/-/k/ (*beak*). Their task is to blend the sounds to say a word and "tell us all."
  Say /b/-/ee/-/k/ while the children listen. Then sing the following song:

  When you think you know the word, tell us all.
  When you think you know the word, tell us all.
  When you think you know the word,
  Please tell us what you heard.
  When you think you know the word,
  Please tell us all.

  Repeat the verse using words of varying sounds and length.

- Sing the lyrics of "The Bear Went over the Mountain." Sing the first four lines of the song with the children:

  The bear went over the mountain,
  The bear went over the mountain,

The bear went over the mountain
To see what he could see.

Then name something the bear might see—for example:

The bear could see a /r/-/a/-/n/-/b/-/o/ isolating the sounds in the word *rainbow*. Give the children time to blend the sounds to form *rainbow*. Then repeat the song and name a different item.

Sound Segmenting Activities

Sound segmenting involves isolating the sounds in a spoken word. It is a difficult phonemic awareness task. Introduce segmenting activities when you notice students attempting to do this as they write. Tell them you have noticed that they are trying to listen for the sounds they hear in words when they are writing, so you are going to help them do this.

Involve the children in modeled, shared, and interactive writing where they listen for the sounds in words and help you write them. Discuss how listening for sounds in words will help them with their own writing.

Before segmenting words into isolated sounds, help the children break spoken language into more easily perceivable units of words and syllables, and match these to physical movements, such as marching in place or clapping. Begin by segmenting sentences into words. Then break compound words into the smaller words within them, segment words into syllables, and divide syllables into onsets and rimes.

Segmenting Sentences into Words   Here are two activities to help children segment sentences:

- *Tapping words.* Tell children to listen carefully as you say each word in a sentence, and ask them to give one tap for each word they hear. Demonstrate: say the sentence, then repeat it and tap once as you say each word. Once children understand, let individuals say some sentences for the others to give a tap for each word heard.
- *Counting words.* Tell children to listen carefully. Explain that you will say a sentence normally, and then again more slowly, pausing after each word. Provide children with counters, explaining that they are to put a counter down for each word they hear. Say the sentence, and have children count the counters they have for the sentence. Repeat the sentence and count the words together so that the children can check their response. Once children understand the task, let them say some sentences, first as they normally would, and then word by word.

Segmenting Words into Syllables   To help children differentiate syllables, activities similar to the sentence-segmenting ones above can be used.

- *Clapping syllables.* Explain to the children that you will say some words and that they are to clap once for each syllable or beat they hear. Demonstrate the task. Using children's names and other words familiar to them, say a word, then repeat it and clap once as you say each syllable. Repeat using words of two, three, and four syllables. To give children the sense that longer words have more syllables than shorter words, refer to class charts with children's names, months, days of the week, and so on, and clap the number of syllables or beats in these words. Discuss the relationship between the number of syllables and word length. Demonstrate how listening for each part of the word when writing can help with spelling.

- *Counting syllables.* Tell the children to listen carefully. Explain that you will say a word normally, and then again more slowly, pausing after each syllable. Provide children with counters, explaining that they are to put a counter down for each syllable they hear. Say the word, then have the children count their counters. Repeat the word and count the syllables together so that the children can check their responses. Once children understand the task, let them say some words, first as they normally would, and then syllable by syllable. Vary the task by adding one syllable at a time to sets of words—for example, *mat, mat-ress, mat-ress-es.* Demonstrate saying each word in the group and tapping out each word. Have the children repeat the words as you tap them out. Repeat the activity for other word groups.

- *Names and syllables.* Seat the class in a circle with one player in the middle. Explain that the player in the middle will clap out a rhythm for a name, and if it matches their name, they should clap it back.

Segmenting Syllables into Onsets and Rimes   Instruct the children to listen as you say a one-syllable word consisting of an onset and a rime—for example, *pick* (/p/-/ick/). Explain that they are to break each word you say into the first and last parts. Assist them by doing the following:

- Say the word, pause, then say just the onset, and have the children add the rime.
- Begin with words that have different onsets but the same rime—for example /th/-/ank/, /s/-/ank/, /b/-/ank/, and /dr/-/ank/; or the same onset and a different rime—for example, /b/-/ake/, /b/-/ug/, /b/-/ell/, and /b/-/ack/.

When the children are ready, increase the complexity of the task by introducing one-syllable words with a variety of onsets and rimes—for example, /p/-/ain/, /s/ -/ide/, /j/-/oke/, and /b/-/est/—or having children segment the whole word without assistance.

Segmenting Phonemes   How many sounds do you hear?

Demonstrate to the children how words can be broken into sounds. For example, say a word (*dog*), then say the individual sounds, pausing slightly between each one (/d/, /o/, /g/). Explain that the children are to listen and break the words you say into sounds and count the number of sounds. Gradually increase the number of phonemes to be listened for.

Singing and Segmenting   Introduce segmenting activities sung to tunes like "Here We Go Looby Loo." This activity involves children in separating each sound they hear in a spoken word. For example, sing the following lyrics to the tune of "Here We Go Looby Loo," and have the children complete the following task:

> Listening to the sounds
> Listening to the sounds
> Tell me the sounds you heard
> The sounds you heard in my word: *night*

(Say the word slowly.)

> /n/ is the first sound
> /igh/ is the next
> /t/ is the last
> These are the sounds that I heard: /n/-/igh/-/t/—*night.*

Elkonin Boxes   During interactive or independent writing sessions, use Elkonin boxes to assist children in thinking about the number and order of sounds in words. (Make sure that the words you use are familiar to the children.) In an Elkonin box (named after D. B. Elkonin), a picture of a word is placed above a series of connected boxes, each representing a sound (not a letter) in the word illustrated. For *shell,* for example, there would be three boxes under the picture of a shell, for the three sounds /sh/-/e/-/l/.

Demonstrate the task by saying the word (for example, *shell*) slowly, while moving counters into the boxes, sound by sound. Encourage the children to join in the process, by either moving counters into the boxes for each sound articulated or by saying the word slowly while you move the counters.

As children become more proficient, allow them to assume greater responsibility for completing the task, and simultaneously increase its complexity. For example, have the children both say the word and move the counters, and remove the boxes and pictures.

Make sure that children understand that the purpose of the activity is to help them learn how to isolate and order the sounds in words. Later, you can use Elkonin boxes in teaching the children that letters represent sounds in spoken words. For example, when your students attempt to spell unknown words in their writing, you may want to use the boxes to help them identify and write the letters that represent the sounds they hear by having the number of boxes correspond to the number of sounds in the word.

Sound Isolation Activities

Although it is technically impossible to isolate many of the phonemes, it is helpful to have children listen for sounds at the beginning, middle, and end of words. This is a strategy used by beginning writers.

Name the First Sound Demonstrate to children how to listen for the first sound in a word. Do this during shared and interactive writing, with children helping you write a word or trying on their own to write the letter that represents the beginning sound of a word.

Alliteration Introduce literature that features alliteration, the repetition of the initial sounds in neighboring words or stressed syllables—for example, "Richly robed rhinoceroses riding in rickety red rickshaws" (from *Animalia*, Base 1986). Present one or two alliterative pieces each day. Say them, then have the children repeat them after you and identify the repeated sound.

Exaggerate and Repeat Introduce activities in which sounds are exaggerated and repeated to help children hear sounds in speech. These may include repeating sounds at the beginning of words; for example, when singing "Old Macdonald Had a Farm," you may want to modify some lines to include repetition. For instance, instead of singing "With a moo-moo here, and a moo-moo there," you would sing "With a m-m-moo here, and a m-m-moo there." While having fun repeating sounds, the children will also learn about the smaller units of speech.

Children's Names Ask the children to form groups according to the first sound in their name—for example, *Christy, Karen,* and *Coban.* Have the children say all the names clearly and identify the first sound in each name.

Vary the game by asking a group of children whose names begin with different sounds to be leaders—for example, Naoko, Moses, Luis, and Sue. Explain to the children that each leader, for example Naoko, will take turns in asking a child, "Do you know a word that begins with the same sound as Naoko?" Children who have a correct answer join that team. The biggest team at the end of the session wins.

When the children are confident in listening for and forming groups according to the initial sound of their names, help them do the same using the final sound in their names.

Shopping Collect pictures of items that can be bought at a supermarket—for example, cakes, ketchup, and cauliflower; and toothpaste, tomatoes, and tarts. Select a leader to distribute several pictures to each player. Give the leader a shopping basket and a card with a picture—for example, a picture of a cookie. Explain to the children that the leader will say, "Who bought something that begins with the same sound as the first sound in *cookie*?" and each child who has a card with a picture of something beginning with a /k/ sound will then name the item and place the picture in the shopping basket. The leader changes after each sound. The next leader then shows a picture beginning with a different sound and repeats the question "Who bought something that begins with the same sound as . . . ?" The children continue the game until the "shopping" is completed.

Vary the game according to the topic the children are studying. For example, if they are studying animals use pictures of animals who are placed in zoos, farms, and so on. Another variation could be to group the items according to their middle and final sounds.

Sound-to-Word Matching   Help children identify words that begin with a given sound from a series of pictures of familiar objects (boy, boat, house) and select those that begin with the sound, for example, the /b/ sound.

Name the Final and Middle Sounds   When children can confidently isolate beginning sounds in words, start to focus on the end sounds. Demonstrate listening for sounds at the end of words; for example, *dad, hold,* and *made* all end in the /d/ sound. As soon as children can identify sounds in both the beginning and the end positions of words, have them listen for sounds in the medial positions. For example, model listening for the /u/ sound in the middle position of *cut, blood,* and *brother.*

Singing and Isolating Sounds   Using the tunes of simple songs, such as "Skip to My Lou," "I'm a Little Teapot," and "Old Macdonald Had a Farm," change the lyrics to focus on phonemes in the beginning, ending, and medial positions of words.

For examples, to the tune of "Skip to My Lou," you would sing:

Who has a /k/ word to share with us?
Who has a /k/ word to share with us?
Who has a /k/ word to share with us?
A word that begins with the /k/ sound.

The children then suggest words. For example, if a child suggested *cut,* the class could sing the following.

Cut is a word that starts with /k/
Cut is a word that starts with /k/
Cut is a word that starts with /k/
Cut begins with the /k/ sound.

The sound focused on may instead be in the final position. The question sung might be:

Who has a /k/ word to share with us? . . .
A word that ends with the /k/ sound.

with the answer

Duck is a word that ends with /k/ . . .
Duck ends with the /k/ sound.

The song can also be used to explore medial sounds.

Another song that can be adapted for sound exploration activities is "I'm a Little Teapot." Have children take turns suggesting a word and selecting a sound to be listened for. For example, if a child suggested *puppy* and the /p/ sound, the class could sing the following lyrics to the tune of "I'm a Little Teapot":

Puppy, puppy, puppy
/p/, /p/, /p/
We can hear the /p/ sound,
/p/, /p/, /p/.

The teacher or child then asks/sings:

Who has another /p/ word
/p/, /p/, /p/?
Please tell us your /p/ word
/p/, /p/, /p/.

As well as listening for sounds, have children identify the position or positions in which the sound occurs—at the beginning, end, or middle of a word.

"Old Macdonald Had a Farm" is another adaptable song. Have children identify the sounds in the initial, final, and medial positions of words by singing lyrics similar to the following.

Which sound comes first in these words:
Five, fat and *fish?*

Pause for the children to respond: /f/. Then sing:

/f/ is the first sound in these words:
Five, fat and *fish.*
With a /f/, /f/, here, and a /f/, /f/ there,
Here a /f/, there a /f/, everywhere a /f/, /f/.
/f/ is the first sound in these words:
Five, fat and *fish.*

Then continue:

Which sound is last in these words:
Bell and *tail* and *hole?* . . .

Or

Which sound is in the middle of these words:
Plant and *plaid* and *trap?*

Which Consonant Blend Is Different?   Have children discriminate between words beginning with consonant blends. For example, tell them, "I am going to say words that begin like *brown*. If you hear a word that begins a different way, clap your hands." Then say *brother, bread, blink, brush*. Repeat the words if necessary. Vary the game by saying, "The word is *grass*. Which is different: *green, gray, chicken, grow?*"

Tongue Twisters   Tongue twisters are fun to say and provide children with practice in listening for repeated sounds. Introduce one or two tongue twisters each day. Say them, then have the children repeat them after you. Challenge the children to say them as quickly as they can, and at other times as slowly as they can. Have them identify and locate the position of the repeated sound.

Secret Sounds   Place a number of objects that begin with the same sound in a box. Explain to the children that they are to identify the sound that each object begins with. Ask them to name the object, listen for the beginning sound, and place the object on a line. As each object is added, repeat the names of the previously placed objects, having children listen carefully to the first sound in each word. Vary this activity by placing objects in the box that end with the same sound or have the same sound in the middle.

Assonance   Read literature containing assonance (the repetition of vowel sounds within words)—for example, the /ay/ sound in "It rains and hails and shakes the sails," (Shaw 1986).

Consonance   Read literature containing consonance (the repetition of consonant sounds within words)—for example, the /p/ sound in "Clippity-clop, . . . Plip-plop," (Allen 1994).

Odd Word Out   Ask children to listen carefully to four words. Explain that one word begins with a different sound from the others. Model the task: *same, seven, fork, salt.* Have children repeat the words, identify the word that is different, and explain why.

Sound Deletion Activities

Tasks requiring children to remove phonological units from words and to say the newly formed word require a high degree of phonological awareness. When children are ready, introduce activities similar to the following, which involve deleting syllables or phonemes from varying positions in words.

- *Deleting syllables.* Have the children do the following:

  > Say *rainbow* without *rain* or *toothbrush* without *brush.*
  > Try to say *bookcase* without *book.*
  > Say *sitting* without *ing.*
  > Say *kangaroo* without *roo.*

- *Deleting phonemes.* Try the following:

  > Say *sat* without /s/.
  > What word would be left if the /m/ sound was taken away from *man?*
  > Try to say *tin* without the /t/.
  > What sound do you hear in *stake* that is missing in *take?*
  > What sound do you hear in *plant* that is missing in *plan?*
  > What sound do you hear in *plant* that is missing in *pant?*
  > Say *made* without /d/.
  > Try to say *digs* without /z/.

Continue to observe children's invented spelling in their writing to gauge the extent of their phonemic awareness, and help those who are not developing strategies to try to spell unknown words.

Sound Manipulation Activities

Adding or substituting sounds in the words of familiar rhymes and songs helps children focus on sounds in speech. Repeated lines lend themselves to sound additions and substitutions.

Sing and Substitute   Help children form substitutions with repeated lines of known songs, such as "Hokey Pokey," "Old Macdonald Had a Farm," "The Farmer in the Dell," and "This Is the Way We Wash Our Clothes."

For example, change the chorus of "Hokey Pokey" from:

Oh, the Hokey, Pokey, Pokey!
Oh, the Hokey, Pokey, Pokey!
Oh, the Hokey, Pokey, Pokey!
Knees bend,
Arms stretch, Ra! Ra! Ra!

to:

Oh, the Nokey, Nokey, Nokey!
Oh, the Nokey, Nokey, Nokey!
Oh, the Nokey, Nokey, Nokey!
Knees bend,
Arms stretch, Na! Na! Na!

In "Old Macdonald Had a Farm" you can change the repeated line from "E-I-E-I-O" to "me-mi-me-mi-mo," "fe-fi-fe-fi-fo," and so on.

For "The Farmer in the Dell," adding or substituting sounds may result in a different line. "Heigh-ho, the derry-o" may change to "Feigh-fo, the merry-o," and so on.

"This Is the Way We Wash Our Clothes" may be sung to the tune of "Here We Go Round the Mulberry Bush" and may be changed from:

This is the way we wash our clothes,
Rub-a-dub-dub, rub-a-dub-dub.
Watch them getting clean and white,
Rub-a-dub-dub, rub-a-dub-dub.

to:

This is the way we wash our clothes,
Scrub-a-scrub-scrub, scrub-a-scrub-scrub . . .

Trade Books That Play with Sound in Language

Allen, P. 1983. *Bertie and the Bear*. Melbourne: Picture Puffin. (Alliteration)
———. 1994. *Clippity-Clop*. Melbourne: Picture Puffin. (Consonance)

Armitage, R., and D. Armitage. 1985. *Grandma Goes Shopping.* Middlesex, UK: Puffin. (Alliteration)

Base, G. 1986. *Animalia.* New York: Harry N. Abrams. (Alliteration)

Carlstrom, N. W. 1994. *What Would You Do If You Lived at the Zoo?* Boston: Little, Brown. (Alliteration, phoneme substitution)

Cole, J., and S. Calmenson. 1991. *Eentsy, Weentsy Spider: Finger Plays and Action Rhymes.* New York: Mulberry Books. (Rhyme)

———. 1992. *Pat-a-Cake and Other Play Rhymes.* New York: Mulberry Books. (Rhyme)

———. 1993. *Six Sick Sheep: 101 Tongue Twisters.* New York: A Beech Tree Paperback. (Alliteration, assonance, consonance)

Cope, W. 1988. *Twiddling Your Thumbs: Hand Rhymes.* London: Faber and Faber. (Rhyme)

Corebett, P., and S. Emerson. 1993. *Dancing and Singing Games.* New York: Kingfisher Books. (Rhyme)

de Paola, Tomie. 1988. *Hey Diddle Diddle and Other Mother Goose Rhymes.* New York: G. P. Putnam's Sons. (Rhyme)

Fortunata. 1968. *Catch a Little Fox.* New York: Scholastic. (Rhyme)

Galdone, P. 1968. *Henny Penny.* New York: Scholastic. (Phoneme substitution)

Geraghty, P. 1992. *Stop That Noise!* New York: Crown. (Phoneme substitution)

Gordon, J. 1991. *Six Sleepy Sheep.* New York: Puffin Books. (Alliteration, rhyme)

Hague, K. 1984. *Alphabears.* New York: Henry Holt. (Alliteration)

Hawkins, C., and J. Hawkins. 1986. *Jen the Hen.* New York: G. P. Putnam's Sons. (Phoneme substitution)

———. 1986. *Mig the Pig.* New York: G. P. Putnam's Sons. (Phoneme substitution)

———. 1986. *Pat the Cat.* New York: G. P. Putnam's Sons. (Phoneme substitution)

———. 1986. *Tog the Dog.* New York: G. P. Putnam's Sons. (Phoneme substitution)

Hutchins, P. 1972. *Don't Forget the Bacon!* New York: Morrow. (Phoneme substitution)

Kellogg, S. 1985. *Chicken Little.* New York: Mulberry Books. (Phoneme substitution)

Larkin, J. 1993. *Alphabet and Number Rhymes.* Melbourne: Macmillan Education. (Rhyme)

Mahey, M. 1987. *17 Kings and 42 elephants.* New York: Dial. (Phoneme substitution)

McCloskey, R. 1941. *Make Way for Ducklings.* New York: Viking. (Phoneme substitution)

Obligado, L. 1986. *Faint Frogs Feeling Feverish.* New York: Picture Puffin. (Alliteration)

Seuss, Dr. 1963. *Dr Seuss's ABC.* New York: Random House. (Alliteration)

———. 1965. *Fox in Socks.* New York: Random House. (Assonance, phoneme substitution)

———. 1974. *There's a Wocket in My Pocket.* New York: Random House. (Phoneme substitution)

Shaw, N. 1986. *Sheep in a Jeep.* Boston: Houghton Mifflin. (Assonance)

———. 1989. *Sheep on a Ship.* Boston: Houghton Mifflin. (Assonance)

———. 1989. *Sheep in a Shop.* Boston: Houghton Mifflin. (Assonance)

Sturges, P. 1996. *What's That Sound, Woolly Bear?* Boston: Little, Brown. (Phoneme substitution and addition)

Tallon, R. 1979. *Zoophabets.* New York: Scholastic.

Van Allsberg, C. 1987. *The Z Was Zapped.* Boston: Houghton Mifflin. (Alliteration)

References

Adams, M. J. 1991. "Beginning to Read: A Critique by Literacy Professionals and a Response by Marilyn Jager Adams." *The Reading Teacher* 44, 6.

Elkonin, D. B. 1973. "USSR." In J. Downing, ed., *Comparative Reading,* 551–580. New York: Macmillan.

Griffith, P. L., and M. W. Olson. 1992. "Phonemic Awareness Helps Beginning Readers Break the Code." *The Reading Teacher* 45, 7.

Moustafa, M. 1997. *Beyond Traditional Phonics: Research Discoveries and Reading Instruction.* Portsmouth, NH: Heinemann.

Yopp, H. K. 1992. "Developing Phonemic Awareness in Young Children." *The Reading Teacher* 45, 9.

Weaver, C., ed. 1998. *Reconsidering a Balanced Approach to Reading.* Urbana, IL: National Council of Teachers of English.

6

Onsets and Rimes

The components of an English syllable are known as onsets and rimes. The *onset* is the part of the syllable that comes before the first vowel and the *rime* is the part of the syllable from the first vowel onward.

The terms *rime* and *rhyme* refer to spoken language, not print. They both refer to sounds in words. *Rhyme* is used in poetry to refer to words that have the same ending sound, such as *wandering* and *pondering*. *Rime* is used in linguistics to describe a unit of speech within a spoken syllable. Linguists would say that the words *pie, sky,* and *high* have the same rime; poets would say that they rhyme. Poets would say that the words *wandering* and *pondering* rhyme; linguists would describe *wandering* as having the onset /w/, the rime /and/ (pronounced /ond/), the rime /er/, and the rime /ing/, and *pondering* as having the onset /p/, the rime /ond/, the rime /er/, and the rime /ing/.

Here are some examples of onsets and rimes to help illustrate their meaning:

- In the word *bat* the onset is /b/ and the rime is /at/.
- In the word *bricks* the onset is /br/ and the rime is /icks/.
- In the word *to* the onset is /t/ and the rime is /o/.
- In the word *on* there is no onset; the rime is /on/.
- In the word *contact* the onset in the first syllable is /c/ and the rime is /on/ and the onset in the second syllable is /t/ and the rime is /act/.
- Words such as *beak* and *break* have the same spelling pattern or letter string, but they do not rhyme so they have different rimes.

- The word *dogs* has four phonemes (/d/, /o/, /g/, /z/), but only one onset (/d/) and one rime (/ogs/).

Although onset-rime explorations are part of phonological awareness, their importance in helping children with spelling and reading is such that we devote a separate chapter to them in this book. Researchers such as Treiman (1983, 1985), Goswami and Bryant (1990), and Moustafa (1995) have suggested that children first learn to split spoken syllables into onsets and rimes before they analyze words into their constituent phonemes, when onsets or rimes consist of more than one phoneme. So they can break down *flat* into /fl/-/at/ before they can separate it into the phonemes /f/-/l/-/a/-/t/. Goswami (1986) also found that children use their knowledge of how to say some print words to help them figure out how to say other print words, and Moustafa (1995) found that children use their knowledge of onsets and rimes in words they already know how to pronounce, rather than their knowledge of letter-sound correspondences, to pronounce unfamiliar words. Thus, if they knew the words *green* and *black* they could use onset-rime analogy to produce a made-up word *grack*. Goswami discovered that all children, regardless of reading level, have a natural ability to make these analogies between words.

We have found that when children are encouraged to apply these same strategies to spelling they are able to spell many new words based on the knowledge they have about how to spell other words. For example, knowing how to spell *can* helps them work out how to spell other words with the same rime and the same spelling pattern or letter string, such as *fan, man, pan, ran, tan, van, than, plan, span*. When work with such onsets and rimes is coupled with significant amounts of shared reading, particularly if children learn to make a one-to-one match with what they are reading, children's use of analogies to figure out the spelling of new words is enhanced. And when children learn to recognize and write many high-frequency words, this added knowledge is even more helpful. Just as in reading, the number of print words from which children can make analogies is important.

Once children have been immersed in shared reading and writing, understand the concept of a word, and are given opportunities for independent reading and writing, they have both the experience and the motivation to explore the ways words work through the notion of onsets and rimes. This exploration may be going on while they are still learning about letters and learning some high-frequency words, and will be among the experiences that help them develop phonological awareness. The use of onset and rime analogy will continue as children discover sound/symbol relationships and learn about spelling patterns.

Although onset and rime theory applies to English, Moustafa (1997) points out that it does not apply to all languages. In Spanish, for example, syllables may begin with either a consonant or a vowel, but when they begin with a consonant, the initial consonant and vowel cannot be divided.

Knowledge of onsets and rimes can also be limited in English words because phonemes in English can be represented in more than one way. For example, knowing that the onset in *win* is represented by the letter *w* and that the rime in *feet* is represented by the letter string *eet* does not help you to spell the word *wheat* (/w/-/eet/). However, scholars such as Dombey et al. (1998) claim that rimes are much more reliable in their sound-spelling relationships than are individual phonemes. We find that it is useful for children to explore the various representations for each of the phonemes in the English language so that they know the possible ways to represent an onset or a rime. Chapter 7 explains how to get children involved in sound explorations, but they also need extensive encounters with print if they are to know whether a particular spelling looks right.

Common Onsets and Rimes

The lists of onsets and rimes provided here are useful to remind you of the range of work you may do with them, but they are not intended to be used in a set order. The study of onsets and rimes will occur throughout your students' reading and writing experiences and the building of word lists in your classroom. Although many words are listed below for each of the rimes, it is more meaningful if the children suggest words for the various onsets and rimes and you discuss their meaning when necessary.

Onsets

All of the consonants are possible onsets as well as the following digraphs and blends, some of which are more common than others:

Digraphs   Digraphs consist of more than one letter, but together they represent one sound. This sound may vary in different words. They include the following:

ch	cheese, Charlotte, choir
gh	ghost
gn	gnat
kn	know
mn	mnemonics
ph	photo
pn	pneumonia
ps	psalm
sc	scissors
sh	shed
th	this, think
wh	when, who
wr	wrong

Blends   Blends have more than one letter and more than one sound—for example:

bl	bleed
br	bread
cl	clock

cr	creep
dr	drop
dw	dwarf
fl	flew
fr	friend
gl	glow
gr	grow
gw	Gwen
kl	kleptomania
kr	krill
pl	play
pr	press
qu	quack
sc	scare
sk	skate
sl	slow
sm	smack
sn	snap
sp	spin
st	sting
sw	swim
tr	trap
tw	twin
chl	chlorine
chr	chrome
scr	scrap
shr	shrimp
spr	spring
squ	squad
str	strong
thr	throat

Rimes

According to Fry (1998), the most common rimes, represented by the following spelling patterns, in order of frequency in monosyllabic words, can make more than 650 one-syllable words. Some of these rimes can be represented by spelling patterns other then those given here, so when you are developing a list of words that have the same rime your students may suggest words other than those listed. For example, if you are developing a list of words with the rime /eed/ children might also suggest words such as *bead;* if you are developing a list of words with the rime /y/ as in *cry,* children might suggest words such as *my, high, die, I,* and *buy.* You should accept such alternative words, agreeing that they have the same sound but explaining that they have a different spelling pattern and so could be listed in other columns. However, many of the following rimes are sometimes referred to as "dependable" rimes because they tend to be represented most of the time by only one spelling pattern.

/ay/ ay	bay, day, Fay, gay, hay, jay, Kay, lay, may, May, pay, ray, Ray, say, way, spray, tray, play, pray, slay, cray, clay
/ill/ ill	bill, Bill, dill, fill, gill, hill, Jill, kill, mill, pill, quill, sill, till, will, drill, frill, grill, shrill, still, krill
/ip/ ip	dip, hip, kip, lip, nip, pip, quip, rip, sip, tip, zip, chip, clip, ship, skip, strip, trip, whip
/at/ at	bat, cat, fat, hat, mat, pat, rat, sat, vat, brat, chat, flat, that, splat
/am/ am	dam, ham, jam, Pam, ram, Sam, clam, cram, sham, tram, pram, wham
/ag/ ag	bag, gag, lag, rag, sag, tag, wag, brag, stag, crag, drag, flag
/ack/ ack	back, hack, Jack, lack, knack, pack, quack, rack, sack, tack, black, shack, slack, smack, snack, stack, track, whack
/ank/ ank	bank, dank, lank, rank, sank, tank, drank, Frank, prank, shank, stank
/ick/ ick	Dick, hick, kick, lick, Mick, Nick, pick, quick, Rick, sick, tick, wick, brick, chick, click, crick, prick, slick, stick, trick
/ell/ ell	bell, cell, dell, fell, hell, quell, sell, tell, well, shell
/ot/ ot	bot, cot, dot, got, hot, jot, lot, not, pot, rot, tot, blot, clot, shot, slot
/ing/ ing	ding, king, ping, ring, sing, wing, bring, cling, fling, sling, sting, string, thing, wring
/ap/ ap	cap, gap, lap, map, nap, rap, sap, tap, zap, chap, clap, snap, strap, trap, wrap
/unk/ unk	bunk, dunk, gunk, hunk, junk, punk, shrunk, sunk
/ail/ ail	bail, fail, flail, frail, hail, jail, mail, nail, pail, rail, sail, tail, trail, wail
/ain/ ain	bain, brain, drain, gain, grain, pain, rain, stain, train
/eed/ eed	deed, feed, greed, heed, need, seed, speed, steed, weed
/y/ y	by, cry, dry, fly, fry, my, ply, pry, shy, sty, thy, try, why
/out/ out	about, bout, clout, gout, lout, pout, snout, shout, stout
/ug/ ug	bug, hug, jug, mug, plug, rug, shrug, slug, thug, tug
/op/ op	bop, cop, chop, clop, crop, flop, hop, mop, plop, pop, shop, slop, stop, top
/in/ in	bin, din, fin, grin, kin, pin, sin, shin, tin, thin, twin, win
/an/ an	an, ban, bran, can, clan, Dan, fan, flan, Jan, man, pan, plan, ran, span, Stan, tan, than, van
/est/ est	best, jest, nest, pest, quest, rest, test, west

/ink/ ink	brink, chink, clink, drink, link, mink, pink, rink, sink, shrink, slink, stink, wink
/ow/ ow	bow, brow, cow, how, now, pow, prow, row, sow, vow, wow
/ow/ ow	bow, blow, crow, flow, glow, know, low, row, show, slow, stow, tow, throw
/ew/ ew	brew, crew, dew, Jew, knew
/ore/ ore	bore, chore, core, more, pore, shore, store, tore, wore
/ed/ ed	bed, bled, bred, fed, led, Ned, red, shed, sled, Ted, wed
/ab/ ab	cab, crab, dab, drab, grab, jab, nab
/ob/ ob	Bob, blob, cob, gob, job, lob, mob, rob, sob
/ock/ ock	block, chock, clock, cock, crock, dock, flock, frock, knock, lock, mock, rock, shock, sock, stock
/ake/ ake	awake, bake, brake, cake, drake, fake, flake, Jake, lake, rake, sake, shake, stake, take, wake
/ine/ ine	brine, dine, fine, line, mine, pine, shine, wine
/ight/ ight	blight, bright, knight, fight, flight, fright, light, might, night, plight, right, sight, tight
/im/ im	brim, dim, grim, him, Jim, prim, rim, Tim, vim, whim
/uck/ uck	buck, cluck, duck, luck, muck, puck, pluck, ruck, suck, stuck, shuck
/um/ um	gum, glum, hum, plum, rum, sum

Exploring Onsets and Rimes

The most useful aspect of knowing about onsets and rimes is that by starting with one word children can work out how to read and spell other words. The more print words children are familiar with, the better able they are to use analogy—for example, not only will they work out how to read or spell *man* because they know *can,* but they will also figure out how to read and spell *smack* because they know the words <u>smile</u> and <u>back</u>.

Children need to be involved in a lot of shared reading and writing so as to become familiar with many words. Although they are all capable of using analogy to figure out words, some will use it intuitively while others will need explicit demonstration and explanation of how it will help them as readers and writers. The best opportunities for you to provide demonstration occur during shared reading and shared or interactive writing, while working with a group in guided reading, and when conferring with a child during independent reading and writing.

When exploring a rime with children be aware that the rime may be represented in different ways, and all will need to be accepted. For example, if they know the word *may* from a shared reading experience, you could ask them to think of other words that the word *may* would help them read and write. Their suggestions may include *say, play, day, neigh,* and *they.* List the words with the different spelling patterns in different columns:

say   neigh   they
play
day

You could write the rime in each word in a different color than the onset and use a different color for each rime. Talk about how the words sound the same but have different spelling patterns, and help children determine whether one of the spelling patterns is more common than the others. Discuss how thinking about words in this way can help the children with their own reading and writing.

Lists of words that have the same rime and the same spelling pattern (referred to by many teachers as *word families*) may be written on charts for children to refer to for reading and writing. You can also make flip books, word wheels, card games, and so on, but these will be much more meaningful if they are developed from work you do with the children during the type of experiences described below. Activities with magnetic letters, such as building words or changing a letter to make a new word, can be used as follow-ups to these reading and writing experiences.

Using Shared Reading

Use familiar Big Books or charts of songs or poems and select a word the children recognize that is suitable for onset-rime analogy. For example, in a grade K or 1 classroom you could select the word *cat* from a known poem and write that word on a chart. Have each child write the word on an erasable board. Then ask them to think of other words they could spell like the word *cat* and have them try words on their boards. Observe what children do so that you can gauge individual understanding, then compile a list of the children's words, with the children reading the list each time a word is added. The rime part of the words (*at*) could be written in a different color. Place the chart where children can refer to it for reading and writing.

A further extension of this activity is to ask children to include words that have *at* words within them, such as *batting.* (Although you won't embark on a major study of the generalizations for adding *ing* to base words, if enough examples are written where the consonant is doubled, children may figure out how to spell similar words.)

You or the children may also make games, flip books, or word wheels using the rime that has been explored, but the most important conclusion to the exploration is for you to talk about how this work will help them with their own reading and writing.

Ask the children to think of sentences that contain any of these words and write them for the children to read. The class may be able to compose a story with many of these words; it will probably be a silly story, however, as it is difficult to compose a rich story when you are trying to use many words with the same rime. Still, the children who wrote it will find it meaningful, and they could make it into an illustrated class book for rereading. Such a story may be likened to books written by Dr. Seuss. For example, a grade 1 class wrote the following story:

One day a fat cat sat on a hat. Splat! The hat went flat! That cat was a brat.

The children enjoyed drawing funny illustrations to accompany the sentences, and the resulting book was much more meaningful for them to read because they had produced it.

You could also have individuals or pairs write some relevant sentences and make a class book such as *Our Book of at Words,* with the first page of the book stating "If I know *cat,* these are some other words I can read and spell," with the appropriate list written underneath, and the rest of the book containing children's illustrated sentences. As a small part of the rich book collection in your classroom, these may be used for reading.

Sometimes individuals or pairs like to write entire books of their own, such as the following, written by groups of four in Shawneen Petersen's class at Pine Springs Elementary School, Fairfax County, Virginia, after they had explored *ip* words together:

Zip and Pip

Once upon a time there was a boy named Zip and a girl named Pip. They were going on a trip on a ship. The flag on the ship had a rip. Zip tried to fix the rip but he took a flip on the ship. Pip found a strip and fixed the rip. They had a good trip. (Gerald, Katy, Kevin, Annie)

My Trip to Planet Flip

I went to Planet Flip. I saw my friend Chip. I tried to do a flip but I tripped and hurt my hip. Our maps started to rip. We jumped ship to take a dip. We started to drip. It was a fun trip. (Dylan, Joe, Amy, Morgan)

When children create their own material, they have the chance to practice thinking of and constructing similar words from a known word.

Another way to demonstrate onset and rime analogy during shared reading is to explicitly show children how to read an unfamiliar word by using what they know about another word with the same rime and letter string. For example, you may demonstrate how to figure out the word *black* in the chant "Mary Mack" by starting with a known word *back,* or how to figure out the word *sheep* in the rhyme "Baa Baa Black Sheep" by starting with the known words *she* and *keep.* Again, explain how children can use this strategy in their own reading, and work with individuals who need more help during independent reading time. You need to demonstrate these concepts regularly and with many different words so that your students will learn how to do this independently to help them figure out words they do not know.

Using Shared and Interactive Writing

When you are being the scribe during shared writing time, demonstrate by thinking out loud how you can figure out how to spell a word by knowing a similar word. For example, if you are writing about the life cycle of chickens, you may demonstrate how to spell *lay* by knowing the word *day*. You could also show how to use the beginning and ending of known words to spell a new word. For example, if the children know *big* and *look* you can show them how to use parts of these words to spell *book*. If necessary, use magnetic letters to show this.

When you are encouraging the children to be the scribes during interactive writing, help them use onset and rime analogy to go from a word they know to an unknown word. For example, you may call on a particular child and say, "Greg, you know how to spell your name, so I want you to use that to help you figure out how to spell the word *leg*." Some children may want to use magnetic letters to construct the word before they write it.

Demonstrate this strategy regularly and with many different words so that the children will understand how to use it for their own writing. Work with individuals who need more assistance during independent writing time.

Use the material you write together for class, group, and independent reading. If the shared and interactive writing material is not reread, a lot of the benefit of that language experience work is lost. It is important for children to frequently read and reread print that is familiar to them. The essence of this language experience is to show children the relationship between the spoken and written word and how they can learn to read from their writing and learn to write from their reading.

Using a Range of Literacy Experiences

One way to link several reading, writing, and oral language experiences with learning about onsets and rimes in kindergarten and grade 1 is described below. This example grew out of the experience of one particular class's daily writing about the planted seeds they were studying, but the same procedure could be used with any other experience that begins with some type of shared or interactive writing. In fact, the greater the variety of writing experiences, the more opportunity there will be for you to model how to write different genres and the more varied the words will be in the children's writing.

With the children sitting in a circle so that they had eye contact with each other, the teacher encouraged them to share what they had noticed about the seeds they had planted. The teacher selected one of the children's observations to write on a large chart, as the children gathered to face the chart. (This could have been done as shared or interactive writing.) A blank space was left for one of the words so that children could attempt to spell it. The word could have been a high-frequency word or any word containing a rime that could be worked with. In this case, the word *crack* was not written:

One of the seeds has some roots coming out of it. The roots made the seed _____.

The chart was left in an accessible place as the class pursued other activities. This allowed children to attempt the word when they wished, writing their names beside their attempts on the chart. Some of the children's attempts for *crack* were:

krak (Amy)
crak (Mohammed)
crac (Fay)
krack (Lee)
krek (Jeffrey)
kerak (Jeffrey)
crack (Edward)

Later in the day the teacher reviewed the chart with the class. All attempts were praised, so that children would realize that good writers try words even when they are not sure how to spell them. The teacher asked the children to share the strategies they had used to try the words. (The first few times you work through this process keep the class together while the children attempt to write the word and immediately talk with each child about what he or she was doing to help figure out how to spell the word. This will give the children ideas about what to do when they are left to do this independently.) Some of the strategies the children mentioned were:

"I sounded it out."
"I stretched it out."
"I tried it different ways because it didn't look right."
"I knew how to spell it."
"I found it in the book about chickens."

The teacher told the students that these were strategies they could use in their own writing when they did not know a word. Together, the class developed a chart listing the various strategies:

Strategies good spellers use

• Listen for the sounds in the word.
• Stretch the word out slowly to listen for the sounds.
• Try it more than one way.
• Think about what the word looks like.
• Find the word in books.
• Learn how to spell some words.
• Try to spell unknown words.
• Do your best.

The teacher then wrote the word *crack* in the sentence on the chart, explaining that that's the way the word would be written in a book. The children were then asked to read the piece of writing as the words were pointed to. They were next asked to circle and read any words they knew or to look for words within words and circle them on the chart.

The teacher rewrote the word *crack,* underlining *ack* (it could have been written in a different color). She then asked the children if they could think of any other words that sounded the same as *crack,* and listed each response. As each word was added the children reread the list as the teacher pointed to the words. Here are the words the children suggested:

back
black
pack
quack
sack
tack
track
smack
whack

One child suggested *yak;* the teacher wrote it in another column to indicate that it sounds the same but is spelled differently. (You may want to show your students how to change from one word to another, using magnetic letters or an erasable board, or have the children do it. You could also show them how to add the letter *s* to words, such as *backs* or *quacks.* When the children are ready you can do the same thing with *ing* and *ed.* Or if children have erasable boards you could ask them to try to write as many words as possible that are like the word *crack.* Once the children are used to this procedure they could do this part individually before you make a class list.)

Next, the teacher rewrote one of the sentences from the original text on a sentence strip and cut it as the children watched, dividing the words into their onsets and rimes or compound words and leaving high-frequency words whole:

The |r|oot|s| m|ade| the |s|eed|s| cr|ack|.|

She then jumbled the word parts in a pocket chart and asked the children to reassemble them into a sentence, one word at a time. As each word was added, children reread the part of the sentence that had been reconstructed, as one child pointed to the words. The word parts were later put into an envelope with the sentence written on the front so that children could work with this sentence independently later.

In the end, all the writing was rewritten into a class experience book—in this case, into a book of observations about plants—and a child illustrated it. (With this type of nonfiction you could demonstrate how the illustration might be in two parts, showing the seed before and after the roots sprouted, with labels indicating the important parts of the illustration, such as *seed, crack,* and *roots.*) The class book was used frequently for shared reading and was also available for independent reading.

Although you may not wish to include all of these experiences at one time or even in one day, every part of this routine is important for children's reading and writing development and should be done frequently. The frequent rereading of what has been written is a vital part of the experience. You may start the sentence-cutting part by just dividing the sentence into words and then, once children understand what a word is, proceed to divide individual words. Cutting words into onsets and rimes and having children reconstruct them are extremely beneficial for children's reading and writing. The process can fit in with any type of shared or interactive writing in any curriculum area.

Learning Words

Remember to refer to the lists of words that you build with the children, asking them if there are any words they think they would use often for their reading and writing. Such words may receive specific attention and be added to the class word wall. Individuals may want to select words they would often use and add them to a list of personal words to learn.

Continuing Evaluation

During reading and writing observe how your students make use of onset and rime analogy. Talk with them about your observations, and make note of children who need more work in this area. Call on these children to figure out relevant words during shared reading and writing, and work with a group during guided reading and with individuals during independent reading and writing. Such children may benefit from reading the books the class made using words with the same rime, although there is no research yet that validates the use of what are called decodable books in developing children's reading ability.

References

Dombey, H., et al. 1998. *Whole to Part Phonics: How Children Learn to Read and Spell.* London: Centre for Language in Primary Education.

Fry, E. 1998. "The Most Common Phonograms." *The Reading Teacher* 51, 7: 620–622.

Goswami, U. 1986. "Children's Use of Analogy in Learning to Read: A Developmental Study." *Journal of Experimental Child Psychology* 42: 73–83.

Goswami, U., and P. Bryant. 1990. *Phonological Skills and Learning to Read.* Hillsdale, NJ: Lawrence Erlbaum.

Moustafa, M. 1995. "Children's Productive Phonological Recoding." *Reading Research Quarterly* 30, 3: 464–476.

———. 1997. *Beyond Traditional Phonics: Research Discoveries and Reading Instruction.* Portsmouth, NH: Heinemann.

Treiman, R. 1983. "The Structure of Syllables: Evidence from Novel Word Games." *Cognition* 15: 49–74.

———. 1985. "Onsets and Rimes as Units of Spoken Syllables: Evidence from Children." *Journal of Experimental Child Psychology* 39: 161–181.

Sounds

Beginning writers often use the sounds they hear when attempting to write unfamiliar words. More experienced writers may use this strategy initially, and then use other strategies to cross-check their ideas.

Children need to know how to use letter-sound relationships when writing, and they need to know that any sound in English may be represented in more than one way. They also need to learn that certain combinations of letters representing sounds occur in predictable positions in words (for example, the /k/ sound is not represented by the letters *ck* at the beginning of a word).

It is also helpful for beginning writers to know how to listen for sounds in the initial, final, and medial positions in words when they attempt to spell unfamiliar words. Some children may be able to identify the sounds in all positions in words, but do not think to do this when attempting to spell words they are not sure of.

The importance of teaching children to listen for sounds in all positions in words, and to find letters to represent these sounds, becomes apparent from the example of one child's progress.

Figure 7.1 was written by Vanessa, a grade 2 student whose only strategy when attempting to write unfamiliar words was to listen for the initial sound in the word and write a letter to represent that sound. Because Vanessa knew that words consisted of more than one letter, however, she padded the words out beyond the sounds she represented, mainly using *n* and *e*, letters in her name.

Vanessa was taught to listen beyond the initial sound in a word, and to write letters to represent the middle and final sounds in words as well. Figure 7.2 was

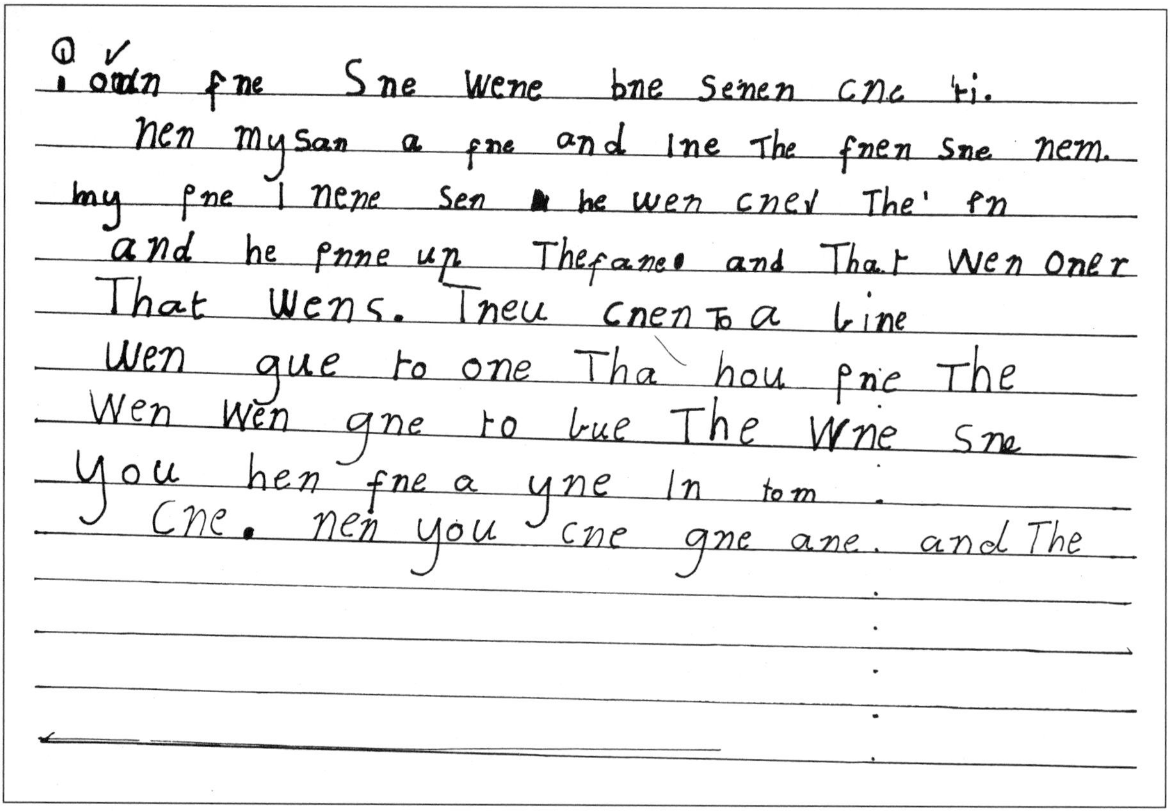

① ✓
. oodn fne Sne wene bne senen cne ti.
   nen mysan a fne and Ine The fnen Sne nem.
my fne I nene sen he wen cnev The' fn
   and he fnne un Thefane and That wen oner
That wens. Tneu cnen To a Line
   wen que to one Tha hou fne The
wen wen gne to bue The wne Sne
you hen fne a yne In to m
   Cne. nen you cne gne ane. and The

FIGURE 7.1 Vanessa's writing representing the initial sound only.

written after one week's instruction and practice in listening for sounds in all positions in words. At first, although there are instances in the writing in Figure 7.2 where Vanessa represented all the distinguishable sounds in words, her writing closely resembles that in Figure 7.1. When she was reminded to listen for and represent sounds in all positions in words, Vanessa proceeded to put two large *x*'s through her writing and began to redraft her piece.

The following day, Vanessa produced the writing shown in Figure 7.3. Here she represented all the sounds she heard in words, using reasonable phonic choices. Note that at the bottom of Figure 7.3 Vanessa wrote some text that closely resembles that in Figure 7.1. However, Vanessa discarded this writing, turned the paper upside down, and resumed.

Vanessa's class had been studying Australian animals, and Vanessa was interested in writing about them. She produced the writing in Figure 7.4 approximately three weeks after that in Figure 7.1.

When comparing the spelling strategies Vanessa used when writing the piece in Figure 7.4 with those she used in writing the piece in Figure 7.1, we can see that she made remarkable progress in three weeks, because the instruction she was given matched her needs. Vanessa continued to become a more competent

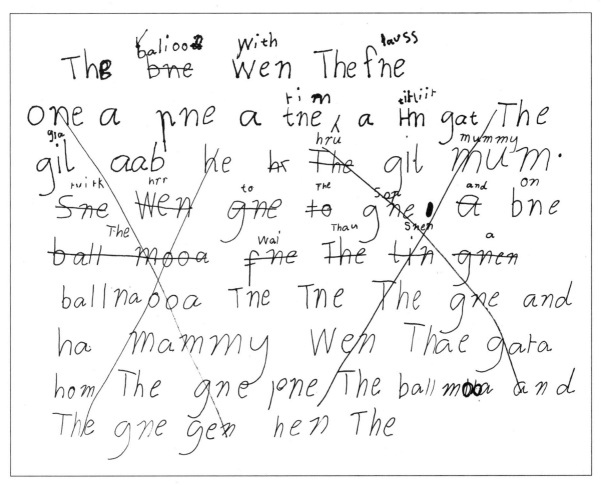

FIGURE 7.2 Vanessa's writing one week later.

speller, and she began to use other strategies when writing unfamiliar words, including thinking about the visual and meaning relationships between words.

Exploration of sounds may occur in the early grades of school; for children whose first language is not English, it may occur during the year they make the transition to English. (Although the examples given in this chapter are for English sounds the same procedure is suitable for sounds in other languages.)

Because English is not a one sound–one symbol language, a purpose of sound exploration is to give children possible options as they try to write words they don't know. They need to develop habits such as attempting a word, trying another way if it doesn't look right, and checking a resource when editing. Although beginning writers will not necessarily be aware that a word is not correct, you should demonstrate the process during modeled, shared, and interactive writing sessions, and make sure that children understand how this knowledge will help them as writers.

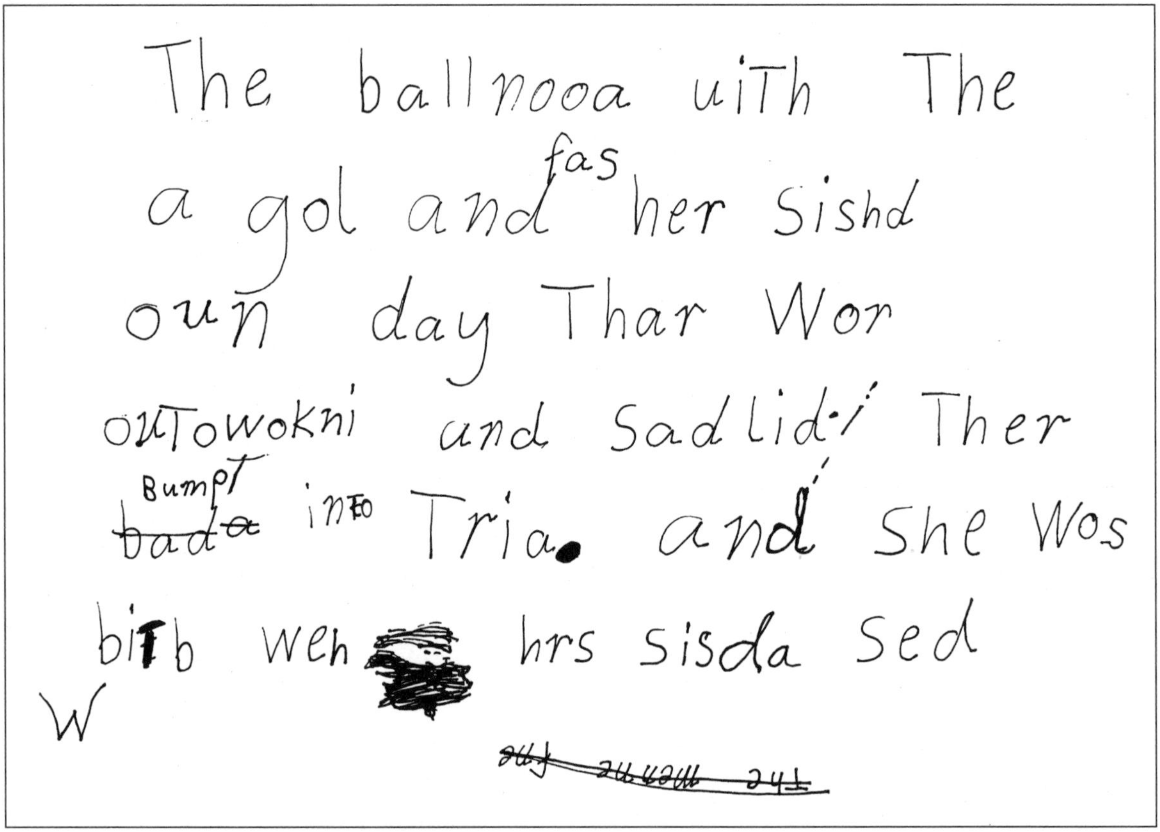

The ball nooa uiTh The
a gol and fas her sishd
oun day Thar Wor
ouTowokni and sad lid·i Ther
Bumpt into Tria and she Wos
bib weh ~~~~~ hrs sisda sed
W

FIGURE 7.3 Vanessa's writing representing all the sounds.

Evaluating Children's Understanding and Needs

Observe your students' writing to gain a general sense of what they know about listening for sounds in words and identifying letters to represent sounds heard. Such observations will assist you in determining your students' overall stage of spelling development—whether they partially or totally map sounds heard in words, that is, whether they are at the semiphonetic or phonetic stage (see Bolton and Snowball 1993). The stage they are at will influence your teaching. For example, if your students are representing only the beginning sound in words, you need to help them listen for and represent all the sounds in all the positions in words. If, however, they are consistently representing a particular sound with the same letter or spelling pattern, they would benefit from learning about the variety of letters or spelling patterns that represent a given sound, and learning how letter choice is influenced by the position of the sound in words.

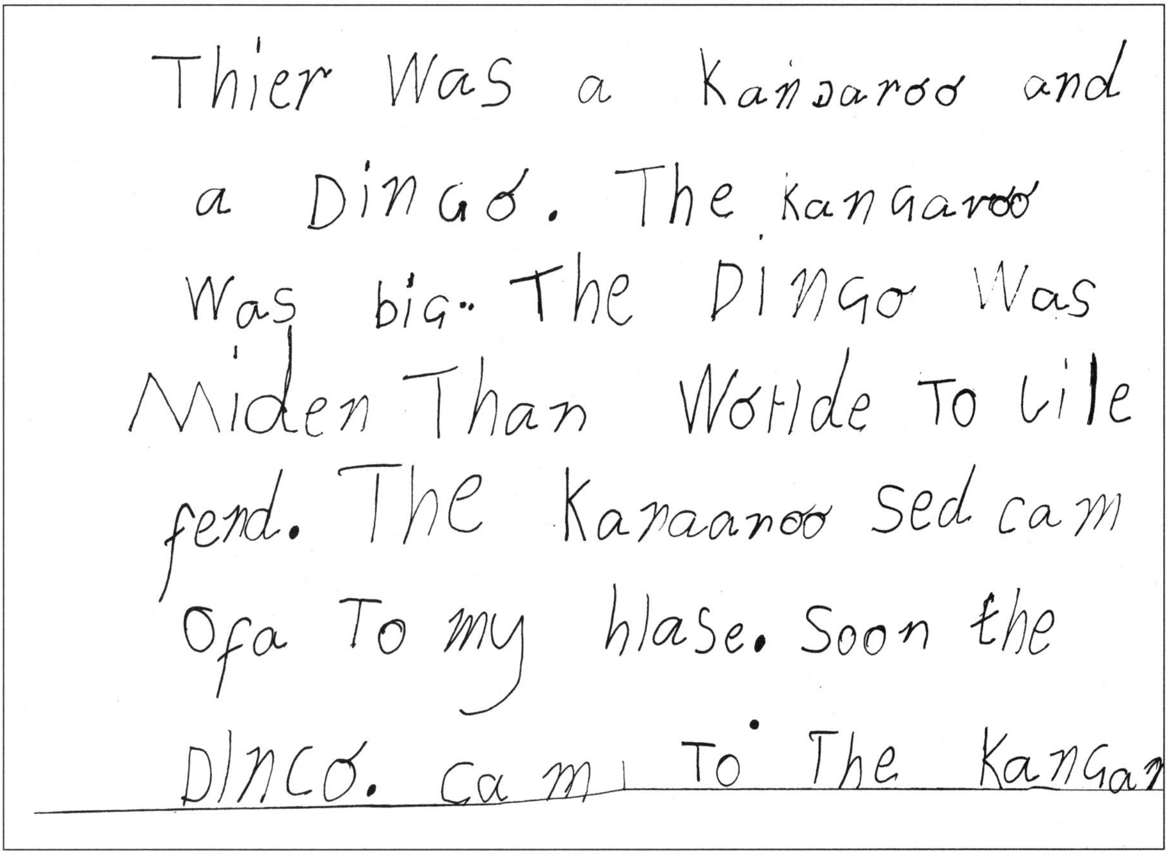

Thier Was a Kanjaroo and a Dingo. The kangaroo Was big. The DINGO Was Miden Than Worlde To Lile fend. The Kanaanoo Sed cam Ofa To my hlaSe. Soon the DINCO. cam To The Kangar

FIGURE 7.4 Vanessa's writing about animals.

When checking children's writing, note their spelling and decide which stage they are at.

The Semiphonetic Stage

The following are characteristics of the semiphonetic stage of spelling development:

- The writer represents only the beginning sounds in words (*b* for *bottom*).
- The writer represents one or two sounds heard in a word (*bt* for *bottom*).
- The writer uses mainly consonants (*cm* for *come*).
- The writer uses letter names to represent sounds (*ne* for *any*).
- The writer represents only easily distinguishable sounds heard (*botm* for *bottom*).

FIGURE 7.5 Semiphonetic spelling ("icing cake")

The semiphonetic spelling shown in Figure 7.5 (meant to represent the words "icing cake") is characterized by the following features:

- The spelling is abbreviated: one or two letters are used to represent a word.
- The letter name *i* is used for *icing.*
- Sounds are represented in correct sequence, left to right.

This writer would benefit from instruction that emphasizes listening for sounds in all positions in words and identifying letters to represent these sounds.

The Phonetic Stage

The following are characteristics of the phonetic stage of spelling development:

- The writer represents all the sounds heard in a word (*botom* for *bottom*) and in correct sequence.
- The writer uses reasonable phonic alternatives.
- Vowels appear in every syllable.
- Nasals (*m* and *n)* appear before consonants.

The phonetic spelling in Figure 7.6 is characterized by the following features:

- All distinguishable sounds are mapped.
- The nasal consonant before a vowel (*dedt* for *didn't, oley* for *only, wot* for *want*) may be omitted.
- The letter *e* is substituted for the letter *i,* based on positions of articulation.
- The /k/ sound is represented consistently by the letter *c.*

This writer would benefit from instruction that emphasizes listening for sounds in words, thinking about the variety of letters that represent these sounds, and considering the position of the sound in the words. In this case, an exploration of the /k/ sound would be appropriate. In addition, this writer would benefit from activities with onsets and rimes where the rime contains a nasal sound before a consonant (for example, /w/-/ent/, /s/-/ent/, /sp/-/ent/, /j/-/ump/, /b/-/ump/, /l/-/ump/, /st/-/ump/, and so on) and is represented by the same spelling pattern (e.g., *ent* and *ump*). Refer to Chapter 6 for a list of onsets and rimes.

When attempting to write unfamiliar words, beginning writers use their letter-sound knowledge in conjunction with how each sound is articulated. Look for examples of this strategy as you evaluate children's writing. For example, children often spell *sc* words such as *school* as *sgool* because the /k/ and /g/ sounds are articulated in similar positions. In addition, children often substitute the letter *e* for the letter *i* when writing because the /ee/ and /i/ sounds are articulated in similar positions. Young writers make many substitutions based on the position of articulation of sounds. Knowing this will assist you in evaluating the logic behind their spelling attempts. Since beginning writers use articulation to

FIGURE 7.6 Phonetic spelling: "I wish that Amy didn't go because she only stayed for 5 days. I want Amy to come back, and she's got to come back. If she doesn't she'll be in big [trouble] because she has to come."

help them when attempting to write unfamiliar words, it is important that they be taught to articulate words and sounds clearly.

Selecting Sounds for Exploration

There are approximately forty-six sounds in the English language, and over a period of two or three years you may wish to investigate each of them. However, helping children use the strategy of listening for and representing sounds in words is more important than covering every sound. If children are able to represent certain sounds in their writing, do not spend time exploring these sounds.

Begin with sounds that are distinctive—those that are not similar to other sounds. The long and short vowels are very difficult to distinguish, as evidenced in beginners' writing (and as explained in Moats 1995). Consequently, short and long vowels are not the most suitable sounds to start with. Children will have many opportunities to work with these vowel sounds in the onset and rime analogies suggested in Chapter 6.

TABLE 7.1		Easily Distinguishable Sounds
Possible Classroom Symbol	*IPA Symbol*	*Possible Representations in Words*
/f/	/f/	*f-fun* (78%), *ff-off, ph-photo, gh-laugh, lf-half, ft-often*
/b/	/b/	*b-bad* (97%), *bb-lobby*
/d/	/d/	*d-dog* (98%), *dd-daddy, ed-called, ld-could*
/k/	/k/	*c-can* (73%), *k-kite* (13%), *ch-school, cc-Rebecca, ck-back, lk-talk, qu-bouquet, kk-Nikki, kh-khaki*
/p/	/p/	*p-pet* (96%), *pp-hopped*
/g/	/g/	*g-get* (88%), *gg-hugged, gh-ghost, gue-vague*
/t/	/t/	*t-ten* (97%), *tt-little, ed-jumped, cht-yacht, pt-receipt, bt-doubt, th-Thailand, ct-indict*
/m/	/m/	*m-man* (94%), *mm-mommy, mb-comb, mn-hymn, lm-calm, gm-diaphragm*
/n/	/n/	*n-nice* (97%), *nn-funny, kn-knee, gn-gnat, pn-pneumonia, dne- Wednesday*
/w/	/w/	*w-walk* (92%), *wh-while, o-one, u-language*
/h/	/h/	*h-had* (98%), *wh-who, j-Jose*
/v/	/v/	*v-van* (99.5%), *f-of*
/z/	/z/	*s-his* (64%), *z-zoo* (23%), *zz-buzz, ss-scissors, x-xylophone, si-business, se-please*
/y/	/y/	*i-Australia* (55%), *y-you* (44%), *ll-tortilla*
/j/	/dʒ/	*g-giant* (66%), *j-joke* (22%), *d-soldier, dge-badge, ge-village*
/l/	/l/	*l-like* (91%), *ll-ball, sle-isle*
/r/	/r/	*r-ran* (97%), *rr-horror, wr-writer, rh-rhyme, rrh-diarrhea, rre-bizarre, rt-mortgage*
/sh/	/ʃ/	*ti-nation* (53%), *sh-ship* (26%), *ch-machine, s-sugar, c-ocean, ss-tissue, sci-conscience, sch-schnauzer, chs-fuchsia*
/zh/	/ʒ/	*si-confusion* (49%), *s-treasure* (33%), *z-azure*
/ch/	/tʃ/	*ch-cherry* (55%), *t-creature* (31%), *tch-catch, c-cello, cc-cappuccino, cz-Czech, te-righteous*
/th/	/ð/	*th-this* (100%)
/th/	/θ/	*th-think* (100%)
/ng/	/ŋ/	*ng-sing* (59%), *n-sink* (41%)
/s/	/s/	*s-bus* (73%), *c-cent* (17%), *ss-hiss, sc-scent, sw-sword, ps-psalm, st-listen*

When selecting sounds to explore, refer to the lists of sounds in Tables 7.1 and 7.2. These include common representations as examples. These lists will help you select sounds to explore that will help meet your children's needs as writers. The first group is easier to distinguish than the second group, but within each group you need not study the sounds in a set order. Nor is it necessary to explore all the sounds if you feel that your students are already representing some of them in their writing without any need for further guidance. This is typically the case for sounds that are not usually represented in more than one way, such as /b/.

The sounds are listed using the International Phonetic Alphabet (IPA) sym-

TABLE 7.2		Less Easily Distinguishable Sounds
Possible Classroom Symbol	*IPA Symbol*	*Possible Representations in Words*
/ay/	/eɪ/	*a-baby* (45%), *a-e lake* (35%), *ai-rain, ay-day, ei-reindeer, ey-they, eigh-eight, ea-great, aigh-straight, e-debut, et-bouquet, ee-matinee, aig-campaign, au-gauge*
/ee/	/i:/	*e-secret* (70%), *ee-feet* (10%), *ea-meat* (10%), *e-e these, ie-piece, y-happy, i-ski, ei-receive, eo-people, oe-amoeba, ey-monkey, is-chassis, ae-archaeology*
/igh/	/aɪ/	*i-tiger* (37%), *i-e mine* (37%), *y-my* (14%), *igh-high, ie-pie, y-e type, eye-eye, eigh-height, ig- sign, is-island, ais-aisle, a-naive, ai-Shanghai, ui-guide, uy-buy, ye-dye*
/oh/	/əʊ/	*o-pony* (73%), *o-e hope* (14%), *oa-boat, ow-snow, oe-toe, owe-owes, oh-oh, ew-sew, eau-beau, ough-though, ot-depot, oo-brooch, ol-folk*
/oo/ (food)	/u:/	*oo-food* (38%), *u-lunar* (21%), *u-e flute, ew-flew, ue-true, ou-soup, ui-fruit, u-Honolulu, o-who, wo-two, ooh-pooh, ut-debut, ough-through, oe-shoe, o-e move, eu-sleuth*
/yoo/	/ju:/	*u-music* (69%), *u-e mule* (22%), *ew-few, ue-value, eu-Europe, eau-beauty, ewe-ewe, ugh-Hugh, iew-view*
/a/	/æ/	*a-can* (96%), *ai-plaid, al-salmon, i-meringue, ua- guarantee*
/e/	/e/	*e-get* (91%), *ea-head, ie-friend, ai-said, u-bury, eo-leopard, ue-guess, ei-leisure, a-any*
/i/	/ɪ/	*i-it* (66%), *y-gym* (23%), *ie-sieve, u-busy, o-women, e-pretty, ui-build*
/o/	/ɒ/	*o-not* (79%), *oh-John, ho-honor, a-was, ow-knowledge, ou-cough, e-entree, au-sausage*
/u/	/ʌ/	*u-but* (86%), *o-front, oe-does, ou-touch, oo-blood*
/oo/ (good)	/ʊ/	*u-put* (54%), *oo-book* (31%), *o-wolf* (8%), *oul-could*
/ou/	/aʊ/	*ou-house* (56%), *ow-cow* (29%), *hou-hour, ough-bough*
/er/	/ə:/	*er-fern* (40%), *ur-fur* (26%), *ir-fir* (13%), *or-world, ear-earth, ere-were*
/ar/	/ɑ:/	*ar-garden, aar-bazaar, ear-heart, are-are, er-sergeant*
/ah/		*a-last, ah-hurrah, al-half, uar-guard, at-nougat*
/or/		*our-four, or-for, ore-more, ure-sure, ar-wharf, orps-corps, oar-board, oor-floor, aur-dinosaur, ort-rapport*
/aw/	/ɔ:/	*augh-caught, a-water, aw-paw, au-because, a-all, al-talk, ough-bought*
/air/	/eə/	*air-pair, ere-there, eir-their, are-mare, ayor-mayor, ear-bear, ar-scarce*
/ear/ (here)	/ɪə/	*ear-hear, eer-deer, eir-weird, eor-theory, ere-here, ier-fierce*
/oy/	/ɔɪ/	*oi-soil* (62%), *oy-boy* (32%), *oig-poignant*
(schwa sound)	/ə/	*o-lemon, a-about, i-pencil, e-taken, u-circus, ia-marriage*
(rounded schwa sound)		*er-father, ar-vinegar, or-doctor, ur-further*

(For more information about the sounds in the English language and their various representations see Wilde 1998).

bols and include possible representations of the sound. The classroom symbols also provided will be more meaningful to children than the IPA symbols. The percentages provided in parentheses following some of the words are based on the work of Hanna and his colleagues, who researched the number of occurrences of letters representing the sounds indicated in the 17,000 most frequently used words. (For further information see Blevins 1998).

Because words are pronounced differently in different locations and in different cultural groups (there are many English dialects in North America), the sounds that children hear in certain words may vary from the way the words are listed in the tables. You need to develop lists for your own classes according to the way that your students pronounce words. Also be aware that for children whose first language is not English, their first language may have different sounds than those here, or their first language may have certain sounds represented by only one symbol. You will need to highlight the differences in English for these children.

Some sounds are very similar (such as /d/ and /t/, /p/ and /b/, /g/ and /k/, /f/ and /v/, and /s/ and /z/), and because of this some children may need help when listening for words with one of these sounds. In particular, children may find it very difficult to hear that the sound in words such as *dogs* is /z/, not /s/. Children may also have been told such misleading statements as "The letter *c* says /k/" or "The letter *s* says /s/" so that when the class is listening for words with a /k/ sound during shared reading and read-alouds, they may suggest a word such as *cheese*. If this occurs, ask the child why he or she gave that word; if the answer is "Because it has a *c* in it," explain that although there is a letter *c* in the word *cheese*, we cannot hear a /k/ sound when we say it.

If you find that many children are having difficulty in hearing isolated sounds in words it may be an indication that you need to help them develop phonemic awareness first.

When exploring a specific sound, you need not introduce children to all the letters and spelling patterns that represent that sound. For example, when exploring the /oh/ sound, children may not learn about the spelling pattern *oo* in *brooch*, because the word *brooch* may not be part of the children's vocabulary. Nor is it expected that children memorize the letter(s) or spelling patterns that represent a sound.

If you wish to deal with beginning and final blends that children encounter when reading and writing, such as *pr, pl, tr, gr, nd, mp, ft,* and *ld,* explore them as you explore each of the sounds and letters in those blends. For example, when finding words with the /g/ sound, words such as *green, grow,* and *grass* will probably be listed, and when finding words with the /r/ sound, these words would again be listed.

Some Misunderstandings

Sometimes sounds are explored in a way that limits children's understanding or confuses them. For example, some teachers explore the sound /ch/ but limit the study to words that have the spelling pattern *ch*, rather than accepting the fact that spelling patterns other than *ch* may have the /ch/ sound, even in children's names and common words. For example, in wi<u>tch</u>, pic<u>t</u>ure, cappu<u>cc</u>ino, and crea<u>t</u>ure the /ch/ sound is represented by a variety of spelling patterns other than *ch*.

Some teachers wonder if it is confusing to show children more than one way to represent a sound. The fact is, it is more confusing to give them statements such as "The /ch/ sound is *ch*" only to have them find other words in their reading and writing where different letters or spelling patterns represent the /ch/ sound.

English Sounds and ESL Students

Some children for whom English is a second language may have difficulty recognizing and producing sounds in English, particularly if they have had limited experiences in hearing and using the English language.

For example, Chinese children may have difficulty with the /b/, /ch/, /d/, /g/, /sh/, /th/, and /v/ sounds, while Spanish children may have difficulties with the /dz/, /j/, /sh/, /th/, and /z/ sounds.

Being aware of the sounds in the children's first language will help you ascertain what sort of additional guidance these children will need in developing knowledge of English language, phonemic awareness, and in exploring sounds. (For further information, see Kress 1993.)

☃ Discovering the Generalizations About Sounds

Children must understand that the purpose of sound explorations is to help them as writers and readers. Tell them that you have noticed them listening for sounds in words to help them when writing, so the class is going to explore sounds together and discover how knowing about sounds and the letters that represent them can help with their spelling and reading.

Sound explorations should be done using the reading and writing occurring in the classroom so that children can listen for sounds in words they know and can say. If they cannot say a word, they cannot hear the sounds in it.

Following are some ways to explore sounds that are relevant to children's reading and writing experiences. Our examples link sound explorations to a shared reading experience and an interactive writing experience.

Using Shared Reading

During initial sound explorations with beginning writers it may be helpful for children to listen only, and not see the print being read during shared reading experiences. This limits possible confusion between the letter names and the sounds they represent. It may be a good idea to proceed in this fashion until the children are familiar with the procedures involved in sound explorations.

If you find children are confusing the meanings of *sound* and *letter,* it may be because you or other teachers are using these words interchangeably, or because published materials such as phonic workbooks, computer programs, or spelling programs are misusing these terms. Remember, a letter is any one of the twenty-six letters in the written alphabet, but a sound is a phoneme that is heard. We *look* for letters and *listen* for sounds. It is important to be consistent and accurate when using these terms.

When thinking about sound explorations, observe children's writing to see what they already know about listening for sounds in words and identifying letters to represent sounds heard. (For more details, see the evaluation section at the beginning of this chapter.) Then observe the children's writing to identify a sound that many of the children are attempting when they write. This sound should become the focus of your exploration.

Notice how the children represent the sound in their writing. Note whether they:

- use one letter consistently to represent a given sound;
- experiment with a variety of letters to represent the sound;
- use the appropriate letter or spelling pattern to represent a sound, given positional constraints (for example, the letters *pp* are not used to represent the /p/ sound at the beginning of a word).

Use familiar materials in shared reading to give children practice in listening for the focus sound, and point out the variety of letters or spelling patterns that are used to represent the sound. Where possible, select more than one story, report, poem, or song containing words that use a variety of letters or spelling patterns to represent the focus sound. Remember, an important goal of sound explorations is for children to discover that a sound may be represented by a variety of letters or spelling patterns.

The following is an example of how a sound was explored in one grade 1 classroom.

From observing the children's writing the teacher had noticed that many of the children were attempting words containing the /p/ sound. She selected the familiar song "If You're Happy and You Know It" to introduce the exploration. She also collected reading materials to further the exploration, including the rhymes "Pease Porridge Hot," "Humpty Dumpty," "Peter, Peter, Pumpkin Eater," and "Jump Rope."

You may remember that "If You're Happy and You Know It" was also used as part of a letter exploration in Chapter 4. Any piece may be used for a variety of spelling explorations. (This may be especially useful to know, given that many schools have limited resources.)

As was customary, the teacher explained to the children why the particular spelling exploration was being undertaken. She explained that many of them were trying to write words containing the /p/ sound, the sound heard at the beginning of *Peter.*

Some children were invited to show their writing containing the /p/ words to the class, and the teacher helped the children say the words and identify the position of the /p/ sound in each written word.

The teacher then displayed the song "If You're Happy and You Know It." She asked the children to point to their ears, since they were to listen for the /p/ sound, and told them that whenever they heard the /p/ sound they were to give a clap.

To ensure that the children understood they were to *listen* for sounds the teacher gave a child a pair of Minnie Mouse ears to wear. She then demonstrated the task by saying a group of words in which the /p/ sound occurred in various positions (*tip, past, bad,* and *apple*) and clapping when she heard the /p/ sound. She then repeated the words and asked the children to clap when they heard the /p/ sound and to identify its position in each word.

Because it is difficult to say some consonants in isolation it might be better when referring to these sounds to say something like "Listen for words that have the same sound we hear at the beginning of *pat.*"

The teacher sang "If You're Happy and You Know It" with the class.

If you're happy and you know it,
Clap your hands
If you're happy and you know it,
Clap your hands.
If you're happy and you know it,
And you really want to show it,
If you're happy and you know it,
Clap your hands.

As the children identified words containing the /p/ sound the teacher listed them on a chart. She asked the children to identify the position of the sound in each word, and as they did she underlined the letter or letters representing the sound. Other rhymes were read to the class, and their /p/ words were added to the list:

happy
Clap
Peter
pumpkin
keep
pease
porridge
pot
Humpty
Dumpty
put

The next step was to group the words according to the letters that represented the /p/ sound. By doing this the teacher was alerting the children to the variety of letters or letter combinations that can represent the /p/ sound, the positions they may take in words, and which were the more common representations.

Once the words were grouped according to the letter or letters representing the /p/ sound, it became apparent to the children that there were two representations of the /p/ sound: the single letter *p* and the letter combination *pp.*

happy   Cla<u>p</u>
          <u>P</u>eter
          <u>p</u>um<u>p</u>kin
          kee<u>p</u>
          <u>p</u>ease
          <u>p</u>orridge
          <u>p</u>ot
          Hum<u>p</u>ty
          Dum<u>p</u>ty
          <u>p</u>ut

The children continued to find other /p/ words in their own reading. This gave the teacher the chance to observe how well each child was able to do this task. Some of the other words they found were *princess, play, open, plant, spray, Pam, spring, hopped,* and *present;* these words were added to the appropriate *p* or *pp* column.

The teacher also made a new list of some words that had blends, such as the *pr* blend in *princess* and *present* and the *spr* blend in *spring* and *spray,* because she noticed some children had trouble reading these types of words. The class read these lists and thought of other words to add, such as *prince.*

(This is a useful way to deal with blends as part of a sound study. Other opportunities to deal with blends will arise during other sound explorations; for example, when exploring the /s/ sound, the blends *st, sl, sm,* and so on may be introduced.)

As the words were being listed throughout the exploration of the /p/ sound the teacher helped the children form generalizations about which letter or letter combination was the most common representation, and the different positions in a word each letter or combination occurred in. These ideas were written on a chart, dated, and read with the children. The children then wrote their initials next to their generalization:

November 5 What we know about the /p/ sound

- The /p/ sound is at the beginning of the words *potato* and *pretty.*   S. T.
- The /p/ sound is at the end of the words *lamp* and *jump.*   S. T. and M. F.
- The /p/ sound is at the beginning and end of the words (*pop* and *pip*).   B. T.
- I heard the /p/ sound in the middle of a word, and in the word *happy* two *p*'s (*pp*) represent the /p/ sound.   L. M.
- There are more words where the letter *p* represents the /p/ sound than *pp.*   A. R.
- The letters *pp* represent the /p/ sound in the middle of words but not at the beginning or end.   V. K.
- The letter *p* represents the /p/ sound in the beginning, middle, and end of words.   V. K.

(If children give inaccurate statements in your explorations, you could cite other words from the children's reading and writing to cause them to rethink their generalization.)

Toward the end of the exploration the teacher referred back to the children's writing that had inspired the sound exploration and asked the children if they had any new ideas about how the words could be spelled. They discussed what they had learned that could help them with their spelling and reading in the future.

The teacher displayed the /p/ class lists and encouraged the children to refer to them when proofreading their writing for words that contained the /p/ sound. The children also reviewed the /p/ class lists to identify high-frequency words that could be added to the alphabet word wall, and the class learned these words. Some of these words were also selected to highlight the meaning relationships between words. For example, the children learned how knowing how to spell *jump* from the /p/ class list would help them spell *jumps, jumping,* and *jumped.*

Class sound lists may also be made into a class spelling journal or class sound book—for example, "Our /p/ Book," containing separate pages for each letter or letters that represent the /p/ sound. Blank pages could be included for children to add more /p/ words as they discover them in their reading and writing. The book could be placed near the writing center for children to browse through and refer to when proofreading their writing.

Using Interactive Writing

Sounds can also be explored during interactive writing sessions. After observing children's writing, and identifying a common need, select a sound to explore. For example, grade 2 children may benefit from exploring the /ee/ sound and the letters and spelling patterns that represent it.

When beginning the exploration, tell the children you have noticed that many of them have been trying to write words with the /ee/ sound. Invite some children to show their writing to the class. Say some of the /ee/ words in these pieces with the children, helping the class identify the position of the /ee/ sound in each spoken word.

Guide the children in choosing a purpose and a topic for interactive writing. Write the piece with them, having them consider whether each word is one the class knows, or (where necessary) using a variety of strategies to attempt new words, such as thinking about letters or spelling patterns that represent the sounds, thinking about what the word may look like, or linking the word to another, perhaps related in meaning. If any words have an /ee/ sound be sure to demonstrate and discuss the possible options for spelling the word. Some of the children's attempts could be written on a "Have a Go" sheet displayed beside the piece of interactive writing (see Chapter 16). The children may want to check their attempts in dictionaries.

The following is what might have been produced as a piece of interactive writing:

We feed our pet canary every morning. It likes to eat bird seed and drink water.

Reread the writing with the children, explaining that the first thing to do is to check that the piece makes sense and sounds right.

Then read it again, or have the children reread the piece, this time to listen for words with the /ee/ sound. List these words:

We	feed	canary	eat
	seed	every	

Since children in grade 2 are likely to already have been involved in many sound explorations, rather than first listing all the /ee/ words in a single list, you may choose to begin by listing the words in groups according to the letters or spelling patterns that represent the /ee/ sound, as shown in the example above. If children have trouble grouping the words this way, you may wish to revert to listing all the /ee/ words together and then help the children form groups according to the letters or spelling patterns that represent the /ee/ sound.

Continue this exploration over the next few days by asking children to find /ee/ words in their own reading, in shared reading, and in interactive writing experiences. The expanded lists may look like this:

ea	ee	I	e	ui	ey	y	eigh	eo	ie
eat	feed	ski	we	quiche	key	canary	Leigh	people	chief
tea	seed	machine	he		keys	every			thief
please	green	taxi	she		turkey	raspberry			believe
bean	greedy		me		turkeys	very			
heat	been		the			jelly			
						greedy			

You may prefer to write all of the words on cards and have the children sort them into groups.

Guide children in forming generalizations about how the /ee/ sound can be represented—for example, that *y* and *ey* usually occur at the ends of words when they represent /ee/, and *i* is not a common way of representing /ee/.

As the lists of words are being developed, you will probably gain insight into your students' understanding of the relationships that exist between words. For example, some children may understand the relationship between *key* and *keys*, and likewise *turkey* and *turkeys*. To help make these relationships explicit to the whole class, ask the children who suggested these words why they thought of them together.

The children could be asked to identify high-frequency words and add them to the alphabet word wall. They could also consider why the word *greedy*, for example, appears in two groups, and be encouraged to locate other words in which the /ee/ sound is represented by more than one letter or spelling pattern. Refer to several of the words, and discuss how knowing one word can help with the spelling of other words in that same family, such as *heat, heats, heating, heated, heater, heaters,* and *reheat.*

The children may not discover the thirteen listed representations of the /ee/ sound listed in Table 7.2, since some of them occur in words that would not be part of the children's vocabulary, for example *oe* in *amoeba.* Remember that the important idea for children to understand is that a variety of letters or spelling patterns can represent a sound, and that they are influenced by the position of the sound in the word. The children may also come to realize that the /ee/ sound has many more letters and spelling patterns that represent it than many other sounds do. Children may consider the implications of this when they attempt to write words containing the /ee/ sound. (Note also that because there are so many representations of the /ee/ sound children will probably take considerably more time in an exploration of this sound than they will for an exploration of a sound with fewer representations.)

You may want to publish the children's /ee/ lists and generalizations in a class book to provide an additional resource for the children, or the class charts could be added to others in a display so that children could continually refer and add to them.

When you explore the /ee/ sound you could also teach the class more about the use of *ei* and *ie* in words such as *receive* and *believe*. To help children form generalizations about these combinations, list words from the /ee/ class list that contain *ie* and *ei* in separate columns to highlight when the *i* comes before the *e* and the *e* before *i*. For example:

bel<u>ie</u>ve	rec<u>ei</u>pt
ach<u>ie</u>ve	rec<u>ei</u>ve
th<u>ie</u>f	dec<u>ei</u>ve
ch<u>ie</u>f	conc<u>ei</u>ted
ch<u>ie</u>fs	conc<u>ei</u>ve
rel<u>ie</u>ve	c<u>ei</u>ling
	s<u>ei</u>ze
	L<u>ei</u>gh

Show children where the spelling pattern *ei* is used and have them write the generalization in their own words. Use the following statement as a guide to what you might discuss with the children and lead them to understand:

If *i* and *e* together have the sound of /ee/ the *i* comes first, except after *c*.

Explain that after the letter *c* the spelling pattern *ei* is used, and that *ei* is also used in words in the *seize* word family—*seize, seized, seizure,* and so on.

Discuss other words the children may find with the *ei* spelling pattern, such as *Leigh,* and help children understand that in these cases it is the spelling pattern *eigh* that represents the /ee/ sound, not the pattern *ei*.

Activities to Develop Letter-Sound Relationships

In addition to sound explorations, children can engage in activities that will help them learn about letter-sound relationships.

Substitution of Sounds and Letters in Words

Talk with children about how knowing how to read and write one word can help them read and write other words. Demonstrate this by saying a word such as *can* and then saying the word *cat* and leading children to understand that the last sound changed from an /n/ sound to a /t/ sound. Write the words and show how the change in sound was accompanied by a change in letter to represent the sound. You may want to use magnetic letters to demonstrate this.

Rimes with Nasal Consonants

Because beginning writers omit nasals before consonants when using the phonetic strategy, they tend, for example, to spell *went* as *wet, band* as *bad,* and *jump* as *jup.* To help them move beyond this, try to include some sound substitution activities, including onsets and rimes in which nasals appear before the final consonants in the rimes. Since *went* and *jump* are high-frequency words, it makes a great deal of sense to include them in sound and letter substitution activities in which you vary the onset but keep the rime with the same spelling pattern—for example, by changing *went* to *rent, tent, spent, sent* and *bent* and *jump* to *bump, pump,* and so on. Have children listen for the changes in sounds and look for the changes in letters that occur in the onsets.

Substitution of Sounds in Rimes

A more complex substitution activity that may be used with more experienced writers involves sound substitution activities in rimes. Using the word /w/-/ent/ again, the children could listen for the changes in sounds that occur when changing the rime /ent/ to /est/, in which the /n/ sound is replaced by the /s/ sound, resulting in the word /w/-/est/. Only make words children know the meanings of. For example, *went* may be changed to form *west* and *wend,* but children are unlikely to know the meaning of the word *wend* or use it when talking. Since it is irrelevant to them it is inappropriate to list. The new words could be formed with magnetic letters, then listed to highlight the changes, as shown below. By doing this the children will readily see that only some words with the rime *ent* can be changed to form real words with the rimes /est/ and /end/; for example, *spent* can be changed to form *spend* but not *spest,* which is not a real word.

-ent	-est	-end
went	west	—
sent	—	send
bent	best	bend
tent	test	—
rent	rest	—
lent	lest	lend
spent	—	spend
—	—	mend

Texts That Play with Letters and Sounds

Play short games with written words the children know. Ask them to say the new word when a beginning, middle, or final letter has changed. Make a list of the words and ask the children to suggest sentences using a combination of these words. Then make class books of these sentences, with the children's illustrations. The children will enjoy reading these silly sentences; they may even be turned into poems. For example:

> The ding, dang, dong
> chased the ning, nang, nong,
> who played ping, pang, pong
> but not for ling, lang, long.
> So long, strong!
> Ding, dang, dong,
> and
> ning, nang, nong.

Class-made material such as this will appeal to the children and make sense to them because it will consist of their ideas, language, and illustrations.

Scheduling Sound Explorations

A sound exploration would generally be the focus of two or three spelling sessions. The amount of time required will depend on the children's familiarity with the procedures involved in spelling investigations, the extensiveness of the investigation, and the children's needs. In the example of the /ee/ sound exploration, more than two or three spelling sessions were necessary. For faster progress, children may be given homework tasks, such as searching for and grouping certain types of words.

You may find it helpful to refer to the list of sounds and the letters or spelling patterns that represent them provided in Tables 7.1 and 7.2 as you estimate the time required for a given exploration.

Sometimes the sound explorations will occur in a daily sequence; at other times they will occur sporadically over one or two weeks, amid other spelling explorations.

Each exploration should move at a reasonable pace to maintain the children's interest. You may need to spend approximately half an hour on introducing a sound. Once the study is under way, however, perhaps a few minutes a day will be sufficient to continue the exploration.

🌀 Learning Words

You may find it helpful to explain to the children and their parents or guardians the purpose of the class sound lists so that everyone understands that they are intended to develop children's understanding of the various letters or spelling patterns that represent a particular sound, and to have children learn about the consistencies in their use. Make it clear that the words are not listed to be learned.

However, you may want to encourage the children to select and learn some of the words from the class lists that they are apt to find useful in their writing. This could be done as either a class or an individual activity. If done as a class activity, select a high-frequency word or a word related to a topic being studied by the entire class. At the same time the children may be shown how learning to spell this one word will help them spell other words. For example, if either the class or an individual child wanted to learn the word *ship* from the /sh/ class list, they should also think of other words that *ship* would help them to spell, such as *ships, shipping, shipped, shipwreck,* and *shipwrecks.*

When children are selecting words to learn, try to make sure that they know the meanings of the words, that they think they would use the words in their writing, and that they do not already know how to spell them. (For further information on children's selecting and learning words, see Chapter 18.)

☞ *Homework Ideas*

Children may be given enjoyable homework tasks related to the sound exploration they are involved in. For example:

- Ask them to bring items from home that their classmates can then name. Once the word is identified, have the class identify the focus sound and its position in the word. The children could then try to spell the word in class by thinking about the position of the sound in the word, possible letters or spelling patterns that represent the sound, the look of the word, and by using other strategies they know. This may be done as an individual or paired activity.

- Have children bring in short lists of words containing the focus sound. In class, have children say and listen for the focus sound, and add each word to the appropriate group on the class list.

- Ask children to make up lines of alliteration. Have their classmates identify the focus sound and its position in the words.

References

Blevins, W. 1998. *Phonics from A to Z: A Practical Guide.* New York: Scholastic.

Bolton, F., and D. Snowball. 1993. *Ideas for Spelling.* Portsmouth, NH: Heinemann.

Kress, J. E. 1993. *The ESL Teacher's Book of Lists.* West Nyack, NY: Center for Applied Research in Education.

Moats, L. C. 1995. *Spelling: Development, Disability, and Instruction.* Baltimore, MD: York Press.

Wilde, S. 1998. *What's a Schwa Anyway?* Portsmouth, NH: Heinemann.

Spelling Patterns

The exploration of spelling patterns builds on the exploration of letters outlined in Chapter 4, and complements the exploration of sounds in Chapter 7. In Chapter 7 we focused on the sounds heard in words and the possible letters or spelling patterns that represent the sounds. In contrast, both in Chapter 4 and this chapter we reverse the focus: letters and spelling patterns are explored to discover the sounds they represent and the positions in which they occur in words.

The exploration of spelling patterns enables writers to focus on groups of letters that represent the sounds they hear in words, and assists them in visualizing and remembering words. Such explorations:

- raise writers' awareness of visual patterns in written English and help them remember the possible spellings of words when writing;

- help children understand that most spelling patterns represent a variety of sounds;

- focus writers' attention on the possible sequences of letters in written English (for example, a word such as *tould* might occur, but not *tluod,* because the latter word does not follow a conventional pattern);

- focus writers' attention on the position of spelling patterns in words (for example, the spelling pattern *ss* occurs in the medial and final positions in words such as *messy* and *business,* but not in the initial position);

- provide children with knowledge in reading so that when they read something that doesn't make sense they can try another way to pronounce the word.

Because English is not a one symbol–one sound language, a purpose of exploring spelling patterns is to give children possible options as they try to write unfamiliar words. They need to develop strategies such as attempting a word, trying another way if their attempt results in letters in a sequence not possible in written English or if their word just doesn't look right, and checking a resource. Beginning and slightly experienced writers will not necessarily be aware that a word is not correct, but it is important that you demonstrate these strategies during modeled, shared, and interactive writing.

Evaluating Children's Understanding and Needs

Observe children's writing to gain a sense of what they know about spelling patterns.

- Do they write acceptable strings of letters?
- Do they think about the look of words and, when proofreading their writing, alter words that don't look right to them?
- Do children refer to class spelling pattern lists or their spelling journals when writing or proofreading their writing?
- Do they realize a spelling pattern represents a variety of sounds?

Also observe children when they are reading to gain a sense of what they know about spelling patterns. Do they comment on spelling patterns in words?

Such observations will assist you in determining your students' knowledge of spelling patterns and allow you to plan for whole class or small-group investigations. For example, it may be that the class as a whole would benefit from an exploration of the spelling pattern *th,* while just a few would gain from an exploration of the spelling pattern *sh.*

Some Definitions

A spelling pattern is a group of letters that represents a sound. Spelling patterns include groups of letters such as *ould* and *ear,* and digraphs, two or more letters that represent one speech sound (for example, the vowel digraphs *eigh* and *ai* and the consonant digraphs *th* and *ch*).

Although some commercial programs use the term *word families* when describing words with the same spelling pattern, such as *ear* in *earth, heart, near,* and *bear,* in this book we use the term differently. In this book, the term *word family* describes a group of words related in meaning. Words in a word family might be derived from the same base word and have different prefixes and/or suffixes added to it. For example, the words *plays, played, playing, replay, players, replaying,* and so on are in the word family based on the word *play.* Compound words may also be part of a word family. For example, the words *playground* and *play group* are related in meaning to the word *play*. Other word families may be based on derivatives. For example, the words *aquatics* and *aqualung* are related in meaning to the root *aqua*.

Although knowing about blends (*fr, br, nd,* and so on) helps writers learn about possible letter sequences in written English, we do not consider blends to be the same as spelling patterns. Blends are the joining of sounds represented by two or more letters with minimal changes to the sounds being blended—for example, the /g/ and /r/ sounds in *green*. If you wish to deal with blends such as *spr, pr, pl, tr, mp,* and so on, do so as you explore each of the sounds in those blends (see Chapter 7).

Before you introduce spelling patterns, children should know the names of the letters of the alphabet, so that they can name the letters within spelling patterns. The time to explore spelling patterns is when you observe children beginning to use them when they write and noticing them when they read. They will probably be aware that there are two vowels together in certain words, but they may have these vowels the wrong way around (for example, *raed* instead of *read*). And similarly with spelling patterns consisting of consonants: children may reverse the order of these letters and, for example, spell *school* as *shcool*, reversing the letters in the spelling pattern *ch*.

Some ESL children's first language may not be alphabetic, so they may require more assistance in learning the names of the letters and in identifying the sounds they represent.

Selecting Spelling Patterns for Exploration

Tell the children that you have noticed them trying to think of spelling patterns in words as well as thinking about the look of words as they write, so together you will explore some spelling patterns that will help them as writers. Explain that you will begin with spelling patterns that will be most useful to them as writers; that is, the spelling patterns found in the most frequently used words.

To assist you in identifying these spelling patterns, refer to Tables 8.1 and 8.2. Table 8.1 lists spelling patterns used most often in English words, and Table 8.2 lists spelling patterns used less frequently in English words. Although we have divided the spelling patterns into two lists, we suggest you draw many of your explorations from Table 8.1 since the patterns listed here are the ones most useful to writers. However, you may notice your children need assistance with spelling patterns in Table 8.2 and decide to explore these. Regardless, you do not need to study the spelling patterns within each group in a set order. (Other spelling patterns or letter strings are listed in Chapter 6, which deals with onsets and rimes.)

When exploring a particular spelling pattern children need not be introduced to all the sounds that the spelling pattern represents. For example, when exploring the spelling pattern *oo* children may not learn about the spelling pattern *oo* representing the /oh/ sound in *brooch*, because the word *brooch* may not

TABLE 8.1	Spelling Patterns Used Most Often in English Words
Pattern	*Sounds the Spelling Pattern Represents*
th	wi*th*, *th*en, *Th*ailand
sh	*sh*e
ch	*ch*air, ma*ch*ine, s*ch*ool, ya*ch*t, *ch*oir, sandwi*ch*
ea	r*ea*dy, gr*ea*t, h*ea*t, cr*ea*te, serg*ea*nt
a-e	h*a*v*e*, m*a*d*e*, *a*r*e*, w*a*r*e*
o-e	h*o*m*e*, c*o*m*e*, m*o*v*e*, g*o*n*e*, p*o*r*e*
i-e	l*i*k*e*, g*i*v*e*, trampol*i*n*e*, rec*i*p*e*
ee	s*ee*n, entr*ee*
ow	n*ow*, fl*ow*, kn*ow*ledge
ai	*ai*m, s*ai*d, pl*ai*d, Th*ai*land, n*ai*ve, capt*ai*n
oo	s*oo*n, l*oo*k, fl*oo*d, br*oo*ch
ou	f*ou*nd, c*ou*ntry, gr*ou*p, b*ou*quet
ar	c*ar*, w*ar*, v*ar*ious, *ar*ound
or	f*or*, w*or*ld, doct*or*, *or*ange
ay	d*ay*, s*ay*s, qu*ay*
ie	th*ie*f, p*ie*, fr*ie*nd, v*ie*w, exper*ie*nce, misch*ie*vous, s*ie*ve, sold*ie*r
igh	l*igh*t
ould	sh*ould*, sh*ould*er
-y	m*y*, bab*y*
oa	b*oa*t, br*oa*d
ew	fl*ew*, n*ew*, s*ew*
e-e	th*e*s*e*, th*e*r*e*, *e*y*e*, w*e*r*e*, n*e*v*e*r, *e*v*e*n
oi	j*oi*n, tort*oi*se
u-e	*u*s*e*, r*u*l*e*, s*u*r*e*, ma*u*v*e*

be part of the children's vocabulary. Nor is it expected that children memorize the spelling patterns and their associated sounds.

Tables 8.1 and 8.2 suggest the possible degree of exploration. For example, if a spelling pattern represents two sounds only, the investigation may be less extensive than a spelling pattern that represents more sounds.

When selecting spelling patterns to explore, consider the sound explorations children have recently engaged in or will soon be engaging in. If you are exploring spelling patterns and common sounds in the same week, try to keep them separate until the children fully understand that they *look* for spelling patterns and *listen* for sounds. For instance, if exploring the spelling pattern *ea* it would

TABLE 8.2	Spelling Patterns Less Commonly Used
Pattern	*Sounds the Spelling Pattern Represents*
oe	shoe, does, goes, poet, amoeba
ir	bird, Iraq, stirrup
ur	turn, rural, injury, hurry
ough	cough, enough, through, though, plough, thought
aw	saw, lawyer
er	her, farmer
ui	build, fruit, guide, guitar, nuisance, genuine, anguish
au	author, aunt, gauge, chauvinist
augh	laugh, caught
oy	boy
ey	they, key
ue	Tuesday, blue, guess, cruel, colleague
ei	seize, reindeer, leisure, either, forfeit
aigh	straight
iew	view
uy	buy
are	are, hare
eau	beautiful, beau
ear	hear, heart, hearth, earth, bear, nuclear
eigh	eight, height, Leigh
eir	their, weird
ere	were, where, here
ua	usual, language, persuade, suave
uar	guard, January, guarantee
our	hour, four, journey
eo	people, leopard, surgeon, video, geography

be better not to study a sound this spelling pattern represents at the same time (for example, the /e/ in *bread* and the /ay/ in *great*).

It is not expected that children will engage in explorations for all the spelling patterns listed in Tables 8.1 and 8.2 in a single school year. Rather, the investigations that take place should relate to the children's writing needs. Spelling patterns may be investigated over a period of two or three years, and some spelling patterns may be explored again in later years as the children's vocabulary grows.

Remember that the important reasons for exploring spelling patterns are for children to learn that a spelling pattern can represent a variety of sounds, and to become aware of possible letter sequences in written English.

Teaching Spelling Patterns

Explorations of spelling patterns should relate to the reading and writing occurring in your classroom so that the children are looking for spelling patterns in words that they know the meanings of. In addition, when spelling patterns are explored in words the children know and therefore can say, they will readily identify the sounds the spelling patterns represent. Thus, it is essential that children be able to pronounce the words in the exploration.

Following are some ways to explore spelling patterns so that they are relevant to children's reading and writing experiences. The explorations are linked to shared reading, a language experience session, and to children's writing.

Using Shared Reading

Observe your students' writing to identify a spelling pattern that many of them are attempting. You may note that many have written the correct letters in words in an incorrect sequence (for example, *nihtg* for *night* or *fonud* for *found*), or that they have written incorrect letters or spelling patterns (for example, *nit* or *nite* for *night, or fownd* for *found*). Or you may notice that the children consistently substitute a letter or spelling pattern for another when they write (for example, the letter *v* for the spelling pattern *th*). If you observe children writing, for example, *ven* and *vere* for *then* and *there,* you may decide to explore the spelling pattern *th*, especially since this pattern occurs in many high-frequency words. It is likely that this particular mistake is a result of the way children articulate *th* words; if so, they need to be shown how to pronounce them correctly. By exploring the *th* spelling pattern and correctly articulating the sounds it represents, you should be able to eliminate this particular substitution.

Once you have identified a common need, review shared reading materials that you can use to have children look for the spelling pattern in question. Try to select texts in which the spelling pattern is used to represent a variety of sounds.

Throughout the exploration be sure to give consistent and clear instructions. Children must understand that they are *looking* for spelling patterns. You may want to make a pair of king-size glasses for a child to wear when the class is looking for spelling patterns.

If you find that the children are confusing the term "spelling pattern" with sound, it may be because you are wrongly using the terms interchangeably. Remember, a spelling pattern is a group of letters that is seen, but a sound is a phoneme that is heard. We *look* for spelling patterns and *listen* for sounds.

The following example suggests how an exploration of the spelling pattern *o-e* might proceed.

Read the familiar Big Books or charts with the children and have them search for words containing the *o-e* pattern (for example, *love, lone, home, one, glove, nose, come, mole, rose, those, hose, hole, some, gone, more, done, phone,* and *alone*). As the children identify the words, list them on a class chart.

Throughout each reading of the various Big Books or charts, add the *o-e* words children identify to the class list. At the completion of each reading say the words on the class list with the children, then have them underline the *o-e* spelling pattern in each word.

Once a sufficient number of words has been listed, have the children identify the various sounds the spelling pattern *o-e* represents. Discuss with them how this knowledge will help them when they write and read.

Next, help them group the words according to the sounds the spelling pattern represents. Begin by writing each word on a card. Organize the children into a circle, and place the cards for the *o-e* words face up in the middle. Have the children say each word and identify the sound the spelling pattern *o-e* represents in the word. If the children are familiar with exploring sounds, some of them could demonstrate how to group the *o-e* words according to sound. Make sure that during the demonstration the children say the words clearly and listen carefully for the sounds.

The resulting groups might look something like this:

/u/	/oh/	/wu/	/o/	/or/
love	lone	one	gone	more
glove	home			
done	phone			
some	alone			
come	hose			
	nose			
	rose			
	those			
	mole			
	hole			

If the children are unfamiliar with grouping words by sound, you may need to show them how to do it. Give each of five or six children a card and guide them in forming pairs or small groups according to the sound the *o-e* represents on their cards. The children in each group could then say their words to check that they sound similar. It may also be necessary to help children realize that the focus should be on the sound the *o-e* represents, irrespective of the letter between the *o-e*. For example, even though the words *home* and *some* have the letter *m* in the middle, they would be placed in two different groups, since the *o-e* pattern represents different sounds in each word.

After the demonstration, each child could be given an *o-e* word card (if there are insufficient cards some children can share a card). They then organize themselves into groups reflecting the various sounds the *o-e* pattern represents. Then, the children in each group say the words on their cards, while the others listen to ensure that the sound that the *o-e* represents is consistent in each word. The groups of cards can then be placed in a pocket chart. Alternately, the grouped cards may be affixed to a class chart using an adhesive such as Blu Tack (which allows the cards to be easily removed for later matching and sorting, and for later reference).

In order for children to be able to form generalizations, many words need to be listed. Throughout the exploration talk with the children about what they have learned about the spelling pattern and how it will help them when writing and reading. Direct their attention toward the variety of sounds the spelling pattern *o-e* represents. Write their generalizations on a class chart. You may want to date the chart, since this facilitates your looking back periodically to see what progress the class has made. It may also be useful to have children write their initials next to their contribution—for example:

April 5 What we know about the spelling pattern o-e

- There are more words with *o-e* representing the /oh/ sound than other sounds.   S. B. and D. S.
- Many *o-e* words have an /u/ sound.   C. R.
- *Ose* is always said with an /oh/ sound.   N. I.
- The spelling pattern *o-e* can represent five sounds.   M. O.
- It is not true that there is a magic *e* that always makes vowels say the long vowel sound, especially in high-frequency words.   D. S.
- I think maybe it is only in the spelling patterns *ove* and *ome* that *o-e* represents the /u/ sound.   H. J.

Initially, some of the children's generalizations may be inaccurate. If this occurs, be sure to cite other *o-e* words from the children's reading and writing that will cause them to rethink the inaccurate generalization. For example, the third generalization above ("*Ose* is always said with an /oh/ sound") does not always hold true, and children could be led to realize this by your introducing the word *whose*.

If children have had limited experience in exploring words containing the *o-e* spelling pattern and have only had activities in which the *e* does cause the preceding vowel to be pronounced as a long vowel, they may have misunderstandings about the oft-referred-to "magic *e*" and the effect it has on a preceding vowel. For this reason investigations of spelling patterns such as *o-e, a-e, i-e, u-e,* and *e-e* may require longer periods of time than others, particularly if they involve redressing children's misunderstandings. Children may discover during the exploration that the "magic *e*" generalization occurs more for *a-e* words. They will probably also discover that the generalization rarely works for high-frequency words.

It is most important throughout this and other spelling pattern explorations that you assist the children in reviewing and revising their generalizations in light of additional words collected. Have children cross out inaccurate generalizations and help them write new ones. Talk with them about how these changes are evidence of their learning, and that they are doing what good spellers do—review and refine their generalizations. Talk with them about how forming generalizations helps them as spellers and readers.

To help children further appreciate what they have learned from the exploration ask them to review some of their earlier pieces of writing to see if they have any new ideas about how certain words could be spelled. Have them think about the sounds they hear in their attempted words and if the spelling pattern they have just explored represents any of those sounds.

Talk with children regularly about how knowing how to spell one word on the class list will help them spell many other words. For example, show children how knowing how to spell *some* will help them spell *somewhere, something, someone,* and *somebody;* knowing *come* will help with *comes, some, home, homes, homework,* and so on. When selecting words to demonstrate these analogies, select words the children will use often when writing or reading. Be sure they understand that thinking about the spelling of a word they know will help them spell a word they do not know when they are writing.

The exploration of the spelling pattern *o* and *e* may be extended by having children explore the spelling patterns within that group, such as *ove, one, ome, ole, ore,* and *ose* and the sounds they represent.

You may want to continue to display the *o-e* charts or make them into a class book, "Our Spelling Pattern *o-e* Book." The book may be divided into two sections, one for the sounds the spelling pattern represents and the other for the children's generalizations. Place the word cards near the book so that children can match and sort the words. Leave some blank pages for children to add words as they discover them when reading and writing. Place the book near the writing center for children to browse through and refer to when proofreading their writing.

Using Language Experience (Talking, Writing, and Reading)

As you should always do, determine children's needs by observing them when they write and/or study their writing, and note the spelling patterns they need to learn about. From these, select a spelling pattern to explore: one that many children in the class are attempting when they write.

The following example suggests how you might investigate the spelling pattern *ch,* perhaps after you have noticed that many of your students are writing *school* as *scool, chip* as *jip,* or *machine* as *mashine.*

To begin the investigation, try to think of an activity that will make the children talk, write, and read about words with the *ch* spelling pattern. For example, the children might make *cheese sandwiches* for *lunch.* Afterward, tell them that together you are going to write about what they did (for example, making cheese sandwiches). Allow the children time to discuss their experience, and help them compose some sentences. Explain that you will be writing, but they will be helping. As you proceed, you might involve them in listening for the sounds in words, finding the letters and spelling patterns that represent the sounds, referring to resources on display such as class spelling lists, or thinking about the meaning relationships between words they know how to spell.

Tell the children that during this writing session you particularly want them to think about the spelling pattern *ch*—the sounds that *ch* represents and its position in words. Explain that you want them to think about this because you have noticed that many of them have been writing words containing the spelling pattern *ch*. It may help the children if you list some of these *ch* words on a chart, but be sure to write the correct spellings only, because incorrect modeling does not help children spell words conventionally.

When writing sentences with the children, leave a blank space for one of the words, ideally a word with the focus spelling pattern, in this case, *ch*. When the sentences are complete reread them, including the missing word, so that everyone can make sure that the piece makes sense and sounds right. Have the children reread the piece and look for words with the spelling pattern *ch*. List these words on a class chart, and have the children underline the spelling pattern *ch* in each word. For example, suppose the sentences the class composed were the following:

At _____ today we made cheese sandwiches for lunch. Cheryl's dad helped us.

In this case the words selected would be these:

cheese
sandwiches
Cheryl's
lunch

Remind children of the word that has been left out of the sentence and have them consider whether or not it may have the spelling pattern *ch*. In this case the omitted word is *school,* which does contain the spelling pattern *ch* and should be added to the list later in the day.

For the rest of the day, leave the chart accessible for children to attempt the omitted word. Have them write their names or initials beside their attempts. Toward the end of the day return to the chart and praise all the children's attempts. Discuss with the children the strategies they used. Then write in the missing word, have children compare their attempts with the conventional spelling, and reread the entire text. The word *school* may then be added to the class chart, learned by the class and added to the alphabet word wall.

To further the exploration of the spelling pattern *ch,* have children search for *ch* words during shared and independent reading sessions, and modeled, shared, interactive, and independent writing sessions. In addition, you may organize other activities that will involve the children in speaking, reading, and writing about words containing the spelling pattern *ch*. For example, you could discuss photographs and pictures found in the children's homes, such as washing machines and chairs or chandeliers.

When several *ch* words have been listed, help children group the words according to the sound *ch* represents. For example, have them listen carefully to the word *sandwiches*. Discuss the two possible pronunciations and how *sandwiches* may be placed in two sound groups, depending on how the *ch* in *sandwiches* is pronounced—as a /ch/ or a /j/ sound. Eventually, the groups might look something like this:

/ch/	/k/	/-/	/sh/	/qw/	/j/
sandwi<u>ch</u>es	s<u>ch</u>ool	ya<u>ch</u>t	<u>Ch</u>eryl's	<u>ch</u>oir	sandwi<u>ch</u>es
<u>ch</u>eese	s<u>ch</u>oolteacher	ya<u>ch</u>ts	ma<u>ch</u>ine		
lun<u>ch</u>			washing		
			ma<u>ch</u>ine		
hopscot<u>ch</u>	s<u>ch</u>oolbag		sewing		
			ma<u>ch</u>ine		
<u>ch</u>ased	s<u>ch</u>oolyard		<u>ch</u>andelier		
mar<u>ch</u>	<u>Ch</u>ristmas		<u>ch</u>auffeur		
cat<u>ch</u>	<u>Ch</u>rist		<u>ch</u>ampagne		
cat<u>ch</u>es	stoma<u>ch</u>		<u>ch</u>ute		
pat<u>ch</u>	<u>ch</u>orus		<u>Ch</u>arlotte		
pat<u>ch</u>es	<u>ch</u>ord		Mi<u>ch</u>elle		
bat<u>ch</u>	<u>ch</u>emist				
lat<u>ch</u>	<u>ch</u>emists				
lat<u>ch</u>es	<u>ch</u>aracter				
stret<u>ch</u>					
fet<u>ch</u>					
<u>ch</u>ocolate					
tea<u>ch</u>er					

Help the children form generalizations about the sounds the spelling pattern *ch* represents and its position in words. Through these discussions the children might learn, for example, that *ch* may occur in any position in a word and that it represents many different sounds. Throughout the exploration help children review and refine their generalizations about the spelling pattern.

Display the *ch* charts and generalizations for children to refer to when proofreading their writing. Encourage them to identify words on the chart that they frequently use when writing, learn them, and add them to the alphabet word wall, and, if appropriate, their personal spelling journals. Also encourage the children to select words to learn for their own writing.

Using Children's Writing

A spelling investigation may also proceed directly from children's writing; it need not always be introduced by another experience, such as shared reading or writing.

The three pieces of writing shown in Figures 8.1, 8.2 and 8.3 were written by children in grade 1, grade 2, and grade 5 respectively. Each piece indicates an attempt to spell words containing the spelling pattern *ea*. We have included this variety of pieces to demonstrate that both beginning writers and older, more experienced writers can benefit from explorations of spelling patterns, and the same pattern may be explored in different grades. The words included in the ex-

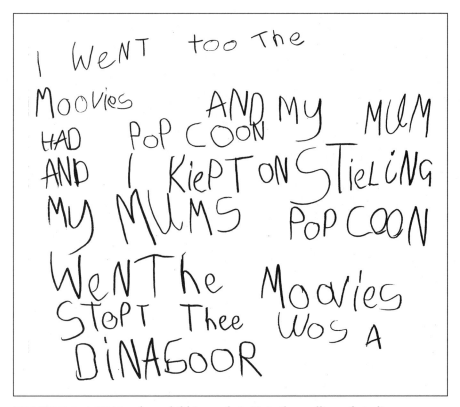

FIGURE 8.1 Writing by a child in grade 1. Note the spelling of *stealing*.

ploration in different grades, however, usually differ greatly due to the older children's more extensive vocabularies. Also, when a spelling investigation is repeated in later years, a more comprehensive investigation usually occurs.

Observe your students as they write and/or collect their writing and note the spelling patterns they use. From these observations select a spelling pattern that many of them are attempting when they write—for example, the spelling pattern *ea*.

Explain the reasons why you will be investigating the spelling pattern *ea* and ask the children to look for words with this pattern as you read familiar material and the print in the classroom generally. List the words as the children find them—for example, *dead, meat, team, ready, create, great, ocean,* and *breakfast.*

Chances are that as they search for words containing the spelling pattern *ea* children will pick out some words containing the spelling pattern *ear*. Similarly, when searching for words containing the spelling pattern *ou*, children may identify words containing the spelling patterns *ough, our, ound,* and *ould.* When this

> Once a upon a time ther was a storog boy ho was the chapen so nobode could defet him. but a nather teme trid to bet them but one boy tacould the storogboy and he codent.

FIGURE 8.2 Writing by a child in grade 2. Note the spelling of *defeat, team,* and *beat.*

happens, list these words, and later review the list, asking the children to look for spelling patterns other than the focus pattern in the listed words. You may have to guide children in identifying the other spelling patterns. Once this is done, group words with the same spelling pattern. You may choose to have the children look for the focus spelling pattern (such as *ea*) and the other spelling patterns (such as *ear*) simultaneously, or you may prefer to deal with each spelling pattern separately.

As the children identify *ea* words, list them and have the children underline the *ea* in each word. When there are several words, help the children group the words according to the pronunciation of *ea*—for example:

dead	meat	great	create	ocean
ready	team			
breakfast				

Some children in the class may pronounce words differently from the majority, perhaps because they come from different English-speaking locations or different cultural groups. Because the words are being grouped according to pronunciation, you will need to help the children group the words according to the way they actually pronounce them. This may result in some different groupings within your own class.

Encourage children to find other *ea* words as they read and write, and add them to the class lists. Discuss and list any useful generalizations, such as "There are not many *ea* words pronounced the same as *ocean.*" You may ask the children to write their names or initials next to their generalizations so that they can compare their present understanding with what they will have learned at a later time.

To make explicit how knowing how to spell one word helps us spell others, you may want to select words from the *ea* lists to form new words. For example:

- Knowing how to spell *dead* helps you spell *deadly, deadlier, deadliest, death, deaths.*

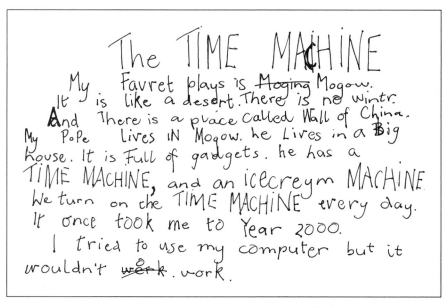

FIGURE 8.3 Writing by a child in grade 5. Note the spelling of *ice cream*.

- Knowing how to spell *team* helps you spell *teams, teamster*.
- Knowing how to spell *great* helps you spell *greater, greatest, greatly*.

Because the lists will be useful resources for children as they write and proof-read, display them for the children to refer to. If children have spelling journals, they may want to write about what they have learned during the investigation and may also select some *ea* words to learn that they think they will use in their writing.

Focusing on ed and ing

Beginning writers may be introduced to *ed* and *ing* as spelling patterns—for example, in the words *red, bed, led,* and *sing, ring, king*. As they learn more about written English they will learn that *ed* and *ing* also have particular meanings when they are added to base words. For example, in the words *played* and *playing, ed* and *ing* are suffixes added to the base word *play*. The addition of the suffixes *ed* and *ing* changes the meaning of *play* to indicate something that is happening now (*ing*) or that happened in the past (*ed*).

Children whose first language is not English, or children who have not been read to often, may have trouble pronouncing words ending with *ed,* because they may not be aware that there are three possible pronunciations. Many children may not know to use *ed* in their writing when they hear /t/ or /d/ in words such as *jumped* or *colored*. Such children need many opportunities in shared reading or reading along with a book and a tape of material that is written in past tense, so that they may have multiple encounters with printed and spoken *ed* words.

For these children it is helpful to deal with the suffix *ed* as you would a spelling pattern, and have them explore the sounds the suffix *ed* represents. Using material that has been read, ask them to help you make a list of words that end in the suffix *ed,* and group them according to the pronunciation of *ed*—for example:

| painted | boiled | hopped |
| wanted | watered | jumped |

Ask them to watch for other *ed* words in their reading and writing, and add them to the appropriate lists. It may be helpful to underline *ed* at the end of these words to help children understand that this particular exploration relates only to the suffix *ed,* and that it can be added to the end of other words.

When they are involved in other word studies, such as sound-symbol groups, spelling patterns, and high-frequency words, ask the children to notice words to which *ed* can be added. There may be some discussion about doubling final letters and other such generalizations, but an in-depth study of these generalizations may not be necessary at this time.

The suffix *ing* may be handled in a similar way.

It would also be helpful during shared reading and writing experiences for you to demonstrate explicitly the strategy of thinking about how to read or write the base word and then add the *ed* or *ing,* and then teach children to use this strategy independently.

Building on Words with a Particular Spelling Pattern

An important benefit of learning about spelling patterns is that knowing how to spell one word with a particular spelling pattern enables you to spell other, similar words. Using a class spelling pattern list, you can show children that as well as their being able to spell many words with the same spelling pattern, they will also be able to spell many other words related in meaning.

For example, in one grade 3 classroom, the children were exploring the spelling pattern *ight*. During the exploration the children found the words *night* and *light* in a book read during shared reading experience.

For homework, the children were asked to build two other words from *night* and *light*. The following day, the teacher listed the words the children found:

night	*light*
nights	lighter
nighttime	lightest
nightie	lightly
nightmare	lighthouse
nightly	candlelight

lamplight
lightning
lighting
relighting
lighten
daylight
flashlight

The children next were asked to build additional words with the spelling pattern *ight*. These were then added to the class list. The children discussed how this word-building activity had helped them as spellers before making an entry on what they had learned in their spelling journals.

Scheduling Spelling Pattern Explorations

As is the case with other spelling explorations, the time required for the first few sessions, when you are introducing the concept, is usually longer than that required for subsequent sessions. As the exploration proceeds, the time spent on it in school may be lessened by having the children search for words as part of their homework. Depending on the children's experience with written English, they may also be able to complete some sound-based grouping activities at home.

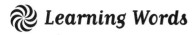 Learning Words

Although class lists are developed to highlight some of the relationships that occur in words in written English, many of these words will also be used by the children in their writing. Encourage the children to learn some of these words, particularly if they are words they often misspell.

When children select words to learn from class lists such as spelling pattern lists, it may be helpful to list other words that contain the same spelling pattern for children to learn. For example, if a child wanted to learn the word *heart* with the *ear* spelling pattern, the words *earth, bear, near,* and *nearly* might also be listed. However, it is important that the children know the meanings of these words, think they would use them in their writing, and do not already know how to spell them. (For further information on children's selecting words to learn and how they might learn words, see Chapters 17 and 18.)

Continuing Evaluation

Observe children's writing continually to note their understanding of spelling patterns. If they continue to misspell words containing spelling patterns that have been explored in class, encourage them to refer to the class charts and their spelling journals to check the spellings of these words, and suggest that they learn these words.

You may also want to collect children's spelling journals on a regular basis, perhaps each child's every three or four weeks. Talk with children individually about their understanding, and have them show you pieces of writing where they have applied their knowledge.

As you note patterns that are misspelled by many children in the class, plan for class investigations. If the pattern is misspelled by only a few, it would be appropriate to plan for small-group or independent explorations.

🌀 Spelling Journals

Personal spelling journals allow children to record the words they are learning and the understanding they develop about spelling patterns. They can also use their journals as a resource, referring to them when proofreading their writing for publication.

A class journal may also be kept. It could have a section for each spelling pattern exploration, and the children may want to have some extra pages in the class journal for regrouping the words according to the sounds the spelling patterns represent and children's generalizations. A contents page could list spelling patterns explored.

☞ Homework Ideas

Plan some homework activities related to spelling pattern explorations. For example:

- Ask children to search for or cut out words in magazines, catalogues, and newspapers that contain the focus spelling pattern in a variety of positions. These words could then be added to the appropriate sound-grouped class chart.

- Have children use cards that have the focus spelling pattern and a variety of letters, prefixes, and suffixes that can be placed in front of or behind the spelling pattern cards to create words. For example, the following letters, the spelling pattern *ear*, and suffixes are written on separate cards. The cards will be used to make words containing the spelling pattern *ear*.

h		t
n		th
d		s
f		ing
g	ear	ed

p	d
r	ly
t	l
w	n
l	er
	est

The children then list the words they can make using the spelling pattern, letters, and suffixes. From the possibilities above, they might come up with the following words:

> hear, hears, hearing, heard
> heart, hearts
> hearth, hearths
> near, nears, nearly, nearing, neared, nearer, nearest
> earth, earthly, earthling, earthed
> bear, bears
> wear, wears, wearing
> pear, pears
> pearl, pearls
> early, earlier, earliest
> dear, dearer, dearest, dearly

Children can then identify the sounds represented by the spelling pattern *ear,* and then can add the words to the appropriate group on the class chart or in their spelling journals.

- Have children make word mazes based on the spelling pattern being explored for other children to complete. This activity will help children develop visual strategies, as they need to *look* for words. For example, children could make the following maze, in which words contain the spelling pattern *th.* Make sure the words are written in the correct direction, from either left to right or top to bottom. Talk with the children about whether or not they wish to list the words players are to look for beneath the maze (as shown in the following example) to help those doing the puzzle to identify the words in the maze.

W	I	T	H	C	T	H	E	I	R
E	T	H	E	T	H	E	R	E	G
A	T	T	I	T	E	T	H	E	M
T	H	A	G	B	Y	M	Y	D	S
H	A	M	R	R	T	O	E	S	E
E	I	O	O	O	H	T	E	I	V
R	L	T	W	T	I	H	T	X	E
C	A	H	T	H	N	E	H	T	N
H	N	F	H	E	K	R	T	H	T
T	H	A	N	R	N	P	A	T	H

with	think	they	there
than	their	the	them
path	growth	moth	weather
brother	mother	sixth	seventh

- Have children prepare activities for others to complete that will get them to think about the serial probability of letters. For example, they could prepare word chains in which a letter is changed in each word to form another word, continuing through a series of changes (*sick* → *silk* → *sill* → *sell* → *well*)

    add-a-letter activities to form new words (*though* → *through*)

    delete-a-letter activities to form new words (*said* → *sad*)

    anagrams, by changing letters in words to form new words (*canoe* → *ocean*)

- Have children find words within words on class lists (for example, from *mother* they might find *moth*, *other*, *the*, *he*, and *her*).

For other ideas about suitable homework and classroom activities, see the references listed at the end of this chapter.

References

Bolton, F., and D. Snowball. 1993. *Ideas for Spelling*. Portsmouth, NH: Heinemann.

————. 1993. *Teaching Spelling: A Practical Resource*. Portsmouth, NH: Heinemann.

Contractions

contraction is the shortened form of a written or spoken expression created by omitting one or more letters or sounds. There are two types of contractions: one formed from two words where the omitted letters are represented by an apostrophe (*we're*); the other being the shortened form of one word where the omitted letters are not represented by an apostrophe (*Dr.*).

It is helpful for children eventually to understand the following about contractions:

• Contractions may be formed from either one word (*Mr.* from *Mister*) or two (*I'm* from *I am*).

• The meaning of a contraction is the same as the meaning of the one or two words it represents.

• The first part of a contraction formed from two words is usually spelled the same way as the first word it stands for (except for *will* in *won't*).

• An apostrophe in a contraction indicates an omission; it usually replaces one (*isn't*) or two letters (*I'll*), but sometimes it replaces more (*o'clock* for *of the clock*).

• In contractions, the apostrophe generally replaces the same letter (or letters) in a given contracted word (for example, the *a* in *are* in the contractions *we're* and *you're*).

• Some contractions have more than one meaning (for example, the contraction *he's* means either *he has* or *he is,* and the contraction *they'd* means either *they had* or *they would*). Their meanings can be determined by the context in a sentence.

119

- A contraction that is a shortened form of a single word ends in the same letter as the word it originated from (for example, *Dr.* for *Doctor*).
- Not all omissions in contractions are indicated by an apostrophe, and contractions formed from single words do not have an apostrophe (for example, *Dr.* for *Doctor*, *Mr.* for *Mister*).
- Shortened forms for names and streets, such as *Mr., Mrs., Ms., Ave., St., Blvd.,* and *Ct.* have a period when written in the United States but not necessarily in other English-speaking countries. However, when addressing envelopes periods should not be used with the contracted words.

At some point you will want to compare contractions with abbreviations, since abbreviations are another form of shortened words. An abbreviation consists of only the initial letter of a word, or the initial letter plus other letters, and usually ends in a period (for example, *anon.* for *anonymous*). Unlike contractions, abbreviations do not include the final letter of the shortened word. To compare contractions and abbreviations, develop class charts of abbreviations and their full forms, as well as contractions and their expanded forms. For example:

Abbreviations (do not include the final letter)		*Contractions (include the final letter)*	
Jan.	January	isn't	is not
Mon.	Monday	govt.	government
vol.	volume	Sr.	Senior
ATM	automatic teller machine		
e.g.	*exempli gratia* (Latin, for example)		

When exploring contractions, discuss the meaning of the verb *contract* and relate it to the term *contraction,* to help students understand that a contraction has fewer letters than its expanded form.

🌀 Evaluating Children's Understanding and Needs

Observe your students' writing to gain a sense of what they know about contractions. Note whether they spell the words that contractions represent consistently when writing and whether or not they understand the consistency with which the apostrophe replaces omitted letters. (For example, some children may spell *couldn't* correctly, but spell *isn't* as *is'nt.*) During writing conferences, talk with the children about their generalizations about contractions.

You may want to have children spell some contractions in order for you to determine their strengths and needs. If so, select words that represent a range of contractions. Words might include:

I'm	he's	she's	we're	they're
I've	he'll	she'll		they've

To help clarify the meanings of the contractions you should both say them in sentences and say their expanded forms.

Such an evaluation will help you determine whether or not a whole-class investigation is required, or whether a number of small-group investigations would be more beneficial.

🌀 *Discovering the Generalizations About Contractions*

Tell the children that you have noticed them using contractions when they write, and that learning about contractions will help them in their spelling and reading.

Explorations of contractions should relate to the reading and writing that is occurring in the classroom. Children should explore words they know the meanings of and can say. If they understand the meanings of the contractions they are more likely to use contractions when writing, particularly when writing dialogue.

Following are two ways to explore contractions during shared reading. The first could be considered a typical session, while the second involves using a familiar Big Book in a readers' theater activity.

Rather than conducting a whole-class exploration of contractions, after an initial class introduction you may consider it more beneficial for children to form groups to investigate a particular group of contractions. For example, some children may be confused about contractions formed with *are,* while others may not know where to place the apostrophe in contractions related to *not.* Individual children may also benefit from investigating contractions related to their personal needs.

Whether children work in groups or independently, have them search familiar reading materials and list examples of the contractions they are investigating. Be sure to provide time for the class to come back together so that groups or individuals can tell the others what they have learned from their exploration. In this way, children learn from each other.

When planning for contraction explorations, you may find some titles more suitable than others. Narratives that contain a great deal of dialogue are good choices, because contractions are more prevalent in spoken than in written English.

Using Shared Reading

Establish the reasons for a contraction exploration with the children, and provide examples of contractions to discuss. Have the children suggest some as well. Be sure they understand that the exploration is being undertaken because you have noticed from their writing that they are confused about certain contractions. To clarify the meanings of the contractions it helps to use them in sentences. This is particularly so when investigating contractions that have more than one meaning, such as *he'd,* which could mean either *he had* or *he would.*

Demonstrate how contractions that children know are formed. An easy way of doing this is to write some individual letter cards for the expanded forms of several contractions together with cards for apostrophes—for example, the letter cards for *did not* and an apostrophe card:

Then, hand out the letter cards and the apostrophe card, one per child. The children then stand in a straight line and form the words *did not,* with a space in between. You may want to suggest that the child with the apostrophe card stand behind the child holding the letter *o* card, and discuss the reason why. Once children have formed the words *did* and *not,* gently squeeze them together, assisting them to *contract,* and in doing so demonstrate how the letter *o* pops out and is replaced by an apostrophe when the words *did not* form a contraction. Repeat this procedure for other contractions children know and suggest that they try this in small groups, providing the letter cards and the apostrophe cards in envelopes, with the contractions written on the outside of the envelope.

Write the contractions formed by the children on a class contractions chart. Include both the expanded and the contracted form of each, and underline the letter or letters the apostrophe replaced. For example:

did n<u>o</u>t	didn't
I <u>a</u>m	I'm
is n<u>o</u>t	isn't
o'clock	<u>of</u> <u>the</u> clock

As you list the contractions discuss the spellings and meanings of the expanded forms and their relationship to the spellings and meanings of the contractions. Use the contractions in sentences, and make sure the children understand the role of the apostrophe in contractions.

Following this initial discussion, invite some children to show their writing to the class, or have the children search the classroom print for contractions. Have children discuss their reasons for identifying words as contractions, focusing the discussion on the meaning and spelling of the contractions, the meaning and spelling of their expanded forms, and the significance of apostrophes.

To provide children with a point of reference, write a definition of the term *contraction* on a class chart, using the children's language.

Introduce one of the familiar Big Books you selected previously, explaining to the children that you will read the book (or part of it), and they are to look and listen for contractions. Then, as you read the book, list the contractions the children identify on a class chart. If they suggest words that are not contractions, list them in another column.

The children may identify words in which an apostrophe is used to indicate possession. These you should list with the words that precede and follow them, and then discuss the role of the possessive apostrophe. It will not be necessary to provide a thorough exploration of the possessive apostrophe at this point; such an exploration is usually more suited to children in their fourth or fifth year of schooling. However, you should provide enough information for children to clarify their understanding of the role of apostrophes.

When you have finished reading the Big Book, return to the list of contractions and ask the children to explain why each word is a contraction. Help them write the contractions in the form of word sums, as shown below. The more children are actively involved in developing the class lists, the more they will engage with the exploration and develop a curiosity about the patterns and consistencies in written English.

wasn't	= was	+ not
I've	= I	+ have
isn't	= is	+ not
you're	= you	+ are
they're	= they	+ are
didn't	= did	+ not

Initially, the children will probably identify common contractions that represent two words and that contain an apostrophe. If common contractions of one word, such as *Mr.*, also occur in a book used for shared reading, you may want to point out this other form of contraction.

Encourage the children to participate in the exploration by listing other contractions they know or find during class, group, and independent reading and writing sessions.

Throughout the exploration, the children could rewrite words from the class lists on individual cards, using one card for the contraction and another for the expanded form. These cards could then be used for sorting and matching activities. The children could sort the cards according to the two types of contractions (with and without apostrophe) as well as by the second contracted word within the contraction.

By sorting the cards according to the second word within the contraction, the children will see more readily the letter or letters the apostrophe replaces in specific words—for example, the *woul* in contractions of *would* (*he'd* for *he would*, *I'd* for *I would*, and *she'd* for *she would*). If you model or get the children to model these sorting activities before they begin working independently in small groups or pairs, they are more likely to experience greater success.

For example, here are some contractions sorted according to the second word the contraction represents:

is or *has*	*had* or *would*	*will*	*not*	*have*	*are*	*am*
he's	I'd	I'll	couldn't	I've	they're	I'm
she's	you'd	you'll	wouldn't	you've	we're	
it's	they'd	he'll	shouldn't	we've	you're	
that's	we'd	she'll	didn't	they've		

is or *has*	*had* or *would*	*will*	*not*
there's	he'd	we'll	don't
how's	she'd	they'll	doesn't
where's			hasn't
what's			hadn't
here's			haven't
why's			wasn't
when's			weren't
who's			isn't
			aren't
			can't
			won't

When grouping the words the children may move beyond the notion of contractions and group the words according to word families, spelling patterns, or common sounds—for example, words in the word family based on the word *do* (*don't, doesn't,* and *didn't*) or the spelling patterns in words such as *couldn't, wouldn't,* and *shouldn't.*

Encourage children to verbalize their generalizations about contractions; have them initial their observations. For example:

March 15 We know a lot about contractions.

- Most contractions have apostrophes to let us know some letters are missing.   H. L.
- When *have* is the contracted word the two letters *ha* are always replaced by an apostrophe.   L. B.
- *I'm* means the same as *I am.*   R. N.
- Lots of contractions have *not* in them, and it looks like this: *n't.*   D. B.
- The meaning of the two smaller words is the same as the contraction.   A. B.

Contractions that are high-frequency words may be added to the alphabet word wall, written on a colored piece of cardboard, or displayed on an alphabetical list, such as the following:

can't	can not
couldn't	could not
didn't	did not
doesn't	does not
don't	do not
. . .	. . .
you'll	you will

By grouping contractions in different ways the children will be better able to access them according to their needs as they write and read. For example, if they are unsure of which letters the apostrophe replaces, they can discover this by referring to the list of contractions grouped according to the contracted word. If they want to find all the contractions beginning with a particular word, such as *they,* the children may do so by referring to an alphabetical list of contractions.

Because the contractions *can't* and *won't* do not follow the general rules of how contractions are formed, encourage the children to speculate about why they are spelled the way they are. The children may suggest that it would look strange if there were three consonants together in *cann't* and four consonants together in *willn't,* since the English language doesn't usually have three or four consonants together. They may also consider why the letter *o* is introduced in the contraction *won't*—whether it follows the same pattern as *did* and *don't,* or whether the original word for *will* was *woll* and its pronunciation has changed over the years.

It also would be interesting to have the children explain which *n* has been retained and which has been omitted in the word *can't.* For example, they could consider whether the initial word *can* has been left intact (as in other contractions) and whether the apostrophe replaces the *no* in *not.* Alternately, they may propose that the omitted *n* is from *can,* and *not* is spelled as it normally is in a contraction (*n't*).

In these cases the children should realize that there may not be one right or wrong explanation.

Readers' Theater

Another contraction exploration that can grow out of shared reading is known as readers' theater. Here a familiar Big Book that contains a lot of dialogue is marked up as a script for the children to perform. The idea is to use dialogue incorporating contractions. On other occasions, rather than using a Big Book for readers' theater, you may choose to adapt a narrative to create a puppet play, a radio play, a stage script or a video script for a similar purpose.

To facilitate adaptation, use Post-it notes and nonpermanent glue, so that your notes and alterations can be removed from the book when the class has completed the activity.

Use the Post-it notes to indicate which character is to speak, and the glue to paste strips of paper over clauses such as "her father roared when she told him" and "she said" (see the example below). The only print remaining visible in the book will be the print to be read by the narrator and the dialogue to be spoken by the various characters.

For example, consider the following extract (from pp. 10–11 of *The Frog Who Would Be King* by Kate Walker):

> His efforts were rewarded. Her answer was "yes." She would marry him, frog or not.
>
> "Marry a frog?" her father roared when she told him. "You can't be serious. Don't you know that the man you marry will one day become king in my place?"
>
> "Yes, Father," she said, "I know, and I think Reginald would make a wonderful king. He's wise and courageous and kind."

"I don't care if his blankets are made from boy scout badges," cried the king. "He's still a frog, and he's not going to sit on my throne!"

In order to adapt this text as a readers' theater script, you would insert Post-it notes to the left of the lines of dialogue to indicate who is speaking, and cover the text that is not dialogue with strips of paper (indicated below by strikeouts):

Narrator	His efforts were rewarded. Her answer was "yes." She would marry him, frog or not.
The King	"Marry a frog?" ~~her father roared when she told him.~~ "You can't be serious. Don't you know that the man you marry will one day become king in my place?"
Lil	"Yes, Father," ~~she said,~~ "I know, and I think Reginald would make a wonderful king. He's wise and courageous and kind."
The King	"I don't care if his blankets are made from boy scout badges," ~~cried the king.~~ "He's still a frog, and he's not going to sit on my throne!"

If necessary, begin the readers' theater activity by introducing or revising the meaning of the term *contraction*. If you are introducing the term, provide the children with examples in sentences and be sure they understand the relationship in spellings and meanings between the contractions and the words they stand for, and the role of apostrophes.

However, if your exploration of contractions is already in progress, encourage children to explain what they have learned so far about them. Throughout these explanations encourage other children to comment upon and question what is being said, and ask the children providing the explanations to refer to the class lists of contractions and generalizations to clarify statements they make.

Explain that as a class you are going to write a readers' theater script to perform before an audience. Present the children with some familiar narratives that contain dialogue and a variety of characters. Allow them to select one to perform.

Help the children adapt the book into a script. Tell them they will be turning the narrative into a readers' theater script by identifying who is talking and what each one will say.

When the script is complete, have the children practice reading it. Consider taping it, so that they can evaluate their performance. Help them plan sound effects; model the use of the letters *FX* to indicate sound effects in the script.

During this activity, have the children identify contractions and list them on a class list. Encourage them to remain watchful for contractions as they read and write, and continue to add those identified to the class list. When there are several contractions, have the children suggest ways of grouping them (as described earlier, this may be according to the two types of contractions, by the second contracted word, or in alphabetical order).

Throughout the exploration, have children identify high-frequency words and select contractions to learn for their personal writing needs. Also, help them form, review, and refine their generalizations about contractions. During writing sessions, encourage the children to refer to the displayed class contraction lists and the relevant generalizations.

Scheduling Contraction Explorations

A contraction exploration would generally occur over a period of one to two weeks, although not necessarily every day during that time. This will vary depending upon your students' needs and how quickly you locate a variety of contractions. It is better to spend whatever time is necessary to ensure that the children understand the concepts involved than to finish the exploration quickly.

Sometimes the contraction explorations will occur daily for a period of time; at other times they will occur amid other spelling focuses.

As is the case with most other spelling explorations, longer sessions of 20 to 30 minutes may be necessary in the early stages of a contraction exploration. Children will need time to develop a knowledge base from which they can start forming generalizations. As the exploration progresses, less time is usually needed.

🌀 Learning Words

Throughout the exploration encourage the children to review the class lists regularly to identify high-frequency words. Guide the children in understanding that the expanded forms of most contractions consist of high-frequency words.

By grade 2 most children will be able to spell most of the high-frequency words and their associated contractions, particularly if the school has implemented a planned spelling program similar to the one we outline in this book. Children in grade 2 who cannot yet spell all of the high-frequency words should be encouraged to identify and learn some of them. If some of these words may be combined with others to form contractions, these children should be taught explicitly about these relationships. For example, they could be shown how the high-frequency words *they, I, we,* and *have* may be combined to form the contractions *they've, I've,* and *we've.* (You would also need to point out the letter or letters the apostrophe replaces in the contractions they were learning.) By making explicit the meaning relationships, students will learn to spell high-frequency words they are unsure of and will further their understanding of contractions.

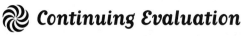 Continuing Evaluation

Observe your students' writing to note how they spell contractions. If they continue to misspell contractions they use frequently when writing, you should work together to ensure that the children learn them. If you want additional information to ascertain their progress, you may ask them to respell some of the contractions they tried to spell at the beginning of the exploration.

Spelling Journals

Children may want to keep a record of contractions and their understanding of them in personal spelling journals. Help them see the value of their spelling journals as a resource to refer to when proofreading their writing.

☞ Homework Ideas

A variety of homework tasks can relate to contraction explorations. For example:

- Have children search for and bring short lists of contractions to add to the class list.
- Ask them to make letter and apostrophe cards to use in making simple crosswords.
- Prepare cards and paper for playing Contraction Bingo. The children would need to select eight pairs of words (contractions and their extended forms) and list them. For example:

didn't	did not
isn't	is not
I've	I have
I'm	I am
they've	they have
o'clock	of the clock
we've	we have
you're	you are

Each player would then be provided with a list of the eight pairs and a piece of paper containing sixteen squares. The players are to write each contraction or its extended form in one of the sixteen squares wherever they choose. For example, here are two different players' placements of the listed words:

did not	*didn't*	*isn't*	*I have*	*I've*	*isn't*	*did not*	*you are*
I've	*I am*	*of the clock*	*I'm*	*didn't*	*they have*	*o'clock*	*we've*
they have	*you are*	*is not*	*you're*	*we have*	*of the clock*	*they've*	*you're*
we have	*o'clock*	*they've*	*we've*	*is not*	*I have*	*I'm*	*I am*

To commence play, a leader reads out each contraction or expanded form and on a given call out the players mark both the contraction and its expanded form on the sheet. The first player who has a row or diagonal filled calls "Bingo," reads the words aloud and wins the game.

• Have children use the contraction cards with their expanded forms to play games such as Memory. In this game the words are spread out, face down, and children take turns turning two cards face up. As the children turn the cards over, they say what is written on each card. If a player matches a contraction with a card that has its expanded form, that player keeps the pair of cards and can continue picking up cards as long as they are matching pairs. When this is no longer possible, the next player has a turn. The player with the greatest number of cards at the end of the game is the winner.

Reference

Walker, K. 1994. *The Frog Who Would Be King.* Greenvale, NY: Mondo.

Compound Words

here are two accepted definitions of the term *compound word*. A widely held understanding is that a compound word combines the meaning of the two or more smaller words within it. For example, the meaning of *breakfast* relates to the meanings of the smaller words *break* and *fast* within it: to *break* a *fast*.

This definition contrasts with Crystal's (1997) definition of a compound word: that it "consists . . . of two or more free morphemes," the smallest units of meaning (p. 76). According to Crystal's definition, words such as *butterfly*, *carpet*, and *legend* are also compound words, even though the meanings of these words do not relate to the meanings of the smaller words within them.

Because the first definition is more relevant when considering spelling strategies, this is the definition we will use in this chapter. Keep in mind, however, that seeing the smaller words within a word, even if they are not related in meaning to the larger one, can be a useful strategy in remembering how to spell them.

It is helpful for children to be aware of compound words when writing, because knowing how to spell the smaller words within compounds, as well as the compound words themselves, assists children in being able to spell other words or terms that are related in meaning. For example:

• If children can spell *life* in *lifesaver* it will help them spell *lifeboat*, *lifestyle*, *lifelike*, *life cycle*, *life jacket*, and so on, all words related in meaning to the word *life*.

- If children can spell a compound word—for example, *someone*—they can spell the smaller words *some* and *one* within it, as well as other words related in meaning to *some* and *one*, such as *something* and *anyone*.

To introduce the exploration, explain the three types of compounds:

- a single, closed word, such as *breakfast, birthday,* and *bookworm;*
- hyphenated words, such as *fire-eater, make-believe,* and *brother-in-law;* and
- separately written words (called open compounds), such as *book club, White House,* and *life jacket.*

Clarify children's understanding of the different types of compound words by having them:

- identify the smaller words within a word;
- consider the meaning of each smaller word;
- consider the meaning of the word containing the smaller words;
- consider whether the meaning of the smaller words relates to the meaning of the word containing them.

Write children's explanations of the term *compound word* on a class chart, using the children's language. For example:

- Compound words have two small words in them.
- Some compound words have three or four small words in them.
- Compound words are like word sums: ear + ring = earring, hair + brush = hairbrush.
- Meaning is important: a compound word usually means the total of the meanings of the smaller words.
- Knowing how to spell compound words helps you spell lots of other words.

For hyphenated compounds, discuss how hyphens are used to clarify meaning for readers, and that whether or not hyphens are used sometimes depends on the personal view of an author or editor or the writers of dictionaries. Children could check the hyphenation of words in more than one dictionary, since variations can occur. Tell the children that when they consult the dictionaries, they should determine the most common rendition of the compound (hyphenated or not), think about the clearest way of writing the word for their readers, and spell the word accordingly.

⟳ Evaluating Children's Understanding and Needs

Observe your students' writing to gain a general sense of what they know about compound words. Note whether they spell the smaller words that make up compound words consistently when the words stand alone or are part of compounds. For example, children may spell *some* conventionally when used by itself and in the compound *something,* but misspell it as *sum* in *sumone* (*someone*); or they may spell *no* conventionally by itself and in *nobody,* but misspell it as *nu* in *nuthing* (*nothing*).

Before beginning the compound word exploration you may decide to check children's spelling of some compound words and the smaller words within them, particularly the high-frequency compound words. For example, you may ask children to write the words *day, birth,* and *birthday,* or *cup, board,* and *cupboard* to see if they understand the relationships between the spellings and meanings of the compound words and the smaller words within them.

In this way, you will be able to determine whether the class as a whole would benefit from an exploration of compound words or whether only a small group would benefit.

🌀 Discovering the Generalizations About Compound Words

Explorations about compound words may be done incidentally throughout the year as a compound word occurs in children's reading and writing, but initially you may want to have the children undertake a more in-depth study.

Tell the children that you have noticed that they use compound words when they write, and explain that learning about compound words can help them with their spelling and reading. It may help to illustrate this point by pointing out how some children have not understood the meaning relationships between some words—for example, when they spell *some* correctly in *something,* but incorrectly in *sumone.*

Explorations of compound words should be done using the reading and writing that occurs in the classroom so that children will be studying words they understand and can say. If they know the meaning of the compound words they explore there is a greater possibility they will use them when writing. But if they cannot pronounce, and do not know the meaning of, a compound word and the smaller words within it, they will not be able to identify a word as being a compound.

Following are two ways to explore compound words so that they are relevant to children's reading and writing. The examples given link explorations of compound words to shared reading and interactive writing. Read-aloud sessions may also be used to further an exploration of compound words, though the children will not be able to see the words.

When thinking about exploring compound words within shared or interactive writing sessions, you may find that some topics are better suited to the use of compound words than others. The human body; cars, trucks, and bicycles;

rooms in a house and appliances in homes; or fires and firefighters are all topics where you are likely to encounter many compound words.

Using Shared Reading

Search familiar materials used for shared reading that will give children practice in looking and listening for compound words.

Having established the reasons for the compound word exploration with your students, demonstrate the meaning of the term *compound word* by providing children with examples and having them suggest their own. Try to introduce compound words consisting of two or more smaller words, such as *eyebrow, double-decker* (bus), and *jack-in-the-box*. Write the compound words on a class chart; then count the number of smaller words in the compound words and discuss the spellings and meanings of the smaller words and their relationship to the spellings and meanings of the compounds.

Invite some children to show their writing to the class or have the children search the classroom print for compound words. Have them discuss their reasons for identifying certain words as compound words. Focus the discussion on the meaning of each smaller word and the meaning of the compound word, and the spelling of each smaller word and the spelling of the compound.

Introduce a familiar Big Book, explaining to the children that you will read the book (or part of the book) and they are to look and listen for compound words.

To assist children, demonstrate the task by saying a group of words—for example, *bathroom, bath, key,* and *keyhole*—and clapping when you hear a compound word. Ask them to explain why *bathroom,* for example, is a compound word but *bath* is not, and to take turns in identifying other compound words from a set of words, identifying the smaller words within them and explaining their related meanings.

List the compound words the children identify on a class chart. If they suggest words that are not compound words (for example, words with prefixes and suffixes), list them to one side of the list, but not in the column of compound words. These noncompound words will provide opportunities for you to clarify the children's understanding of compound words.

When you have finished reading, return to the list of compound words and ask the children to explain why each word is a compound. Refer to dictionaries that give the derivations of some words to show how a compound word and the smaller words within it are related in meaning, since at times the meaning connections may be a little obscure.

The compound words may be listed as word sums, as shown below. You might write the compound words in the left-hand column and have the children complete the remaining columns by writing the word sums on strips of paper and, once checked, adding them to the class list. Generally, the more the children can be responsible for developing the class lists, the more they will learn.

Here is an example of a compound words chart:

earphones	= ear	+ phones	
earring	= ear	+ ring	
hairbrush	= hair	+ brush	
father-in-law	= father	+ in	+ law
toothbrushes	= tooth	+ brushes	
toothpaste	= tooth	+ paste	
fireplace	= fire	+ place	
newspaper stand	= news	+ paper	+ stand

Encourage the children to participate in the exploration by listing other compound words they know or find during class, group, and independent reading and writing sessions.

Throughout the exploration, the children could rewrite words from the class lists on individual cards, using one card for the compound word and another card for the smaller words within the compound. For example:

birthday	*birth + day*
great-grandmother	*great + grand + mother*

Show children that using parts of compound words can help them spell other, related compounds, such as:

- birthday: daybreak, daytime
- great-grandmother: grandstand, mother-in-law

Encourage the children to use a word book or dictionary to help them build lists of compound words, and have them write the words that make up the compounds on cards.

The children could use the cards for sorting and matching activities. If the children are not familiar with sorting activities, involve the class in a number of such activities before having them work independently in pairs or small groups. As they are working independently and sorting the compound words, observe the criteria they employ and challenge them by suggesting different criteria for sorting or having them identify other criteria of their own. For example, they may choose to sort compound words according to the number of smaller words within them, or group them according to the type of compound the word is— open or closed, hyphenated, or a combination (found, for example, in the word *great-grandmother*).

When they are grouping the words, children may move beyond the boundaries of compound words and group them according to spelling pattern or common sound, using, for example, the *ea* spelling pattern or the /e/ sound in *gingerbread* and *breakfast,* or the meaning relationships in words such as *lifeguard* and *lifeboat.*

The children may also use the cards to play games. For example, they may place the cards face up, one by one on top of each other. When a compound word is followed by the card with the smaller words within it, the first player to call "Match" and name the compound word and the smaller words within it wins the pile of cards. The player with the greatest number of cards at the end of the game is the winner. (To maximize children's learning when they play spelling card games, encourage them to say the word or words on each card before they play it.)

If the children are not experienced in forming generalizations you may choose to write them as a class. However, if the children are competent in formulating and writing generalizations, you might demonstrate writing one together as a class and then have the children break into pairs or small groups to write their own, which they will subsequently share with the class. Once the children have shared and tested their generalizations with the class, those who have written similar generalizations could then get together as a group to refine and clarify their generalization. All the generalizations could then be written and displayed for the children to refer to, with the date included on the chart as a record of the children's understanding at that particular time. The list can be reviewed periodically, with the children encouraged to change or add to them as their knowledge grows.

Here is an example of such a list:

March 15 We know heaps about compound words!

- If you can spell *birthday,* you can spell *birth* and *day.*
- If we can spell *rain* in *raincoat,* we can spell *rain* in *rainbow, raining,* and *rained.*
- The word *cupboard* has *cup* and *board.* Long ago, cups were put on boards. Now we will remember the letter *p* in *cupboard.*
- We know compound words can have two, three, or four words. We're looking out for compound words with five smaller words.
- Some compound words, like *damage,* have smaller words in them (*dam* and *age*) whose meanings do not add up to mean the same as *damage.* These are another type of compound word.

Review the class lists regularly to identify and learn high-frequency words or current topic words to add to the class alphabet word wall.

Since by grade 2 almost all children should be able to spell most of the high-frequency words, they may only be involved in activities that get them to learn how to spell other words related in meaning to the compound words. For example, show children how knowing how to spell *no* will help them spell *nothing, no one, nowhere,* and *nobody,* or by knowing how to spell *birthday* they can also spell *birth, births, day,* and *days.*

In particular, discuss how the high-frequency words *some, one, with, in,* and *out* may be combined to form the compound words *someone, without,* and *within.* This activity could then be extended to demonstrate how to spell other compound words containing these words, such as *outside, everyone,* and *anyone.*

In this way children can learn to spell high-frequency words they may be unsure of and at the same time further their understanding of compound words.

The compound word charts may be made into a class compound word book, organized in alphabetical order, with at least one page for each letter of the alphabet. Alphabetical order highlights the fact that knowing how to spell one word in a compound can help you spell other words (though obviously this is limited to the first word of the compounds). For example, on the *a* page the words *anybody, anyone, anything,* and *anywhere* might be listed in sequence, while on the *l* page *lamplight* and *lamppost* might be listed.

Using Interactive Writing

If necessary, begin the exploration by introducing or revising the meaning of the term *compound word*. If introducing the term, provide children with examples, and be sure they understand the relationship in spellings and meanings between compound words and the smaller words within them.

If your exploration of compound words is already in progress, encourage some children to explain what they have learned so far about compounds. Throughout these explanations encourage other children to comment upon and question what is being said, and ask the children providing the explanations to refer to the class lists of compound words and generalizations to clarify statements they make.

Tell the children that you are going to write a piece together about the current topic you are studying, and guide the children in choosing a purpose for writing. For example, if the children are studying the topic of transportation, they may want to write descriptions of different forms of transportation and the features of each, explanations of how the different forms of transportation work, or an account of a transport-related excursion, such as to a bus depot or airport, they themselves took.

Assist the children in composing their thoughts and writing them down. Tell them they will all help to write the class piece by writing words they know how to spell, and they will try to spell words they are not sure of by thinking about the relationship of the unfamiliar word to words they do know how to spell. For example, explain that they could:

- listen for the sounds in words and think about the letters and spelling patterns they know that represent the sounds;
- think about letters and spelling patterns they know and the sounds they represent; and
- think about the meaning relationships between words and how this can help them spell other words; for example, if they can spell the compound word *boathouse* it will help them spell *boatyard* and *boatbuilder,* or if they can spell *happy* it will help them spell *unhappy.*

Explain that although you need them to help you write all the words, you want them to think particularly during this writing session about compound words and their relationships in spellings and meanings to the smaller words within them.

When the draft is complete, reread the completed piece with the children to check that it makes sense and sounds right; then reread the piece to look and listen for compound words. Ask the children to justify their choices and add the compound words to the class lists.

Following is an example of a piece of interactive writing, in this case an account a class wrote after visiting an airport:

Visiting the Airport

Last week we visited an airport. Lots of different airlines use the airport.

We saw the Radar Center at the Control Tower and learned this was where air traffic controllers tell pilots what to do when they take off and land planes.

We went into a special room near the check-in section. The lady told us about the work that immigration officers do to make sure no criminals enter the country.

She also told us how custom officers check passengers' bags to make sure there is nothing dangerous in them.

We walked around the terminal and a man showed us some airline tickets and boarding passes. He explained that planes were now non-smoking and that there were films for in-flight entertainment.

We walked past the duty-free shop to the bus stop, where we hopped into the school bus and came back to school.

Once the piece was written, the children identified and discussed the meanings of the compound words and how they related to the meanings of the smaller words within them. The compound words were then listed on a class chart:

airport	= air	+ port	
airlines	= air	+ lines	
Radar Center	= Radar	+ Center	
Control Tower	= Control	+ Tower	
air traffic controllers	= air	+ traffic	+ controllers
take off	= take	+ off	
check-in	= check	+ in	
immigration officers	= immigration	+ officers	
custom officers	= custom	+ officers	
nothing	= no	+ thing	
airline tickets	= air	+ line	+ tickets
boarding passes	= boarding	+ passes	
in-flight	= in	+ flight	
duty-free	= duty	+ free	
bus stop	= bus	+ stop	
school bus	= school	+ bus	

The teacher then showed the children how knowing how to spell one word within a compound word would help them spell other words—for example, if they knew how to spell *air* in *airport* it would help them spell *airline, airlines,* and *airbus,* or if they know how to spell *check* it would help them spell *checkbook, checker, checked,* and *checking.*

Encourage students to remain watchful for compound words as they read and write and have them add the compound words they find to the class lists.

Throughout the exploration, get children involved in searching for examples of compound words and forming, reviewing, and refining their generalizations.

Scheduling Compound Word Explorations

The initial compound word exploration should occur over a period of one to two weeks, although not necessarily on a daily basis. Since compound words are not hard to understand, the children may grasp the concepts fairly quickly.

Sometimes you may explore compound words on a daily basis as a sole spelling exploration for a period of time; at other times you may want to study them amidst other spelling explorations.

Like most other spelling explorations, longer sessions of 20 to 30 minutes may be necessary in the early stages, so that children can develop a knowledge base from which they can start forming generalizations. As the exploration progresses, the time required may be less.

After the major exploration is completed, encourage children to continue to notice compound words. They may want to add newly found compounds to the class list or word book.

🌀 Learning Words

The entries on class compound word lists should be listed in a way that highlights the relationships in spellings and meanings between compound words and the smaller words within them. Children need not learn the words on the lists. However, some children may be directed to learn some high-frequency compound words for their writing and to consider how this will help them when spelling other words. For example, if a child was to learn the word *everything* from the compound word class list, he or she should also think about how knowing that word will help them spell the words *everyday, everywhere, everybody, everyone, nothing, something,* and *anything.* Children should choose to learn listed compound words they know they will use often in their writing.

🌀 Spelling Journals

Children may want to keep a record of compound words and their understanding of them in their personal spelling journals. The journals may have a section for compound word explorations, and the children may wish to have a column for each letter of the alphabet, in order to facilitate their finding the compound words they will want to use as they write.

Children should also be led to appreciate the value of their spelling journals as a resource to refer to when proofreading their writing.

☞ *Homework Ideas*

Children may be given enjoyable homework tasks related to compound words. For example:

- Have children bring items from home for their classmates to name— *saltshaker, nailbrush, toothbrush,* and so on. Have them identify the smaller words within the compounds.
- Have them search for and bring in short lists of compound words to add to the class list.
- Have them refer to their spelling journals, word books, dictionaries, and class compound word charts to make crosswords for their classmates to complete. You may have to teach children the basics of making crosswords by modeling how to construct one. Initially, it would be best to keep the crossword simple by using only a few compound words. For example:

```
              B
              I
              C              S
              Y              E
       R      C              A
  H    E  A  D  L  I  G  H   T
       A      E              B
       R      P              E
       L      U              L
       I      M              T
       G      P
       H
       T
```

Clues

Across

4 head + light =

Down

1 bicycle + pump =

2 seat + belt =

3 rear + light =

Reference

Crystal, D. 1997. *A Dictionary of Linguistics and Phonetics.* 4th ed. Oxford, UK: Blackwell Publishers.

Homophones

n the English language there are many *homophones*—words that sound the same, but are spelled differently and have different meanings. It is important that children learn how the spelling and meaning of such words depend on their grammatical function.

You may extend sound explorations to include the investigation of homophones with children who are ready to understand their usage, those who are, perhaps, in their third or fourth year of school. Younger children may acquire some incidental learning about homophones, but understanding their grammatical usage requires knowledge of written English. Although the explorations described in this chapter involve a class, the same process could be used with a small group. An individual child could also be guided to find out about particular homophones, but in this case there would not be the opportunity to compare ideas with other children.

Because children often misspell or misuse frequently used homophones it may be useful to limit the exploration of homophones to the ones children use most often in their writing, such as *there/their/they're, two/too/to, which/witch, its/it's,* and *here/hear.*

Homophones must be explored within the context of a clause or a sentence, because context determines the meaning and spelling of homophones. The context of a homophone also provides insight into its grammatical role. For example, in the following sentences containing *hear* and *here* the meaning and grammatical function of each homophone becomes apparent.

Here is the park. Put the painting here.
I can hear the music. I hear you are moving.

The homophone *here* is an adverb whose meaning relates to a place, while the homophone *hear* is a verb whose meaning relates to the ears.

In the initial stages of exploring homophones, you may wish to discuss the differences between homophones, homonyms, and homographs:

- *Homophones* are words that sound the same, but are spelled differently and have different meanings—for example, *hear* and *here*.
- *Homonyms* are words that sound the same and are spelled the same, but have different meanings—for example, *table* (furniture) and *table* (math).
- *Homographs* are words that sound different, but are spelled the same and have different meanings—for example, *minute* (time) and *minute* (small).

It may help if you explain that the word *homophone* is formed from the two roots *homo* (same) and *phone* (sound), *homograph* is formed from the two roots *homo* (same) and *graph* (writing), and *homonym* is formed from the two roots *homo* (same) and *nym* (name).

Since some children may still not understand the meaning of the term *homophone* provide them with examples, and have them suggest their own, encouraging them to use each homophone in a sentence. It may also be helpful to write an explanation of the term *homophone* on a class chart, using the children's language. For example:

Homophones sound the same.
There are lots of homophones, but you have to know which one to use in your
    writing because they sound the same but are not spelled the same.
Homophones have different meanings.

To summarize this explanation, you may want to have children draw a visual representation as shown, for example, in Figure 11.1

🌀 Evaluating Children's Understanding and Needs

Observe your students' writing to gain a general sense of what they know about spelling homophones within a set, and knowing when to use each. Such observations will assist you in determining a child's needs. For example, if the children do not know how to spell and when to use certain homophones that are on the list of high-frequency words, you might begin with them. For example, you may find that the children either misspell or misuse the commonly used homophones *to, too,* and *two; its* and *it's; there, their,* and *they're;* or *here* and *hear.*

To help you to quickly determine whether this is the case, dictate some sentences for the children to write containing a set of homophones—for example:

- *They're* going to the movies tonight.
- Where is *their* house?
- I put the pen over *there*.
- I wonder where *they're* going.

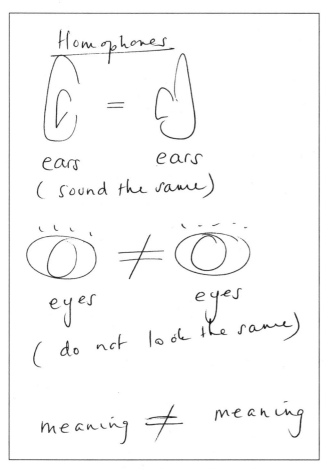

FIGURE 11.1 A visual definition of homophones.

- They left *their* books behind.
- I will be *there* soon.

By noting how well the children spell the homophones in these sentences, you will be able to determine whether a class exploration is necessary or whether a group exploration of a particular homophone set would be beneficial.

You may also want to discuss with children and observe how they use resources to proofread their writing and find the correct spelling and usage of homophones, and note their needs.

🌀 Discovering the Generalizations About Homophones

When introducing a homophone exploration, make sure the children understand that the purpose of the exploration is to help them as writers and readers.

Tell them that you have noticed that they sometimes use an incorrect homophone when they write, so you are going to explore homophones together and learn how knowing about homophones can help them with their spelling and reading.

Homophone explorations should be done using the reading and writing that is already occurring in the classroom so that children will be learning about homophones they can say and know the meanings of. If they cannot say a word and do not know the meaning of a word, they will not be able to distinguish homophones.

It is unusual for multiple examples of homophones within a particular set (for example, *too, two,* and *to*) to occur in a piece of modeled, shared, or interactive writing. For this reason, both examples of homophone explorations given in this chapter are linked with multiple shared reading experiences. This does not mean that the use of homophones would not arise during modeled, shared, interactive and independent writing sessions in various curriculum areas. When this happens, the homophones could be added to the class lists and their spelling and usage discussed.

The examples we provide that link homophone explorations to shared reading represent two different forms of organization. The activities related to the homophone set *to, too,* and *two* reflect one way of planning a whole-class exploration, while the exploration of the homophones *there, they're,* and *their* combine whole-class and small-group activities.

Regardless of your organization, you must first observe your students' writing to note their use of homophones, and identify one set of homophones on which to focus. The set you select should be homophones that many of your students are attempting. Once the set is selected, you should then select familiar texts in which those homophones occur.

You may also select titles to read to the class in order to create a general interest in homophones—for example, Fred Gwynne's humorous books, including *The King Who Rained* and *A Little Pigeon Toad.*

In addition, consider placing copies of word books, such as the *Writer's Word Book* (Snowball 1997), in the writing center for children to refer to. In this word book the meanings of homophones are conveyed in illustrations crossreferenced to assist writers in selecting the appropriate homophone (see Figure 11.2).

Using Shared Reading to Explore To, Too, and Two

When beginning a study of homophones—for example, *to, too,* and *two*—tell the children that you have noticed many of them using these homophones when they write, and that they are often able to spell these words conventionally but do not always know which one to use.

You may wish to show a child's piece of writing to the class and have the children identify the homophones *to, too,* and *two* in the piece. Have the children discuss their reasons for identifying words as homophones, focusing the dis-

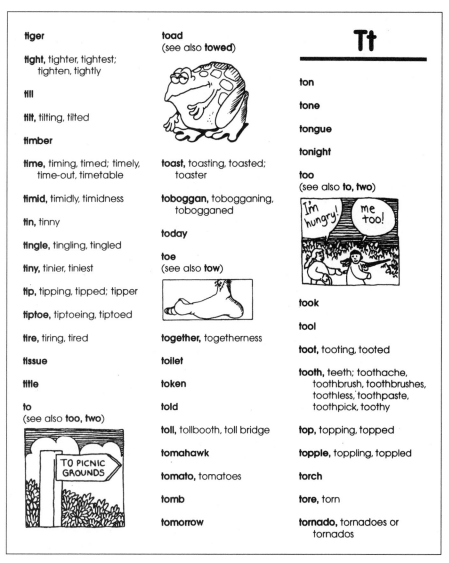

tiger

tight, tighter, tightest; tighten, tightly

till

tilt, tilting, tilted

timber

time, timing, timed; timely, time-out, timetable

timid, timidly, timidness

tin, tinny

tingle, tingling, tingled

tiny, tinier, tiniest

tip, tipping, tipped; tipper

tiptoe, tiptoeing, tiptoed

tire, tiring, tired

tissue

title

to
(see also **too, two**)

toad
(see also **towed**)

toast, toasting, toasted; toaster

toboggan, tobogganing, tobogganed

today

toe
(see also **tow**)

together, togetherness

toilet

token

told

toll, tollbooth, toll bridge

tomahawk

tomato, tomatoes

tomb

tomorrow

Tt

ton

tone

tongue

tonight

too
(see also **to, two**)

took

tool

toot, tooting, tooted

tooth, teeth; toothache, toothbrush, toothbrushes, toothless, toothpaste, toothpick, toothy

top, topping, topped

topple, toppling, toppled

torch

tore, torn

tornado, tornadoes or tornados

FIGURE 11.2 A page from the *Writer's Word Book,* showing *to* and *too.*

cussion on the sameness of the sound and the differences in meaning and spelling.

Read parts of the familiar books you selected, asking children to listen and look for the homophones *to, too,* and *two* and think about the meaning of each. Then list the three homophones and the sentences or clauses containing each on the appropriate chart as children identify them. Children could underline the homophones in each line of print and explain the differences in meaning and spelling of the three. For example:

to	two	too
lowering her voice <u>to</u> what she thought was a whisper	walked for <u>two</u> hours	She was <u>too</u> tired to even smile.
ran up <u>to</u> a house	I'll bring <u>two</u> books.	I've got a cat and a dog, and mice <u>too</u>.
They walked where they wanted <u>to</u>.	I have <u>two</u> brothers and <u>two</u> sisters.	Can I come <u>too</u>?
It was fun <u>to</u> play.		but it was <u>too</u> much <u>too</u> soon

There may be an insufficient number of examples of the use of *to, too,* and *two* in the books you initially chose for the children to form accurate hypotheses about these homophones, but encourage them to form hypotheses from the examples available and to revise their ideas throughout the study.

From this point, there are various ways you may choose to proceed. For example, the class may continue working together throughout the exploration, or the children could break into three groups, with each investigating one of the three homophones. Each group could collect examples of the homophone in context, and the groups could then come together to share what they have learned. The class then continues working together in exploring the three homophones.

When working as a class, you may wish to ask the children which homophone they want to begin with. Perhaps there is one whose meaning they find easier to distinguish, and therefore are better able to use. For example, the class may decide that in this set of homophones *two* is a useful starting point. Children could then search reading materials and their own writing for examples of the homophone *two* and illustrate the *two* items listed, for example, two hours, two books, and so on, reinforcing their sense that the homophone *two* is a number.

The children should be encouraged to suggest ways to help them know when to use *two*. Some may suggest that there is usually a noun or an adjective after *two*, while others may link *two* with other number words containing the letter combination *tw*—*two* tens in *twenty*, *two* plus ten equals *twelve*, *twice*, and *two twins*. Write children's ideas on the *two* section of the homophone chart and review all the points as each new idea is added.

This exploration should be followed by investigations of the homophones *too*and *to*. Have children speculate about ways of knowing when to use these homophones, directing their thinking toward the meaning of the two homophones and the words preceding and following them. Accept all suggestions; encourage children to comment on others' hypotheses. For example, some children might suggest that *too* never comes before a noun or a verb, that it means *also*, especially when it is at the end of a sentence, and that it can mean *really, really*. Write children's ideas on the *too* chart and review them as each new example is added.

When thinking about *to*, some children might suggest that it comes before verbs, for example, *to play, to skip,* and so on, or that its meaning sometimes has to do with moving in a direction (*to* a house). Write children's ideas about *to* in the appropriate place on the *to* homophone chart and review them as each new example is added.

As the exploration progresses, children may think of some questions to ask themselves when writing, to help them differentiate the homophones *to, too,* and *two.* For example:

- Is it a number? Then *two.*
- Does it mean *also* or *really, really?* Then *too.*
- Is it none of these? Then *to.*

Some children may need many examples in order to understand when to use the homophones *to, too,* or *two.* Continue adding to the class lists during the following weeks as the children search for and encounter examples when reading and writing, and have them review and refine their generalizations.

To help children understand the relevance of the exploration, refer back to the writing that originally suggested the homophone exploration. Ask several children to tell the class what they have learned about the homophones *to, too,* and *two,* and how this will help them spell these and other sets of homophones in the future, and how it will assist them when reading.

For easy reference, display the set of *to, too,* and *two* homophone lists together, or make the lists into a class spelling journal or homophone book. Leave some blank pages for children to record additional examples of the use of these homophones in their reading and writing. Place the book near the writing center for children to refer to when they proofread their writing.

You might add the children's generalizations about each set of homophones to a class spelling journal, homophone book, or generalization book. Ask children to write their own statements about homophones in their spelling journals, and have them share their personal explanations.

Since children need to be able to check the use and spelling of homophones in their writing, refer them to dictionaries and word books, such as the *Writer's Word Book* (Snowball 1997), and help them locate sets of homophones in addition to *to, too,* and *two.* Suggest that children refer to these references when they think about homophones and when they are proofreading their writing.

Using Shared Reading to Explore There, They're, and Their

Rather than conducting a whole-class exploration as was done for the study of the homophones *to, too,* and *two,* after the initial class introduction you may prefer that children form small groups when investigating a set of frequently used homophones—for example, *there, they're,* and *their.* In some instances, forming groups may be a more effective way to meet children's writing needs. For example, some children may use the homophone *there* conventionally when writing, but not *their* or *they're,* while others may use *their* and *they're* conventionally but not *there.* In such cases it is more beneficial for children to explore the homophones they are still unsure of.

Begin the exploration by telling the children you have noticed that many of them often use the homophones *there, they're,* and *their* when writing, and that they will work in groups to investigate when authors use each one of these words.

When each of the children has decided which of the three homophones to explore, have them form three groups. Read one of the Big Books you selected and write sentences containing the homophone *there, they're,* or *their.* For example:

there	*they're*	*their*
The view is better from over <u>there</u>.	<u>They're</u> behind a tree.	<u>Their</u> bag is heavy.
We knew <u>there</u> was a house.	While <u>they're</u> hiding	Where are <u>their</u> shoes?
They walked <u>there</u>.		Where's <u>their</u> green book?
<u>There</u> once was a girl who lived in a forest.		It could be <u>theirs</u>.

Then have the groups search reading materials and list other examples of the homophones they are investigating. Toward the end of the session bring the class back together. Have each group present its list and tell the others what they have learned about the homophone they explored. In this way children learn from each other about the use and spelling of homophones.

By listening to the children's conversation you will gain valuable insight into their understanding and will have a better sense of how the exploration should proceed. For example, if you determine that the groups are making good progress you may decide to allow the class to continue their group investigations. If not, you may decide to reconvene the class for a period of time, and then have the children return to their groups.

An exploration such as this could continue over a period of two to three weeks, alternating between whole-class and group activities. You will know when it is appropriate to conclude the exploration by listening to the children's questions and comments about *there, they're,* and *their,* noting their generalizations, and observing the use of this homophone set in their writing.

For example, here are some generalizations about the homophone set *there, they're,* and *their* that children might suggest:

- There is often a noun after *their.*
- There is often an adjective and then a noun after *their.*
- *Their* means owning or belonging to: they played with *their* teddy bears.
- *Their* comes in front of what they own.
- It's not mine so it must be *theirs.*
- You won't find *their* at the end of a sentence, but you will find *theirs.*
- *They're* means *they are,* and you never find *they're* at the end of a sentence.
- I can spell *here,* which is a place, so I can spell *there,* which is another place.

- *There* is pointing *there.*
- You know when to use *there* by thinking about *ere* in *here* and *where.*

In addition, throughout the exploration focus attention on *there, they're,* and *their* during independent, modeled, shared, and interactive writing sessions. Also encourage students to refer to the class lists, dictionaries, and word books.

If the class uses a computer when writing, alert children to the limited capacity of spell-check programs in identifying incorrect homophones. Such programs can only detect misspelled, not misused, homophones.

Ask children to orally describe their understanding of *there, they're,* and *their;* it helps for children to hear their peers explain their ideas in their own way. When children feel ready, they could write their explanations in their spelling journals. Pairs or small groups could meet to read each other's explanation and to borrow ideas if they think it would help their own explanations. Figures 11.3, 11.4, and 11.5 show what three children in grade 5 wrote on the homophone set *there, they're,* and *their.* Written pieces like these could themselves become subjects of discussion, on what qualities in the children's explanations might be useful for other writing they do, such as the use of examples.

Refer children to their own writing and tell them that you expect them to think about the correct usage of these homophones in the future. At first some children may want to refer to examples on the charts, comparing them with their own use of homophones. Others may wish to refer to the explanations done in class or written in their personal journals until they are automatically using the words correctly.

their – You would use their when you are telling that something belongs to someone.

there – You would use there when you are talking about a place such as There is a ball over there.

they're – You would use they're when you are stating something that you are going to do. Contraction for they are.

FIGURE 11.3 A student in grade 5 learning about the homophones *there, they're,* and *their.*

> When I use the word there I usually use it when I'm trying to tell someone a location. I also use it when I am referring to someone.
>
> When I am using the word their it's when I am saying something belongs to them.
>
> When I am using the word they're it is when I am describing what a group of people are doing. It can also be used to describe how something is feeling.
> they're = they are

FIGURE 11.4 Another grade 5 student's ideas.

> I would use their when I am talking about someone. For example: But all the same it was their home.
> I would use they're when I am talking about someone and they are doing an action. For example: They're going to the park.
> I would use there for many reasons. One reason could be picking someone out of a crowd. example: There is Joanna. Another reason is when I point to someone or something. or at a specific location.

FIGURE 11.5 A third student on the homophone set *there*, *they're*, and *their*.

Scheduling Homophone Explorations

Because some homophone sets are used frequently in written English, it is important that sufficient time be set aside to ensure that children fully comprehend their use and spelling. By conducting an in-depth investigation of homophones in grades 3, 4 and 5, children can move on through middle school confident in their use of homophones.

You may find that the exploration of a homophone set requires a period of approximately two or three weeks, depending on your students' needs. During this period, the actual time spent on homophones may vary greatly. For example, when homophones are first introduced, you might want the class to spend some time on them daily so that the children can quickly build up some knowledge and develop hypotheses for testing. After the first week the exploration may not have to be done every day; perhaps two or three brief spelling sessions a week will be sufficient.

The duration of each session may also vary. When introducing the exploration, and during the initial stages, a period of 20 to 30 minutes may be required. In the final stages of the exploration, when fewer words are being listed and generalizations refined, sessions may be very brief.

🌀 Learning Words

Some children may already know how to spell the homophones in a set and need instruction in their usage only, while others may not be spelling the homophones conventionally. Because the words on the class homophone lists are words often used in writing, children who cannot spell the homophones should learn these and other related words.

If some children needed to learn the word *some* from the homophone set *some* and *sum*, for example, you could show them how knowing how to spell *some* would also help them spell *somehow, something,* and *someone,* or other words with the same spelling pattern such as *come, comes, home,* and *homes.* You might have them draw a picture or write a sentence depicting the meaning of the homophone, since the spelling of a homophone depends on its meaning.

Some children may come up with memory aids of their own to help them remember how to spell and when to use the different homophones. For example, when learning about the homophones *piece* and *peace* a child may remember their correct spelling and usage by referring to the sentence *I would love a piece of pie.* Children can share these ideas.

Because there are many homophones in the English language, they will turn up often as children read and write, and as they explore sounds and spelling patterns. For example, when exploring the sound /air/, you may list such homophones as *hair/hare, mayor/mare, where/wear, bear/bare, stare/stair, pear/pair,* and *fare/fair,* and discuss their meanings with the children.

If you wish to develop a book or chart about homophones as the class discovers them, be sure to provide a sentence or illustration with each one so that children can use such a class resource to help them with their writing.

Above all, children need to be guided to realize that when they are not sure of the correct spelling or usage of such words when they are writing, the best strategy is to check a book or other source of information.

🌀 Continuing Evaluation

Observe your students' writing to note their use of homophone sets that they have explored as a class or in groups.

You may want to prepare cloze exercises using familiar reading materials in which homophones have been covered or deleted, and have the children write in the missing homophones. The children could prepare these activities for others to complete. Just be sure that the children are able to read the passages of print that are selected. Here is an example of such an exercise on the use of *to, too,* and *two:*

Well, today was my second day at my new school. The only girl I spoke _____ all day was Mary, and she was _____ shy _____ speak much.

She showed me around the school, and the _____ of us sat together in class. We went _____ the library at lunch time because it was _____ hot _____ play outside.

At home time, Mary walked with me _____ the gate. The _____ of us said "Goodbye."

I started _____ walk in one direction, and Mary began _____ walk in the other direction.

A variation on cloze activities would be to have children complete rebus activities. Rebus involves the use of pictures to represent the meanings of words. Within a passage of print, homophones could be replaced with pictures depicting their meaning, and the children could then write the correct homophone, possibly below the picture.

Rebus cloze, however, is limited to homophones for which drawings can be made. The passage above would not be suitable for rebus, because children could draw an illustration only for the homophone *two.* However, cloze rebus might be suitable for the homophone set *hair* and *hare.*

The children could also prepare rebus activities for others to complete. They could either illustrate or cut out pictures from magazines depicting the meanings of the homophones.

✿ Spelling Journals

Children may keep personal spelling journals to record the homophones they are learning and their understanding of their spelling and usage. Make sure that children enter homophones in their journals with either words that explain their meaning and usage or illustrations that convey their meaning.

Encourage the children to refer to their personal journals when they proofread their writing.

☞ Homework Ideas

Have children suggest homework they could do that is related to the homophone explorations they are involved in, and have them explain how doing the activities will help them learn about homophones. For example, they may do the following:

- Make cards for the game Homophone Match. Help children select homophones for the game. Suggest that they include more than one homophone within a set. For example, if a child wanted to include the homophone *would*, make sure that cards are also prepared for the homophone *wood*. For each homophone, make two cards: one for the homophone plus one for its meaning. Each child will need approximately twenty cards. On ten cards they write homophones, one per card. On the other ten cards, help the children write a sentence or phrase or draw a picture to illustrate the meaning of these homophones, again one per card. Have the children underline the homophone in each sentence or phrase. If the children are drawing the meaning of a homophone, have them write the homophone underneath the picture to help the players learn about the homophone and to make it easier for players to make a match.

Then, explain how to play Homophone Match. Tell the children it is a game for two players. The cards are separated into two packs, one for each player. One pack contains cards of the written homophones, the other the cards that indicate their meaning.

When a player turns up a card with a homophone written either by itself or in an example, the player must say the homophone and read the card aloud before placing it on the pile, because an important purpose of the game is to help players understand the spelling and use of homophones. Explain that players take turns in placing turned up cards in a pile between them. Explain the same rule applies to cards with illustrations: players must name the homophone before placing it on the pile.

When two cards that match (that is, a homophone card and a card indicating its meaning) are placed on top of each other the first player to say the homophone and "Match!" wins the pile of cards. The player with the most cards at the end of the game wins.

- Collect pictures of sets of homophones to place in their spelling journals.
- Watch for other examples of homophones in sentences as they read and write and share them with the class.
- Make crossword puzzles for others to complete, using the meanings of the homophones as clues.

Trade Books Containing Homophones

Gwynne, F. 1970. *The King Who Rained*. New York: Prentice-Hall Books for Young Readers.

———. 1976. *Chocolate Moose for Dinner*. New York: Prentice-Hall Books for Young Readers.

————. 1980. *The Sixteen Hand Horse.* New York: Prentice-Hall Books for Young Readers.

————. 1988. *A Little Pigeon Toad.* New York: Prentice-Hall Books for Young Readers.

Reference

Snowball, D. 1996. *A Writer's Word Book.* Greenvale, NY: Mondo.

Plurals

n the English language plurals can be formed in several ways, sometimes determined by the origin of the word (for example, the plural of *larva* being *larvae*, from the Latin). Through study and exploration, children will learn that there are consistencies about the ways plurals are formed, depending on the spelling of the base word. They will also learn that it is important to check spelling in a dictionary or word book, because variations occur (for example, the plural of *handkerchief* is *handkerchiefs*, but the plural of *thief*, another word ending in *f*, is *thieves*). Children should learn generalizations about plurals so that they can apply them when appropriate, but they should also know when it would be better to check a resource.

✪ Evaluating Children's Understanding and Needs

Through their experiences in reading, children notice at an early age that the letter *s* can be added to many words, such as *hat/hats* and *run/runs*. They may even use these different words correctly in their speech and writing (*I have one hat; I have three hats; He can run; They run down the street; He runs down the street*). But they may not really understand the role of the *s* in forming plurals. Children may also start to use the correct spelling for common plurals such as *babies* because they have seen the word in their reading, but they may not realize that there is a generalization about forming plurals of words that end with a consonant plus *y*.

When you notice that your students are spelling many words conventionally and using strategies such as sounding out words and thinking about what words look like, but are making spelling errors such as *puppys, leafs,* and *dishs,* it's a good time to begin to explore the generalizations for forming plurals. You may want to do this with just a group or the whole class.

During their first three years of school there will be many opportunities for children to discuss the spelling of common plurals, but an in-depth study of all the generalizations for forming plurals may not be appropriate until grade 3 and will probably continue for a few years as children discover less common types, particularly in science and mathematics.

🌀 *Discovering the Generalizations About Plurals*

When you observe spelling mistakes such as *boxs, skys,* and *tomatos* in your students' writing, or when you notice that some ESL children do not even add the letter *s* to a plural word, point out these misunderstandings to the children and suggest that it would be worthwhile to study the way to spell words for more than one person or thing. First, help them understand the meaning of the terms *singular* (one), *plural* (more than one), and *noun,* using shared reading materials and mathematics activities to find and discuss examples. You will probably find lots of examples in nonfiction material, such as the following (the plural nouns are italicized):

> *Beavers* are *mammals.* They feed their *babies* milk. *Beavers* are *plant eaters.* They pull the *leaves* off *branches. Beavers* have sharp *teeth.*

You could make lists of singular and plural forms of words from material being read so that the children will notice that a plural is not always formed simply by adding an *s*—for example:

Singular	*Plural*
beaver	beavers
mammal	mammals
baby	babies
plant eater	plant eaters
leaf	leaves
branch	branches
tooth	teeth

Ask the children if any of them know about any generalizations, or statements that are generally true, for ways to spell plurals. Write the children's suggestions on a chart, and throughout your study of plurals compare these statements with the ideas that the children come up with as they find other examples.

The generalizations that you will help your students discover are listed below. If the children are told the generalizations before they have a chance to work them out independently, the information will not be as meaningful and therefore will not be remembered or used as successfully. It is also preferable to have the children explain the generalizations in their own words rather than having them try to understand an adult version.

1. The plural of most nouns is formed by adding *s* to the singular: *dog/dogs, word/words, boy/boys.*

2. The plural of nouns ending with *x, ch, sh, ss, z,* and *s* is formed by adding *es* to the singular: *box/boxes, branch/branches, brush/brushes, loss/losses, buzz/buzzes, bus/buses.*

3. The plural of nouns ending with a consonant plus *y* is formed by changing the *y* to an *i* and adding *es*: *berry/berries, fairy/fairies.*

4. The plural of nouns ending with a vowel plus *o* is formed by adding *s* to the singular: *radio/radios, folio/folios, tattoo/tattoos, kangaroo/kangaroos, rodeo/rodeos.*

5. The plural of nouns ending with a consonant plus *o* is usually formed by adding *es* to the singular: *mosquito/mosquitoes, tornado/tornadoes, potato/potatoes, volcano/volcanoes.* There are many exceptions to this, however, particularly with regard to musical terms (*piano/pianos, cello/cellos, solo/solos*), but also for other words, such as *silo/silos, Eskimo/Eskimos, zero/zeros.* So for words ending with *o* it is wise to check a dictionary or other resource.

6. The plural of nouns ending with *f* (but not *ff*), *fe*, and *lf* is sometimes formed by changing the *f* to a *v* and sometimes adding *es*: *leaf/leaves, half/halves, life/lives.* There are so many exceptions to this generalization, however, that a resource should be used to check the spelling if you are in doubt.

7. The plural of compound words is usually formed by making the significant noun in the compound word plural: *plant eater/plant eaters, father-in-law/fathers-in-law, bystander/bystanders, passerby/passersby, man-of-war/men-of-war.* If none of the words in the compound word is a noun, add the plural to the whole group, such as *tryouts, flypasts,* and *go-betweens.* When you are not sure, use a resource to check.

8. The plural of nouns of foreign origin is formed in the same way that the plural would be formed in the language they originated from, though these may also have alternative, Anglicized plurals: *cactus/cacti* or *cactuses, fungus/fungi* or *funguses, larva/larvae* or *larvas, oasis/oases, hypothesis/hypotheses, chateau/chateaux* or *chateaus.* When you are not sure, use a resource to check.

9. The plural of some nouns is formed by either changing the singular form of the word or by using exactly the same spelling as the singular noun: *man/men, woman/women, mouse/mice, tooth/teeth, foot/feet, sheep/sheep, fish/fish* or *fishes.*

10. Plurals of words ending in *ful*, such as *cupful, spoonful,* and *handful,* are formed by adding *s* in the usual way: *cupfuls, spoonfuls,* and *handfuls.*

There are several ways to conduct an exploration about plurals, depending on children's prior knowledge and the range of plural forms they are encountering in their reading and using in their writing. You may wish to focus first on the more common types of plurals, including some incidental learning about particular words, and leave further studies to later years; or you may wish to continue the exploration throughout an entire year to allow your students to discover all of the generalizations about plurals. Either way, this exploration is likely to take considerable time and should be interwoven with other spelling focuses.

The following is a description of how a typical exploration of plurals might occur. On the day the exploration begins you may spend up to 45 minutes on it, ensuring that the children understand the meanings of singular and plural, having them help you find and list many examples of plurals, and then having them write the singular form for each. After the initial session you may need to spend only a short time each day or on alternate days helping the children categorize the different ways of forming plurals and allowing them opportunities to explain the generalizations that they discover. As the children learn how to search for plurals and write their explanations, much of the work can be done as homework, with time set aside for sharing in school.

First tell the children why you are going to study plurals with them: that you have noticed from their writing that some are unsure about forming some plurals, so the study will help them with their writing. Add that they could learn a lot from other authors' writing, so together you will use the material they are reading to see what can be learned. After shared reading of familiar material such as Big Books, overhead transparencies of published writing, or charts of poems or songs, ask the children to help you locate any plural nouns. It's important to refer to material that children can at least read along with you and to discuss the content so that they understand the meaning of the words. List the plural nouns on a chart and write the singular form for each one—for example:

Plural	*Singular*
turkeys	turkey
knives	knife
thieves	thief
knots	knot
guesses	guess
deer	deer
porches	porch
lives	life
stories	story
frogs	frog
butterflies	butterfly
homes	home

Next, ask the children to search for and list other plural nouns independently in material they read themselves. Observe how the children manage this task, and assist where necessary. This should give you a reasonable indication as to whether the children all know what is meant by a plural noun. Have the children share their findings and add new words to the list as they do so. Encourage the children to help you to write the singular forms. It is important to list many examples so that the children will be able to start to form hypotheses about the spelling of plurals. Ask the children what they notice about the changes that happen to the singular word in forming the plural and whether they see any words they would group together according to the way they change.

You may want to continue the activity the next day with the whole class working together, or you may prefer to have the children work in small groups to categorize the words according to how the plurals are formed. List the words according to the children's discoveries:

turkey/turkeys	knife/knives	porch/porches	story/stories	deer/deer
knot/knots	thief/thieves	guess/guesses	butterfly/butterflies	
frog/frogs	life/lives			
home/homes				

Ask children to return to the independent lists they made and decide which group they would add each of their words to, and why. Again, this may be done with the whole class or in small groups. Some children may have words that do not belong to any of the existing word groups and so may need to form new word groups. The children may continue this task independently for homework and share their findings with the class. They should also continue to search for other examples of plurals, from both fiction and nonfiction reading in all curriculum areas, to add to their personal and class lists.

Encourage the children to try to provide a statement to explain how to change a singular to a plural for one of the word groups. Write their statements on a chart (with a name next to each contribution) and see if others want to revise the statements in any way. Here are some examples of children's statements:

- When a word ends with an *x* if you want to spell the plural of that then add *es* to the word, like *fox* gets changed to *foxes.* (Liam)
- For words that end with a *y* with a consonant before it, you take away the *y* and then add an *ies,* but you don't do this if the letter before the *y* is a vowel like *i, e, o, a, u.* (Sue)
- Some plural words are not the same as the singular word, like *tooth* and *teeth.* If you use some of these words you will have to learn them. (Ginnie)
- For lots of words you just add an *s* to make a word mean that there is more than one. (Hirem)

Some of these statements may need to be revised as the exploration continues. Talk about how it helps to give examples when explaining generalizations, and continue the process until all the children are able to provide explanations. Then ask them to write such statements in their spelling journals. By reading their entries, you will gain insight into how each child understands this aspect of spelling and which ones, if any, need further assistance. Discuss how this study is helping the children with their writing and determine what your expectations will be for future writing. During shared and interactive writing, call on children to spell plural nouns so that you can demonstrate how their knowledge can be used when writing.

To encourage children to refer to the class charts if necessary and to enable them to add examples in the future, keep the charts somewhere accessible, perhaps hanging them together in the room. You may also want to make a class book about plurals, with a table of contents listing each type. Place the book in the class library with other writing resources.

If this is the first time the class has discovered spelling generalizations through exploration, you may want to ask the children to reflect on how it has been helpful for them to learn through discovery rather than being told a set of statements that they were expected to memorize and apply. Talk about how they learned by looking for examples in material written by published authors and how they could use this technique, independently or in small groups, for other areas of writing that they think they need to learn more about.

❧ Learning Words

Throughout their exploration ask children to reflect on whether any of the plurals they are listing are words that they use frequently in all their writing or for a particular topic. Such words should be added to the class word wall, and the children who do not know them should learn them. Talk about the best strategies they could use to learn each word. For words that fit into one of the generalizations the best strategy is to remember the generalization; for irregular or unusual words the children may think of a memory aid to use, or try the "look, say, spell, cover, write, check" strategy (see Chapter 17). Whichever of these words individual children do not know they should add to their personal word list to learn. (For more information about learning high-frequency words and children's personal word learning refer to Chapters 17 and 18.) Topic words that have been added to the word wall, such as *butterflies* and *larvae,* may be removed at the end of the topic, but the class may decide to leave common words such as *children* because they are used frequently in all kinds of writing.

❧ Continuing Evaluation

The main way to assess children's learning of plurals is to examine their writing. During writing conferences talk with each child about what the child, or you, notice about his or her spelling of plurals; record what the child is good at and what is still being worked on. Consider involving some children in small-group work as needed.

You may also want to have the children try spelling some different kinds of plural nouns so that you may quickly determine how well they can apply the generalizations they have been learning. Allow the children to use resources, such as class charts, their spelling notebooks, dictionaries, and word books to check their spelling when they are not sure, as this is what you would expect them to do as proficient writers. If children do not consult resources, you will know that this is something you will need to show them how to do; perhaps you need to demonstrate these strategies more during modeled writing sessions.

To get the children involved in evaluating their own learning, you could ask them to reread pieces they have previously written, specifically proofread to check whether plurals are spelled correctly, and correct any misspellings. Children could then discuss the ways their spelling has improved as a result of their study of plurals.

☞ *Homework Ideas*

Throughout this study children may be given many homework tasks, including searching for and listing plural nouns in general, categorizing the plurals they find into different types, finding examples of particular plural types, writing statements about what they are learning about plurals, writing generalizations in their own words, choosing and learning particular plurals that they often use in their writing, and proofreading their writing to make sure that plurals are spelled correctly.

Children may also want to make useful activities for other children to do, such as making word mazes, where all of the words to be found are plural nouns; or making crossword puzzles, where all of the clues are related to plurals.

Parents should be informed about the class's focus on plurals and the fact that you are expecting the children to discover generalizations about plurals through their finding many examples and looking for similarities and differences. Point out that this type of learning encourages children's thinking, cooperative learning, forming and testing hypotheses, and being able to explain and apply what they have learned. Explain also that you will be guiding the children's learning and will be able to observe who needs more individual assistance; and that you will then have high expectations about children applying this aspect of spelling knowledge to their writing. Parents can assist by participating in the word searches and making the exploration an enjoyable family experience. At different times during the study children could also write a newsletter for parents about what they have been learning and how they have been learning it.

13

Prefixes and Suffixes

nglish is a meaning-based language: the spelling of words is determined by their meaning, even though the pronunciation of related words may be different. For example, the beginning parts of *electrical* (e-lec-*trik*) and *electrician* (e-lec-*trish*) are pronounced differently, but they are spelled the same because they are based on the same meaning and are built from the same base word. If children understand this principle and are aware that a useful spelling strategy is to think of the spelling of the base word and then think about adding prefixes or suffixes to build other words, they will be able to spell many words they want to write. In addition, noticing base words with prefixes and/or suffixes enables children to read longer words, and learning the meaning of prefixes and suffixes builds children's vocabulary.

Learning about prefixes and suffixes and the generalizations about how to add them to base words should be the major focus of spelling in grade 3 and beyond. The most common misspellings in this age group are caused by lack of knowledge or misunderstanding of this aspect of written English. As with all other explorations, the more closely studies about prefixes and suffixes are related to children's actual writing needs and the more they are allowed to form their own hypotheses and generalizations by using their reading as a source of examples, the more they will understand and be able to apply what they have learned.

Evaluating Children's Understanding and Needs

Use your students' writing to gauge their understanding of prefixes and suffixes. In general, children in grade 3 and older may not realize that when spelling words containing prefixes and suffixes they should first determine the spelling of the base word and then add the prefix(es) and/or suffix(es), and they may not know all of the generalizations for adding suffixes. For example:

- If you see misspellings such as *eregula* (irregular), *remberd* (remembered), *discuverd* (discovered), or *hopt* (hopped), this tells you that the writer is using a sounding-out strategy rather than starting with a base word and then adding prefixes and suffixes.

- If you see misspellings such as *realy* (really), this tells you that the writer does not understand that the base word is *real* with the suffix *ly* added.

- If you see misspellings such as *unecessary* (unnecessary), this tells you that the writer does not understand that the base word is *necessary* and the prefix *un* is added.

- If you see misspellings such as *happyness* (happiness), *heatted* (heated), and *stared* (starred), this tells you that the writer does not understand generalizations for adding suffixes.

If you observe these types of spelling errors, even though the children are at the stage of spelling development where they are spelling many words the conventional way and are able to use visual and phonetic strategies to attempt words, you should spend considerable time exploring prefixes and suffixes with your students.

Discovering the Generalizations About Prefixes

The most useful prefixes for children to learn first are *re* and *un* because they occur frequently, and the way they change the base words to which they are added is easy to see. This allows children to quickly understand the function of a prefix and that it comes before the base word. You may come across words such as *recycle, rewrite, replay, retell, unhappy, undo, unemployed, unfair, unreal,* or *unusual* in material you are reading with the children. This will give you an opportunity to explain that these words are formed by adding a prefix to the beginning of the base word and how the prefix changes the meaning of the base word. (You will also have to help children understand what is meant by the term *base word* if they are not familiar with it.)

You could make class lists of words with these prefixes by having children think of them or find them in their reading and dictionaries or word books. Guide the children to discover that *re* means *again* or *back again* (*fill/refill*) and that *un* means *not* (*happy*/*unhappy*) or reverses the action (*lock*/*unlock*). Talk about how some words may begin with the letters *re* or *un,* but in these words these letters do not act as a prefix added to a base word. For example, *rebel* does not mean "to bel again" and *unite* does not mean "not ite." As the lists develop over a number of days ask the children if they can discover a generalization for how these prefixes are added to the base words.

The following is a list of words that children discovered in a multiage class of grades 2–3, how they wrote their charts, and the generalizations they discovered:

> *re* = "again" when it is added to the front of a base word
> *redo* = *re* + *do* = do it again
> *rebuild* = *re* + *build* = build it again
> *replay* = *re* + *play* = play it again
> *reappear* = *re* + *appear* = appear again
> *rethink* = *re* + *think* = think again
> *recapture* = *re* + *capture* = capture again
> *remodel* = *re* + *model* = model it again
> *re-enter* = *re* + *enter* = enter again
> *re-elect* = *re* + *elect* = elect again

> We think that you just add *re* to the base word and the base word stays the same. When the base word starts with the letter "e" we think the hyphen is put there to help the reader say the word properly.

> *un* means "not" when it is added to the front of a base word or to make the action the opposite
> *unhappy* = *un* + *happy* = not happy
> *uneven* = *un* + *even* = not even
> *undo* = *un* + *do* = to reverse what has been done
> *unequal* = *un* + *equal* = not equal
> *unlucky* = *un* + *lucky* = not lucky
> *undress* = *un* + *dress* = the opposite of *dress*
> *unnatural* = *un* + *natural* = not natural
> *unnecessary* = *un* + *necessary* = not necessary
> *unnumbered* = *un* + *numbered* = not numbered
> *unlined* = *un* + *lined* = not lined

> We think that you just add the prefix *un* to the base word. This means that if the base word begins with the letter *n* then when the prefix is added the word will have *nn*.

The charts were displayed and children were encouraged to add other words containing these prefixes as they found or thought of them and to keep checking to see if their generalizations remained true. The class also reflected on how learning about these prefixes would help them with their reading and writing, and children recorded personal statements and examples of words with these prefixes in their spelling journals.

The teacher frequently used opportunities to show children how to build families of words, including words formed by adding these prefixes, such as *play, playing, played, plays, replay, replaying, replayed, replays;* and *dress, dressing, dressed, dresses, undress, undressing, undressed, undresses.* The class discussed how knowing how to spell one word can help with the spelling of many words.

Beyond re and un

In a similar way you can explore how the prefixes *dis, il, im, in,* and *ir* are added to base words. As they all mean "not" or "to do the opposite" the children may find it interesting to discover when these prefixes are used instead of *un.* The lists that you build with the children may look something like this:

discontinue = dis + continue
disagree = dis + agree
disregard = dis + regard
disqualify = dis + qualify
disown = dis + own
disallow = dis + allow
dissatisfaction = dis + satisfaction
dissimilar = dis + similar

illegal = il + legal
illegible = il + legible
illiterate = il + literate

immature = im + mature
immobile = im + mobile
immoral = im + moral
immortal = im + mortal
immovable = im + movable
impatient = im + patient
imperfect = im + perfect
impersonal = im + personal
impolite = im + polite
impossible = im + possible
improbable = im + probable
immeasurable = im + measurable
impure = im + pure

inability = in + ability
inadequate = in + adequate
inappropriate = in + appropriate
incapable = in + capable
incompetent = in + competent
incorrect = in + correct
independent = in + dependent
ineffective = in + effective
informal = in + formal
insecure = in + secure
insignificant = in + significant
intolerant = in + tolerant
invincible = in + vincible
innumerable = in + numerable

irresponsible = ir + responsible
irregular = ir + regular
irrational = ir + rational
irrelevant = ir + relevant
irreplaceable = ir + replaceable

When the children have enough examples to see a trend they may notice that:

- The prefix *ir* is used only when the base word begins with the letter *r.*
- The prefix *im* is used only when the base word begins with the letter *m.*
- The prefix *il* is used only when the base word begins with the letter *l.*
- The prefix is always added to the base word with no change to the base word.

Talk about how helpful these generalizations are for the spelling of words such as *illegal, dissatisfaction, innumerable, irregular,* and *immobile* when the last letter of a prefix is the same as the first letter of the base word. Encourage children to use this information when they write.

Other Prefixes to Explore

Other common prefixes and their meanings are listed in Table 13.1. (For more examples, see Bolton and Snowball 1993.) All can be explored over a period of three or four years, with children coming to realize that all prefixes are added to the base word with no change to the base word. It's not likely that you will find many examples of each prefix in the material you are reading at any one point in time; the study of prefixes is likely to be supported by the use of dictionaries and word books, and children will continue to find examples over an extended period. You will probably need to help the children understand that when they are looking in a dictionary for words containing a prefix, they need to check the meaning to be sure that the word actually contains a prefix (for example, *disco* and *dish* do not begin with the prefix *dis*).

Continually reflect with the children on how their explorations help them read and write. Build word families using the prefixes to show how useful it is to think of words in this way (for example, *satisfy, satisfies, satisfied, satisfying, satisfaction, satisfactory, dissatisfied, dissatisfaction, unsatisfactory*).

🌀 Discovering the Generalizations About Suffixes

Suffixes are a more complex topic than prefixes because there are many different generalizations about how suffixes are added to base words. The process of exploring suffixes will probably take longer in order for children to gather enough examples to be able to form hypotheses and draw conclusions.

The Suffixes ed and ing

Through their reading, children learn to correctly write many words ending with the suffixes *ed* and *ing*, such as *hopped* and *hopping* or *hoped* and *hoping,* but this does not mean that they fully understand the generalizations for adding these endings to any base word. This is evident in misspellings such as *visted, remberd,* and *whispring,* where the writers are not thinking first about how to spell the base word and then how to add the suffix. They may rely only on the strategy of listening for sounds in the word.

For example, some children may not add *ed* to some words at all, using only the sounds they hear instead, resulting in such spellings as as *hopt* or *numberd*. To help children overcome this misunderstanding you should explore the spell-

TABLE 13.1	Other Common Prefixes	
Prefix	*Meaning*	*Examples*
anti	against, opposite	anticlimax, anticlockwise, antisocial
auto	self, same	automatic, autobiography
bi	two, double	bifocal, biennial
circum	round	circumference, circumnavigate
co	together	co-author, co-pilot, cooperate
de	remove from, break down	defrost, decipher, decompose
en	in, on, into	entitle, encircle, encase, enlist (makes a noun into a verb)
em	same as *en*, but used when base word begins with *b* or *p*	empower, embody
ex	away from, out, no longer	exhale, export, exhaust, ex-president, ex-king
fore	before, in front of	forecast, foretell, foreground, foreword
inter	among, between	interstate, intersect, interchange
intra	within, inside	intrastate, intravenous
hemi	half	hemisphere
micro	small	microscope, microfilm, microwave
mis	incorrect, astray	mismanage, mislead, misprint
mono	one, single	monopoly, monologue, monotony
multi	many	multitude, multimillionaire
pre	before, in front of	prejudge, precook, prejudice, preview
semi	half	semifinal, semicircle
sub	under, lower	subway, subcommittee, subtitle
super	more than, extra	supernatural, superhuman, supermarket
tele	distant	television, telecast, telegraph
trans	across	transport, translate, transcontinental
under	insufficient, below	undercooked, underground

ing pattern *ed* at the end of words (in examples where the *ed* is acting as a suffix) so that they can discover that this spelling pattern may be pronounced three ways: /t/, /ed/, and /d/ (see Chapter 8). Also, during exploration of the /t/ sound children will learn that one way to represent this sound is with the letters *ed*, and during the exploration of the /d/ sound they will discover that one way to represent this sound is *ed* as well. Children whose first language is not English often need more assistance with the pronunciation and spelling of verbs that end with *ed* than native English speakers do, particularly if their first language is a phonetic language and does not have the inflectional endings such as those in English words. Ensure that these children have many opportunities to be involved in shared reading experiences with material that has many verbs with *ed* endings, such as in folk tales, so that they can see, hear, and read these words at the same time.

It is usually in grades 3 and 4 that children are ready to explore and thoroughly understand the generalizations for adding *ed* and *ing*. By then they are correctly spelling many more base words, they are ready to understand the grammatical function of words with inflectional endings, and they are able to articulate their hypotheses about how these endings are added to base words. Samples of children's writing in these grades show that students are still experimenting with how to add the suffixes *ed* and *ing*, however, because their most common spelling mistakes include words ending with these suffixes. Starting with children's own writing can be a useful entree to an exploration of these endings. Of course, if you find writing in older grades that indicates that some children still do not understand this aspect of spelling, you will want to continue exploring these generalizations with the class. In this case, children who are knowledgeable about suffixes can contribute to the class's learning. Alternatively, you may prefer to work just with a small group of children with this particular need.

Because there are several generalizations relating to the inflectional endings *ed* and *ing*, it usually takes several weeks to explore this aspect of spelling before most of the children can understand the main generalizations and apply them in their writing. It is worth spending time to make sure children can do this because these endings are essential in written English. Also, once these generalizations are understood the children will find many similar generalizations for other suffixes. More time may be spent during the first couple of days of the study, but once under way the exploration requires only a little time each day for words to be added to lists, for children to share their thoughts, and for ideas to be refined. It is more fruitful to take the time to do this study well the first time, rather than spend just one or two weeks for it, only to have to repeat the study year after year. Also, bear in mind that children who are simply told the generalizations do not understand and apply them as well as children who are guided to work out the generalizations themselves and write them in their own words.

Adding ed   Explain to the children that you have noticed that some of them are not sure about the spelling of words that end with *ed*. Write several such words on a chart, such as *jumped, carried, regretted, visited, whistled*. Try to show some samples of children's own writing with some misspellings of *ed* words. Ask children if they know the function of words ending in *ed* and what the *ed* indicates. If necessary, read a story told in the past tense and have the class search for the *ed* words so that the children can understand that the words are action words, or verbs, and the *ed* indicates that the story took place in the past. Children may need to find many examples of such stories and locate many *ed* words before they understand this concept.

Return to material that children are familiar with and reread it together, watching for verbs that end with *ed*. Begin to make a class list of these words on a chart and write the base word next to each, encouraging children to help you. Some may need help understanding what is meant by the term *base word*. Point out that sometimes the *ed* is just added to the base word and sometimes the base word is changed, and ask them to figure out the rules or generalizations for adding *ed* so they can use such information for their own writing. The class may discover *ed* words that are not verbs, such as *left-handed*. This will give you an opportunity to discuss the function of adjectives, and that *ed* can be added to a noun to make an adjective.

Once you have the list of words, there are several ways that you can proceed. You may work with the children to classify the listed words according to the types of changes to the base words, or you may give this task to the children, who will work in small groups and then share their findings with the class, or you may classify some words together as a class and then have groups complete the lists. Make sure to have children explain why they think particular words should be grouped; and have the children find other *ed* words on their own in their reading, adding the words to the appropriate groups and explaining why each word has been placed in its group. Children can also locate and group words for homework. This should continue for several days, until you feel that there is a sufficient number of words in the groups for children to form hypotheses about how *ed* is added to the words.

Ask children to provide oral explanations or generalizations for each group, and write some of their statements on a chart to accompany the word lists. (If children do not know the terms *short vowel*, *long vowel*, and *consonant* this is an appropriate time to introduce these terms; otherwise the children will have a hard time describing their generalizations even though they may not eventually need all of these terms to describe the accurate generalizations. Having the children hear the others' explanations is very helpful, and they should also attempt to write their own explanations, possibly giving some specific words that exemplify each generalization. A spelling journal would be an ideal place for the children to record their thoughts. Having the children write the statements in their own words is much more meaningful and therefore useful to them than having them copy a textbook statement of the generalization and expecting them to remember it.

The generalizations that children usually discover are these:

- For many base words just add *ed*, like *rent/rented, wish/wished, whisper/whispered*.
- When the word ends with a silent *e*, drop the *e* and add *ed*, such as *whistle/whistled, dye/dyed, free/freed, issue/issued*. (If children say that only a *d* is added to the base word you need to remind them about the meaning of *ed* as an addition to the base word.)
- When the word ends with a consonant plus *y* change the *y* to an *i* and add *ed*, such as *carry/carried*. If the word ends with a vowel plus *y*, just add *ed*. (If the children think that the generalization of changing *y* to *i* applies to any word that ends with a *y* you may need to guide them to refine their generalization by showing them words such as *convey/conveyed, enjoy/enjoyed*.)

- When a word ends with a single vowel and a single consonant (except *x*) and the stress is on the last syllable of the base word, double the consonant before adding *ed*, such as *hop/hopped, regret/regretted, star/starred, occur/occurred, control/controlled.*
- When a word ends with the letter *c* add a *k* before adding the *ed*, such as *frolic/frolicked, mimic/mimicked, picnic/picnicked.*

Usually children at first think that the generalization of doubling the consonant is for all words ending with a short vowel plus consonant, but after a while they may discover that this explanation is not quite right because it does not work for words such as *edit/edited, travel/traveled, budget/budgeted,* or for words where the short vowel is more than one letter, such as *head/headed.* It may take some guidance and several examples for the children to work out all the details of this generalization (even many adults do not know this generalization completely). Usually children can work out some of the basic principles fairly quickly, but the refining of the generalization takes a long time. As the children work through this puzzle they usually wonder if it has something to do with the number of syllables in a word, but then they find that the consonant is doubled for two-syllable words such as *regret/regretted, submit/submitted, repel/repelled* as well as for single-syllable words. Some find it difficult to notice that only when the stress is on the last syllable in the base word is the consonant doubled. They also may not realize at first that the vowel before the consonant does not need to be short, and only when they notice words such as *occurred, starred,* and *warred* do they realize that they need to revise the generalization they have formed.

Stress or emphasis on a particular syllable may be difficult for some children to distinguish, and they will need a lot of practice pronouncing words and listening for emphasis. Start with names of more than one syllable. Write the names on a chart and ask the children to say them, to notice which part is emphasized or stressed, and to consider how the pronunciation would change if a different syllable were emphasized. Having access to a dictionary that includes pronunciation guides for each word also helps. One of the fundamental strategies to teach children is that good spellers use a resource to check when they are not sure of how a word is spelled; and each individual needs to be aware of the particular types of words that he or she needs to check.

There are various ways to conclude an exploration of the suffix *ed*. You may make a class book about what has been learned, with statements of the generalizations and lists of each of the types of *ed* words. This may be placed in the reference area of the class library for children to refer to as they write or proofread; they can continue to add examples to each section as they discover new words in their reading. You may ask children to write their own statements and examples in their spelling journal. Perhaps you would like to give a type of test, explaining to the children that having them spell different kinds of *ed* words will help you know how much they have understood and who may need more help. Another good idea is to have the children help you prepare a newsletter to explain to parents what the class has been doing and what the children have learned.

Here is an example of how an exploration of *ed* occurred in a grade 4 class.

The teacher began by rereading part of a familiar Big Book with the class. They listed the *ed* words on a chart and then wrote the base word beside each one.

ventured	venture
hopped	hop
cried	cry
roamed	roam
giggled	giggle
croaked	croak
rumbled	rumble
wished	wish
married	marry
dropped	drop
happened	happen

Then the teacher asked the children to find something they could read by themselves, to individually list more *ed* words, and to write the base word for each one. During this time she roamed the class, checking to make sure that each child understood the task. After a time, the class gathered together again, and the teacher asked them what they had noticed about the base words and what happened when *ed* was added. They grouped the words according to what they had noticed:

ventured	venture
giggled	giggle
rumbled	rumble
hopped	hop
dropped	drop
cried	cry
married	marry
roamed	roam
wished	wish
happened	happen

Each child selected a word from his or her own list to add to one of the groups, explaining why it would be placed with that particular group. The teacher then said that there were some rules or generalizations (statements that are generally true, she explained, but for which there may be an exception) about how *ed* is added to base words, and that their task now was to work out what these generalizations were. During the next day children worked in small groups, pooling their individual lists of words and taking turns suggesting possible generalizations about how *ed* is added to base words. They came together as a class right after the group work, and the teacher recorded some of their ideas on charts, even if they were not entirely accurate at this stage, and noting who provided each one:

- When a word ends with an *e* you throw the *e* out the window and then add *ed*. (Abigail)

- When you get a word such as *rot* (ends with short vowel written with only one letter and then a consonant) and add the suffix *ed* you get *rotted,* but when you get the word *heat* (ends with a long vowel and then a consonant) you don't double the final consonant to get *heated.* (Rachelle)
- *shopped = shop + p + ed.* The short vowel is before the final consonant so you double the final consonant. (John)
- If you have a look at the word *heat* and then say it you will find that you can't really hear the letter *a* but you can hear the sound *e.* So it is a long vowel. So you don't double the last consonant. (Lin)
- In *shop* the *o* is a short vowel so you have to double the final letter so you still get a short vowel sound in *shopped.* It's the same for *hopped, shipped, webbed, manned.* (Michael)
- If there is a word ending with a consonant and then a *y* you change the *y* to an *i* before you add the *ed,* like *carry* and *carried.* It doesn't happen for *monkeyed* because *monkey* ends with a *vowel* and the *y.* (Josie)

The teacher asked the class to find more *ed* words for homework; the next day some of these were added to the class word charts and the recorded statements checked to see if any of them needed to be changed or if new statements had to be written. This process continued for two weeks, with just a few minutes being spent each day for the class to add words and check the charts until the children felt confident that they had grasped the main ideas. They were then asked to write their own explanations in the back section of their spelling journals. They were also expected to think about the spelling of *ed* words in their writing, using a dictionary or word book if necessary to check the spelling of base words, and reviewing the word charts to help them make decisions about which generalization applied to the word they were writing.

One child wrote the following in her journal:

What I've learned about the "ed" suffix

I have learned that when adding "ed" to a word like race you drop the "e" and add "ed."
race − e + ed = raced
NOT race + d = raced
When there is a "y" after a consonant change it for an "i" and add "ed."
cry − y + i + "ed" = cried
NOT cry + ed = cryed
When a word ends with a short vowel and a consonant you double the consonant but I'm not sure about all of this yet.
hop + p + ed = hopped
NOT hop + ed = hoped

Most of the children quickly understood when to drop an *e* or when to change the *y* to an *i,* but they were not sure about some aspects of the doubling of consonants. Although the major part of the study was completed in a few weeks, the children remained interested in figuring out the details of the doubling generalization, and it was several weeks later before they realized that only when the stress is on the last syllable in multisyllabic words ending with a vowel plus a consonant is the consonant usually doubled. This idea became evident to the children only when they had a number of examples of *ed* words so that they could form a workable hypothesis:

The consonant is not doubled	*The consonant is doubled*
happened	regretted
traveled	embedded
orbited	rebelled
edited	submitted
modeled	referred
budgeted	occurred
gardened	
visited	
blossomed	
benefited	
conquered	

As a conclusion to the study the teacher asked the children to try to spell several *ed* words as a quick check to see which children could apply all of the generalizations and who needed more assistance. During future reading and writing experiences she was able to draw attention to examples that the needy children found useful to further guide their understanding. Also, because the class explorations about *ing, er,* and *est* that followed were similar to the *ed* study, she was able during those explorations to focus on the children who needed more help.

Because the children had developed such a sense of inquiry through this process, one of them noticed the word *boxed* in a book several weeks later and realized that the *x* had not been doubled. At first the class decided that this must be an exception to their generalization about doubling the consonant. Then they thought about other similar words such as *waxed, fixed, mixed, outfoxed,* and *faxed,* and decided that they needed to revise their generalization to state that if the consonant at the end of the word is an *x* it is not doubled. Eventually some children in the class also found some other exceptions to their generalizations, such as *handicap/handicapped, kidnap/kidnapped, equip/equipped, zigzag/zigzagged,* and *format/formatted,* where the last syllable in the base word is not stressed but the final consonant is doubled; but it was only because they had such a deep understanding of the generalizations that they were able to notice the exceptions.

When this exploration takes place in English-speaking countries other than the United States children discover a further refinement to this generalization. In countries such as Canada, Australia, and England, words that end with the letter *l* always double the *l,* regardless of whether the last syllable is stressed or not (*travelled, modelled, signalled, rebelled*). It may be worth discussing this with children in the United States because they will probably read material that has been published in other countries and will need to understand why these words are spelled this way. Even U.S. dictionaries sometimes give such a spelling as an alternative spelling for some words.

Children may also notice that sometimes in publications from other countries words are not always spelled with an *ed* ending even though they would be in the United States—for example, *spelt* instead of *spelled* and *dreamt* instead of *dreamed.* With the Internet and e-mail easily linking people from many countries spelling variations are becoming more visible.

Other Ways to Form Past Tense   As you read stories with the class to find verbs that end with *ed,* point out verbs where the past tense is written differently, such as *built, thought, said.* List these on a chart with their base words and ask children to add others to the list as they find them in their reading and writing. As the list grows ask children to watch for ways to group the words to highlight similarities in the base words. For example:

creep/crept	say/said
sleep/slept	pay/paid
weep/wept	lay/laid

This activity may encourage children to link words with the same spelling pattern, but if they form any hypotheses about generalizations encourage them to test out their ideas with other words. For example, they may think that if the base word ends with *eep* the past tense is formed by deleting an *e* and adding a *t* (*ept*), but this does not always hold true—as in *beep/beeped, peep/peeped,* and *seep/seeped.* Help children understand that if they are not sure about the spelling of a past tense verb they should check in a dictionary or word book. No one can be expected to learn every word, and the children should learn that the best strategy for spelling is to check a reliable source when they are not sure.

Encourage children to continue to notice unusual past tense verbs in their reading and to add them to the class list. An alphabetized book of these words could be made and placed in the class library as a reference.

A study of the different ways to form past tense will take place incidentally over a long period of time; children whose first language is not English may need more guidance and more time to understand the various forms. Involving such children in shared reading of material written in the past tense is the most fruitful way to help them develop their understanding of both oral and written language structures because they will see, hear, and read the words at the same time. Use Big Books that are intended for older children, such as *The Frog Who Would Be King* and *Baba Yaga,* and make overheads of passages from stories.

Adding ing   When children have some knowledge of the generalizations for adding *ed* ask them what their thoughts are about adding *ing* to base words, such as *jumping, carrying, picnicking, boxing, regretting, visiting, whistling.* Try to show some samples of their writing with some misspellings of *ing* words and explain that the class needs to explore words of this type to learn more about them for the purpose of writing. Compare words such as *thing, anything, nothing,* and *everything* (which end with the spelling pattern *ing*) with words such as *singing, buying, running,* and *riding* (which are verbs with the *ing* ending indicating that the action is occurring now, or are adjectives such as *singing nuns* or *running water*). This discussion should take place as material containing such words is being read, because the grammatical function of these words depends on their context. Children may need to find many examples to help them to understand this.

Return to material that children are familiar with and reread it together, watching out for verbs that end with *ing*. Begin to make a class list of these words on a chart and write the base word alongside each *ing* word, with the children's help. Ask the children to notice that sometimes the *ing* is just added to the base word and sometimes the base word is changed, and explain that you want them to figure out the rules or generalizations for adding *ing* so they can use such information for their own writing.

Have children review the process they used for their study of *ed*, and have them think about how they could apply the process to this new study. You may work as a class or in small groups as you make lists and group the words. The children could return to the charts they made of *ed* words and add the *ing* form of each word, such as:

happen	happened	happening
hop	hopped	hopping
hope	hoped	hoping
carry	carried	carrying
play	played	playing
mix	mixed	mixing
star	starred	starring
regret	regretted	regretting

This would help children notice whether the generalizations for adding *ing* are the same as or different from those for adding *ed*. Allow time during the next couple of weeks for the children to find examples in their own reading and to write their own statements about the generalizations in their spelling journals. They could also proofread previous writing they have done to check that these types of words are spelled correctly, applying what they now know. Point out that you expect that children will apply their knowledge about adding *ed* or *ing* to base words in their future writing.

As children continue to notice *ing* words in their reading they may find that for some base words ending with *e* the *ing* is added without deleting the *e*, such as *dye/dyeing* and *singe/singeing*. Help them understand that these words are spelled this way to prevent them from being confused with similar words, such as *die/dying* and *sing/singing*. Also draw the children's attention to words such as *hurry/hurries, carry/carries*, and *marry/marries*, and ask if they can use what they know about adding *ed* and *ing* to explain what is happening with these words.

Comparative and Superlative: *er* and *est*

In the same way that children explored adding *ed* and *ing*, help them understand the generalizations for adding *er* and *est*. They will first need to understand the function of these endings for the comparative and superlative forms. Use concrete examples: for example, show the children a *long* piece of string, a *longer* piece, and then a still longer one—*longest* piece. Also use examples from material you are reading ("If only he could grow bigger tomatoes" and "She was the daintiest girl in the entire kingdom," for example) to introduce the notion of comparing two or more things, people, or situations. If children do not know the term *adjective* this would be a suitable time to introduce it; use this term throughout the study.

As children make lists such as the following, and group words where the same generalization seems to apply, ask them how their knowledge of the generalizations for adding *ed* and *ing* can help them.

> big, bigger, biggest
> red, redder, reddest
> fat, fatter, fattest
>
> small, smaller, smallest
> great, greater, greatest
>
> blue, bluer, bluest
> late, later, latest
>
> tiny, tinier, tiniest
> pretty, prettier, prettiest

Also be alert for opportunities to point out that sometimes the comparative is formed by using the words *more* and *most,* such as:

> beautiful, more beautiful, most beautiful
> superstitious, more superstitious, most superstitious

Add to this list as children find other such words from their reading and writing, and discuss the possible reasons for using *more* and *most.* (It is usual to use *more* and *most* when forming the comparative and superlative of most polysyllabic words.) Remind the children that writers use correct spelling and grammar to make their writing easier to read and that words such as *beautifuller* and *superstitiouser* would be difficult to say.

Children could write their own generalizations about formulating comparative and superlative and include examples of adjectives ending in *er* and *est* in their spelling journals. It is helpful to have them read their statements to the class so that the children can compare the different ways they wrote their explanations and have a chance to borrow ideas from their classmates to improve their own writing.

Other Common Suffixes

Throughout grade 4 and onward, continue to guide children to discover the generalizations for adding other suffixes through explorations similar to those described in this chapter. It may not be easy to find many examples of certain suffixes in just one or two pieces of reading, so chances are that the lists will develop gradually over time and children will find it useful to browse through dictionaries and word books. One way to have children watch out for words that relate to a current exploration is to ask them to keep a blank piece of paper as a bookmark in the book they are reading and to make a note of any word they come across that could be added to the class list. Your focus should always be on helping children to understand that good spellers frequently use the following strategy to help them spell words: Think about how to spell the base word *first* and then how to add the prefix and/or suffix.

As each suffix is explored, encourage children to build on what they already know; have them consider the similarities about the generalizations for each suffix. Continually discuss how these studies can help them with their reading and writing, and use typical mistakes from their own writing (such as *realy, beautifull, loveabel,* and *committment*) as examples of why you are helping them to learn about these generalizations.

Some of the knowledge that you will want the children to learn about certain suffixes is described below. Although having the children initiate the inquiry and discovery is always preferable, in some cases it may take too long for them to find a sufficient number of examples of a given suffix in their reading, so you may want to provide some examples; when you do, make sure that the children know the meaning of the words.

The Suffixes ly *and* ally   The suffixes *ly* and *ally* are used to form an adverb from an adjective; for example, "He is a cruel person" and "He treated his dog cruelly." In general, *ly* is added to the adjective, but when the adjective ends with *ic* the suffix *ally* is added to form the adverb. (Children may discover that an exception to this is *publicly.*) By making lists of words with these suffixes, as they notice them in their reading, children should be able to realize that the suffix is usually just added to the base word, but if the base word ends with a consonant plus *y,* the *y* is changed to an *i* before the suffix is added:

real/really	sincere/sincerely
unusual/unusually	complete/completely
near/nearly	basic/basically
practical/practically	automatic/automatically
truthful/truthfully	noisy/noisily
quiet/quietly	happy/happily
personal/personally	
skillful/skillfully	

Understanding these generalizations will help children know how to spell such commonly misspelled words as *really, finally,* and *actually.* Discuss how correct spelling is meant to help readers, and that if *noisily* were written *noisyly* it would distort the pronunciation of the word, so the *y* is changed to an *i.*

Children may eventually discover some exceptions to the above generalizations, such as *terribly, possibly, truly, incredibly, wholly,* and *duly.* In these words the letter *e* is deleted from the base word before the *ly* is added—a change from what normally occurs with this suffix. If children use any of these words frequently in their writing they should learn them.

The Suffixes ance/ence *and* ant/ent   The suffixes *ance, ence, ant,* and *ent* are added to base words to form nouns and adjectives. As children make lists of words ending with these suffixes they may try to form hypotheses about when to use each of the endings; unfortunately, there are no guiding principles for these suffixes. The best strategy for these words is to refer to a dictionary or word book.

However, children will find that some of the generalizations they know for adding other suffixes, such as when to double a final consonant, when to drop a final *e,* and when to change a final *y* to an *i,* apply to these suffixes also:

- Doubling the final consonant:
  occur, occurrence
  admit, admittance
- Deleting the final *e:*
  assure, assurance
  interfere, interference
  guide, guidance
  insure, insurance
  observe, observance
- Changing the *y* to an *i:*
  defy, defiance
  rely, reliance

The Suffixes able *and* ible   Having children discover the generalizations for knowing when to use the suffixes *able* and *ible* will require many examples and a lot of guidance. Because there are so many generalizations to remember children should also be encouraged to check a dictionary or word book when they are not sure. Students who make mistakes such as *acceptabel* need to be reminded that the word means *able* to be accepted.

The suffix *able* is used in the following instances:

- When the part before the suffix is a full word (*acceptable, dependable, available, breakable, fashionable, laughable, passable, workable, predictable, readable, noticeable, changeable*), except when *ion* can be added to the base word without an intervening letter (*collect/collection/collectible,* but *present/presentation/presentable*).
- When the part before the suffix is a full word ending in *e;* in this case the final *e* is deleted before adding the suffix (*believable, desirable, lovable, likable, usable, valuable*).
- When the part before the suffix is a full word ending in *y;* in this case the final *y* is changed to an *i* before adding the suffix (*reliable, enviable, justifiable*).
- When the part of the word, or a form of the base word, before the suffix ends with a syllable with the long *a* sound (*tolerate/tolerable, separate/inseparable*).
- When the part before the suffix ends in a hard *c* or hard *g* (*applicable, despicable, amicable, navigable*).

The suffix *ible* is used in the following instances:

- When the part before the suffix is not a full word (*credible, edible, horrible, audible, visible, terrible, admissible, possible, permissible, sensible*).
- When the part before the suffix ends in *ns* (*sensible, insensible, responsible, irresponsible, comprehensible*).
- When the part before the suffix ends in a soft *c* or *g* (*legible, invincible, negligible, intelligible, producible*).

Children may find some words that are exceptions to these generalizations, such as *formidable, memorable, probable,* and *inevitable.* They should investigate the usual generalizations about when to drop the final *e,* when to change the *y* to *i,* and when to double the final consonant before the suffix is added. For words where the final *e* is not deleted (such as *changeable, manageable,* and *noticeable*) it is useful to discuss how readers may mispronounce the words if the letter *e* was deleted and how writers need to use spelling that will not confuse their readers.

The Suffixes er, or, *and* ar   The most common meaning of the suffixes *er, or,* and *ar* is "one who"; thus, a manager is one who manages, an actor is one who acts, and a burglar is one who burgles. These suffixes can also be used for equipment of some type—for example, *accelerator* and *escalator.* The only way to be sure about which of the three spellings to use is to check in a dictionary or word book. Children could search for words containing these suffixes in their reading and make class lists as a resource. They could also check the words for generalizations about when to delete the final *e,* when to double the final consonant, and when to change the *y* to an *i* before adding the suffix.

Here are some of the words the children may find, categorized by generalization. First, some words with *er:*

Just add the suffix

boarder
employer
murderer
teacher
traveler

Delete the final silent e

adviser
announcer
baker
believer
debater
manager
observer
provider
writer

Double the final consonant

batter
beginner
digger
jogger

Change the y *to an* i

carrier
worrier

Add k *to words ending with* c

panicker
picnicker

Some words with *or:*

Just add the suffix

actor
collector
director
editor
visitor

Delete the final silent e

dictator
distributor
educator
elevator
escalator

And some words with *ar:*

Delete the final silent e

burglar
liar

Double the final consonant

beggar

There are many other words that end in *er, or,* or *ar* where these letters are not suffixes, *alter, partner, harbor, neighbor, dollar,* and *caterpillar.* Students are likely to bring up such words in their study of the suffixes *er, or,* and *ar.*

Other Suffixes to Explore

There are many suffixes to explore, as illustrated in Table 13.2, which lists common suffixes and examples of words formed with each. Help children form generalizations about how these suffixes are added to base words and compare these generalizations for each suffix to look for patterns, such as the dropping of a final *e* before a suffix is added (*waste/wastage, ice/icy*), the changing of a *y* to an *i* (*fury/furious, beauty/beautiful*), the changing of an *f* to a *v* (*mischief/mischievous*), and the doubling of the last consonant when the base word ends with a vowel plus a consonant (*mud/muddy*). It is always a good idea to discuss with children the strategy that good spellers always use: to check a dictionary, particularly for words ending in *ery, ary,* or *ory* and *ise, ize,* or *yze*. Children may also notice when the base word changes, as is the case with *hunger/hungry* and *anger/angry, deep/depth* and *long/length*.

Summary of Generalizations About Suffixes

When the class has completed explorations of several suffixes, ask the children if they can draw any conclusions about how suffixes are usually added and whether a factor is whether the suffix begins with a vowel or a consonant. If they have sufficient examples to compare they may notice the following generalizations for all suffixes:

- For words ending in a consonant plus *y*, you usually change the *y* to an *i* before adding any suffix, except for suffixes beginning with an *i*.
- For words ending with a final silent *e*, drop the *e* before adding a suffix beginning with a vowel, unless the *e* is needed to help with the pronunciation of *g*, such as *manageable*).
- When words of one syllable and those of more than one syllable whose accent falls on the last syllable end in a single vowel plus a consonant, you usually double the consonant before adding a suffix that begins with a vowel.
- You usually add the letter *k* to words ending with the letter *c* before adding a suffix beginning with the letters *e, i,* or *y*.

Children learn best if they are allowed to work in groups or as a class to formulate these ideas themselves and then express them orally and in writing in their own words. Children may write their own statements and examples in their spelling journals.

An alternative approach to understanding these global generalizations is to select one type of word, such as base words that end with a consonant plus *y*, and have children explore what occurs when a variety of suffixes are added. Or you may wish to select just the suffixes *ed* and *ing* first, form generalizations about those, and then explore what occurs when other suffixes are added to other base words with the same feature.

TABLE 13.2	Other Common Suffixes
Suffix	*Examples*
age	orphanage, anchorage, wastage, postage
ary	stationary, dictionary, elementary
cede	concede, recede, precede, concede
ceed	exceed, proceed, succeed
dom	freedom, kingdom
ery	stationery, greenery, monastery
ful	beautiful, harmful, careful
hood	falsehood, neighborhood, likelihood
ise	exercise, disguise, surprise, advise, rise, wise, advertise
ish	boyish, girlish, British, Irish, Turkish, babyish, stylish
ist	realist, motorist, violinist, pianist
ive	productive, effective, negative
ize	apologize, criticize, realize, organize
less	shameless, speechless, lifeless, reckless
ment	commitment, amazement, development, argument
ness	kindness, readiness, greenness, feebleness
ory	laboratory, exploratory, contradictory
ous	poisonous, dangerous, marvelous, mischievous, furious
proof	waterproof, greaseproof, fireproof, bulletproof
sede	supersede
ship	friendship, membership, ladyship, comradeship
sion	confusion, decision, erosion
some	wholesome, cumbersome, twosome, quarrelsome
th	eighth, tenth, health, width, depth
tion	collection, relation, creation
ure	pressure, enclosure, pleasure, failure
y	cloudy, choosy, drowsy, icy, thirsty, muddy
yze	analyze, paralyze

Building Word Families with Prefixes and Suffixes

Throughout these explorations you should provide the children with opportunities to work in groups, pairs, and as individuals to try to build as many words as

possible by adding prefixes and suffixes to base words. As each prefix or suffix is learned, children could return to their lists to see if they can make other words.

Groups or pairs could compete with each other to see who can build the longest lists from a base word (a good example is *direct, directs, directing, directed, director, directors, direction, directions, directive, directives, directly, indirect, indirectly, misdirect, misdirects, misdirecting, misdirected, misdirection*). Children can use dictionaries and word books to assist them with their lists and then reflect on how this exploration is helping them as writers and readers. Extending knowledge of the language is one of the most powerful ways to develop competent spellers.

🌀 Learning Words

Apart from learning useful generalizations, children may want to consider which of the words on their lists they use frequently in their writing. These could be added to a class word wall for everyone to learn, or individuals may choose to learn some that they personally use. Sometimes memory aids are helpful for learning specific words, such as station*ary* (c*ar*) and station*ery* (pap*er*).

👉 Homework Ideas

Throughout the study of prefixes and suffixes children should be continually searching for examples of words related to the class exploration, listing these on a Post-it or a blank bookmark and adding them to class lists. They should explain to their parents the purpose of their searches and how they are forming hypotheses and drawing conclusions that will help them with their writing. Families may wish to work together in the study and compare their findings with ideas they may remember from their own education.

Children could also create spelling games that focus on words containing prefixes and suffixes. They could, for example, make groups of cards with base words that have a variety of prefixes and suffixes. The game would be to have players collect words in the same word family.

Big Books for Older Children

Phinney, M. 1994. *Baba Yaga.* Greenvale, NY: Mondo.
Walker, K. 1994. *The Frog Who Would Be King.* Greenvale, NY: Mondo.

Reference

Bolton, F., and D. Snowball. 1993. *Teaching Spelling: A Practical Resource.* Portsmouth, NH: Heinemann.

14

Derivatives and Origins of English Words

The English language contains many words derived from other languages. Knowing about the sources of words, such as words derived from Greek, Latin, and Old French, helps children in their writing and reading. For example, knowing that words such as *photograph, telephoto,* and *photosynthesis* are based on the Greek *photos,* meaning light, helps children learn the meanings of these words and enables them to spell them.

As well as words in English being derived from other languages, new words are constantly being coined, including acronyms (words formed from the initial letters of other words, such as *scuba,* from *self-contained underwater breathing apparatus*), blended words (such as *brunch,* a combination of *br*eakfast and l*unch*), and eponyms (words derived from the name of a person, place, or institution, such as *sandwich,* named after the Earl of Sandwich).

The main reason to have children study derivatives, acronyms, blended words, and eponyms is to give them a broader understanding of why words are spelled as they are in English, and to enhance their curiosity about the English language.

🌀 Evaluating Children's Understanding and Needs

The main way to evaluate children's understanding of derivatives, acronyms, blended words, and eponyms is to check their writing and to talk with them about your observations.

You may want to have the children try spelling some familiar words derived from the same root. For example, you might have them spell familiar words derived from *tele* (*television, telephone,* and *telescope*) or *thermo* (*thermometer, thermostat*). If the selected root occurs at the beginning of the words, you may ask the children to check their spelling attempts in a dictionary, to see how well they use dictionaries.

However, when checking the children's understanding of acronyms, blended words, and eponyms, rather than having them write examples of each, it may be of greater value to talk with them about their understanding of the meaning of each word and list examples they know of each word type, plus their sources. For example, if you are discussing acronyms and the children suggest *scuba*, list the word *scuba* and its source (*self-contained underwater breathing apparatus*); when you are discussing blended words and the children suggest *smog*, list *smog* and its source words (*smoke* plus *fog*); similarly, when you are discussing eponyms list the eponym (*Ferris wheel*) and its source (named after G. W. G. Ferris, an engineer). If necessary, suggest a few examples; then help children locate them in dictionaries, and help them make connections between the meaning and spelling of each word and its source.

Discovering the Generalizations About Derivatives

A derivative is a word containing a part that originated in another language. Studies of derivatives are likely to occur when students in the class investigate particular topics. For example, if the class is studying the earth and various aspects related to its origin or composition, children are likely to be reading and writing words such as *geography, geology,* and *geologist,* which contain the root *geo.* If they are studying transport they are likely to encounter derivatives from *aero* (*aerodynamics*), *auto* (*automobile*), and *port* (*heliport*). Other derivatives may be more subject-related than topic-related. For example, derivatives from *centum, deca,* and *mille* occur in words children read and write during math sessions.

Following is a list of some roots frequently investigated in elementary and middle schools, with their meanings in parentheses:

aero (air)	*electro* (beaming sun)
aqua (water)	*grapho* (I write)
astron (star)	*hemi* (half)
auto (self)	*logy* (speech, thought)
bios (life)	*meteoros* (high in the air)
chloro (light green)	*metron* (measure)
centum (a hundred)	*mille* (one thousand)
cyclos (circle, circular)	*monos* (one)
deca (ten)	*octo* (eight)
deci (a tenth of)	*photos* (light)
demos (the people)	*video* (see)

Words formed from these roots are only some of the derivatives children will encounter. When exploring derivatives, only bring up those relevant to the children's writing and reading needs. (For a more extensive list see Bolton and Snowball 1993.)

To assist children as they explore derivatives, have dictionaries available that give the derivations of words.

As you observe your students' writing, note the spelling mistakes they make when writing derivatives, such as *tellievision* for *television,* and suggest that it would be helpful for them to learn about the spelling of these words and their derivations.

Help them understand the meaning of the term *derivative,* and discuss derivatives they know. Be sure to discuss their meaning and their relationship to the meaning of the words they are based on.

Have children suggest a particular root they would like to learn about, and search for derivatives originating from that root.

Here is an example of a derivative exploration. A class of grade 5 children were learning about weather, and they decided that knowing about the root *sphero* would be helpful in their reading and writing.

During their study of weather, the teacher had copied and enlarged extracts from books and articles about weather onto overhead transparencies for use during shared reading sessions. Where possible, she also used Big Books and charts related to the topic, weather.

The class revisited these familiar reading materials for the exploration of *sphero.* In preparation for the exploration, the teacher prepared a chart with the headings as shown below. The children searched texts during shared, group, and independent reading sessions for words based on *sphero.* Words they identified were listed and the root underlined in each word.

Once the *sphero* words were listed, the teacher modeled ways of predicting the meanings of some of the words: by thinking about the meaning of *sphero,* and also by thinking about the context clues. The children's predictions were written in the appropriate column on the chart; then, dictionary definitions were checked and recorded in the appropriate column. The children then compared their predictions with the definitions.

Their completed chart looked like this:

Derivatives from sphero (*sphere*)	Predicted meaning of derivative	Dictionary definition
atmo*sphere*	something about Earth being a sphere, like a ball, and the gases around it	the mixture of gases surrounding the Earth, a star, or a planet
tropo*sphere*	like atmosphere, but maybe another layer of gases—a sphere of gases	the lower layers of the atmosphere, below the stratosphere, about 12.5 miles from Earth's surface

| strato*sphere* | like atmosphere and troposphere—a layer of gases | . . . |
| meso*sphere* | . . . | . . . |

Once the children understood the task they formed groups to continue their investigation. The teacher distributed forms containing the same headings as those on the class sheet to each group. Each group searched for other derivatives from *sphero*, predicted the meanings, and then compared the predicted meanings with the dictionary definitions.

The groups then came together to discuss their lists of words, which included *spherical, spheroid, hemisphere, hemispheres, atmospheric,* and *atmospheric pressure.* The words were added to the class list, with the children's predicted meanings and dictionary definitions. The class list was displayed for easy reference.

The teacher then helped the children form generalizations about the relationship between the meaning and spelling of *sphero* and the words derived from it. The children's generalizations included these:

- *Sphero* is spelled almost the same as *sphere.*
- *Sphero* is Greek.
- If you can spell *sphere* in one word it will help you spell many words.
- *Sphere* is in all positions in words.
- *Sphere* is a word, as well as a part of other words.
- *Sphere* always means the same thing—a three-dimensional figure shaped like a ball.

These generalizations were written in a class book about derivatives. The children were encouraged to use this book as a reference when writing.

The students found the topic of weather a rich source of derivatives. As they identified derivatives based on words they had not yet explored, these were listed and investigated over a period of three weeks. Such words and derivatives included *thermo/meter, meteoro/logists, meteoro/logy,* anemo*meter,* baro/*meter, milli/bar, hemi/sphere,* hygro*meter, stratus* clouds, *cyclo*ne, *auto*matic weather stations, *auto*mated aircraft, *geo*stationary satellite, and *photo/graphic* film.

At times the teacher discussed the meaning of a root prior to an investigation. At other times the children identified derivatives based on the same root, and from the meanings of the derivatives predicted the meaning of the root before checking it in a dictionary.

On occasion, several explorations occurred simultaneously. For example, when thinking about the word *thermometer,* which is composed of *thermo* and *meter,* the children explored the two side by side.

As each root was explored, generalizations were formed and added to the class derivative generalization book. After a while it was also decided to add the class charts to this book, and the children were asked to suggest ways of organizing the book. Although some children wanted to organize the root words according to their country of origin, it was finally agreed to organize them alphabetically, and to include a contents page in the book for easy access.

In addition to the class book, throughout the derivative explorations the children were constantly writing, reviewing, and revising their own understanding about derivatives in their personal spelling journals.

𝕽 Discovering the Generalizations About Acronyms, Blended Words, and Eponyms

When you notice children misspelling words such as *scooba* for *scuba*, *hellyport* for *heliport*, or *hambirga* for *hamburger* point out to the children that it would be helpful for them to find out how some words have become part of English.

During the initial discussion introduce and discuss the terms *acronyms, blended words,* and *eponyms* and how these kinds of words evolve and become part of English. Provide children with examples of each word type and ask them if they know of any.

List examples of the three word types on three separate class lists. Using the examples listed, help children define each term in their own words. For example:

- If you take the first letter from each word in a group and put them together, you form an *acronym* (for example, *PIN* for *P*ersonal *I*dentification *N*umber).

- A *blended word* is where you take a bit of one word and put it together (blend it) with a bit of another word (for example, *smog* is *sm*oke plus f*og*, and *sci-fi* is *sci*ence plus *fi*ction). A blended word means the same as the two words it came from.

- An *eponym* is a word that comes from the name of a person, a place, or an institution.

Write these statements on the relevant class lists.

Once you have introduced each term, there are various ways you might approach explorations of acronyms, blended words, and eponyms. Initially you may introduce explorations of each word type separately; then, as children discover examples of acronyms, blended words and eponyms when reading and writing, you may deal with each incidentally. Alternately, you may begin by exploring all three word types simultaneously, again adding to the class charts and teaching incidentally as new words are discovered by children in their reading and writing.

Regardless of the way the explorations proceed, make sure that children understand the reason for the explorations: that the explorations will help them as writers and readers.

Using familiar reading materials, have children find examples of acronyms, blended words, and eponyms, and discuss the meanings of each, as well as the meanings of the words from which they originated. Make sure that children understand these meaning relationships, and discuss how understanding this relationship will help them when writing. For example, if children know that the acronym *scuba* is related in meaning and spelling to the phrase *self-contained underwater breathing apparatus*, it will help them know how to spell *scuba*.

As children discover examples of acronyms, blended words, and eponyms when reading and writing, list them on the relevant class lists. If you need assistance thinking of acronyms, blended words, and eponyms, a useful teacher reference, which contains extensive lists of each word type, is *Teaching Spelling: a Practical Resource* (Bolton and Snowball 1993).

When listing the words the children find, also note the words from which they are derived in order to assist children in understanding the relationships. For example, when listing acronyms write the related words and underline the first letter of each; when listing blended words list both the blends and the words from which they originated; and when listing eponyms indicate the origin of the eponym, whether it is a person's name or a place.

When there are sufficient words—a list approximately as long as the ones in the following examples—help children form generalizations about each word type. Write the generalizations in children's own words.

Acronyms

Explain to the children that if you take the first letter from each word in a group and put them together, you form a new word, known as an *acronym*. For example:

laser: light amplification by stimulated emission of radiation
radar: radio detection and ranging
scuba: self contained underwater breathing apparatus
RAM: Random Access Memory
ROM: Read Only Memory
PIN: Personal Identification Number
Alcoa: Aluminium Company of America

Here are some examples of generalizations about acronyms that children may come up with:

- Lots of acronyms have to do with computers and science.
- Acronyms are born when new things happen in the world, like a PIN number being used with computers. They weren't used before computers were discovered.
- There are lots of new acronyms being formed.
- Some acronyms are written in capital letters, some are not.
- Acronyms written in capital letters often have the same letters as other words with different meanings—for example *PIN* and *pin*. Maybe capitals are used so we don't confuse the meanings.
- Acronyms aren't like initials—there are no periods after each letter.
- Some acronyms like *Alcoa* have a capital letter at the beginning. Maybe that's because it is a company.
- Acronyms are said as a word, not letter by letter.

Blended Words

Explain to the children that a *blended word* is created by taking a bit of one word and putting it together (blending it) with a bit of another word—for example, *brunch* is a blend of *br*eakfast and l*unch*, and *sci-fi* blends *sci*ence and *fi*ction. A blended word has the same meaning as the two words it came from.

Here are some examples:

aerobatics	= *aero*	+ acro*batics*
brunch	= *br*eakfast	+ l*unch*
hi-fi	= *hi*gh	+ *fi*delity
intercom	= *inter*	+ *com*munication
modem	= *mo*dulation	+ *dem*odulation
motel	= *mot*or	+ ho*tel*
motorcade	= *motor* cars	+ caval*cade*
newscast	= *news*	+ broad*cast*
sci-fi	= *sci*ence	+ *fi*ction
smog	= *sm*oke	+ f*og*
telecast	= *tele*vision	+ broad*cast*
walkathon	= *walk*	+ mar*athon*

And here are some generalizations students may come up with:

- Sometimes blended words are formed when two parts of words are put together, like *heliport* from *heli*copter and air*port*.
- Sometimes you take a whole word and put another bit with it to make a blended word, such as *travelogue* from *travel* and catal*ogue*.
- If we know how to spell the blended word it will help us spell the two words it came from.
- If we can spell the two words used for making a blended word it will help us spell the blended word.
- If the language keeps changing, we can make new blended words of our own, like *ginormous* from *gi*gantic and e*normous*. One day *ginormous* might be in the dictionary.

Eponyms

An *eponym* is a word that comes from the name of a person or a place. For example:

August	Augustus Caesar
begonia	Michel Bégon (patron of science)
bikini	Bikini atoll, Marshall Islands
bloomers	Amelia Bloomer (social reformer)
boycott	Capt. Charles Cunningham Boycott (English land agent in Ireland)
braille	Louis Braille (teacher)

brussels sprouts	Brussels, Belgium
canary	Canary Islands
cashmere	Kashmir, India
cereal	Ceres (goddess of agriculture)
denim	Nîmes, France
diesel	Rudolf Diesel (engineer)
Fahrenheit scale	Gabriel Daniel Fahrenheit (physicist)
frankfurt	Frankfurt, Germany
Friday	Frigg (pronounced fry) (goddess of the sky)
hamburger	Hamburg, Germany
January	Janus (god of beginnings and endings)
July	Julius Caesar (born in July)
leotard	Jules Léotard (trapeze performer)
lima bean	Lima, Peru
limerick	Limerick, Ireland
limousine	Limousin, France
loganberry	James Harvey Logan (horticulturalist)
magnolia	Pierre Magnol (botanist)
March	Mars (god of war)
May	Maiea (goddess of spring)
mayonnaise	Port Mahon, Majorca
Morse code	Samuel F. B. Morse (inventor)
ohm	Georg Simon Ohm (physicist)
Olympic	Olympia, Greece
sandwich	Earl of Sandwich (nobleman)
sardine	Sardinia
Saturday	Saturn (god of agriculture)
teddy bear	Theodore Roosevelt (politician)
Thursday	Thor (god of thunder)
Tuesday	Tue (god of war)
volcano	Vulcan (Roman god of fire)
watt	James Watt (engineer)
Wednesday	Woden (god of storms)

Some generalizations the children might offer about eponyms are the following:

- There are more eponyms from people's names than from places.
- As people make discoveries or do something famous, their name might be used as an eponym.
- If I become famous something might be named after me; my name could become an eponym like Louis Braille's did.
- If something famous comes from a place it is sometimes named after that place, like *frankfurters* from Frankfurt.
- Lots of food words are eponyms. They're named after the place they come from.

• If I know where an eponym comes from and can spell that word, it will help me spell the eponym—if I can spell the city *Hamburg* it will help me spell *hamburger.*

Leave the generalizations and class charts displayed for children to refer to. After a while you could publish the generalizations and the class lists for each of the explorations in a class book.

Involve children in suggesting ways of organizing the book. Presumably there would be separate parts for acronyms, blended words, and eponyms. The children may also decide to have sections within each of these parts—for example, separating eponyms into those named after people and those named after places. They may also consider a contents page a useful addition, and some blank pages for words to be added throughout the year.

In addition to their writing class generalizations and lists in the class book, provide time on a regular basis for children to write, review, and revise what they know about acronyms, blended words, and eponyms in their personal spelling journals.

Scheduling Explorations

When introducing derivative, acronym, blended word, and eponym explorations, you might need to take 20 to 30 minutes to ensure that the children understand what each of these terms means and how knowing about each can help them when writing and reading. Once introduced, an exploration may take just a few minutes each day or every two or three days.

Throughout the day, many opportunities will arise to explore derivatives, acronyms, blended words, and eponyms related to specific curriculum areas. For example, during health studies the children may encounter words such as *cardiac* and *cardiology,* based on *cardio* (heart), or *bronchitis* and *bronchial,* based on *bronchus* (windpipe). Similarly, in music sessions, children may encounter the word *auditorium,* based on *audio* (to hear), or *xylophone* and *microphone,* based on *phono* (sound/voice).

It is important to make the most of these opportunities, enabling children to learn about and spell words they encounter when reading and writing about topics in various curriculum areas. Rather than scheduling time in the regular language sessions for spelling explorations, it would be logical to do the spelling exploration when reading and writing about the topic. If specialist teachers are involved in the teaching of other curriculum areas, they should take responsibility for spelling explorations related to the words the children are using in their subject areas.

Class time required for explorations may be reduced by involving children in homework tasks, with the time spent in school used mainly for sharing.

As children discover additional words relating to these explorations, you will want to engage in short episodes of incidental teaching, allowing time for this, and for the addition of the words to the relevant class lists.

Learning Words

Throughout the explorations, ask the children to think about whether any of the words listed are words they have used a lot when writing in general, or now, for a particular topic. Words so identified should be learned by the class using the "look, say, spell, cover, write, check" strategy and added to the class word wall. Ask individual children who require further practice to add the words to their personal lists to learn. (For more information about high-frequency words and learning words refer to Chapters 17 and 18.)

Continuing Evaluation

One way to find out what children have learned, and still need to learn about derivatives, acronyms, blended words, and eponyms is by checking their writing to see how they are applying what they have learned. For example, if you notice a particular root spelled in different ways in different derivatives, have the child check the spelling of the derivatives and the roots on which they are based on the class chart or in a dictionary. Have the child explain how knowing how to spell a particular root word helps spell other words based on that root and how this applies to the currently misspelled words. Suggest that the child add the misspelled words to his or her personal list of words to learn.

Similarly, if children misspell acronyms, blended words, or eponyms, have them refer to the relevant class charts and think about how the words originated and how this will help them when spelling the words. Also encourage children to check dictionaries to find the origin of acronyms, blended words, and eponyms.

You may also collect children's spelling journals on a regular basis, perhaps each child's every three or four weeks. Talk with them about their understanding, and have them show you pieces of writing where they have applied what they have recently learned. During the discussions, have them reflect on their understanding of derivatives, acronyms, blended words, and eponyms and how this knowledge helped them in their writing.

☞ Homework Ideas

The children can be involved in homework tasks throughout the explorations of derivatives, acronyms, blended words, and eponyms. For example:

- Have them search reading materials for derivatives, acronyms, blended words, and eponyms, listing these and adding them to class lists.
- Ask them to bring items from home named after people or places.
- They can play games with a partner, such as Concentration: provide children with numerous cards, approximately 3 inches by 2 inches, and a dictionary. Have children write derivatives, acronyms, blended words, or

Across

2. meteoro + logy =
   (atmosphere)
8. zoo + logy =
   (animal)
9. geo + logy =
   (earth)
10. cosmo + logy =
    (universe)
11. eco + logy =
    (house)
13. theo + logy =
    (God)
14. minera + logy =
    (mineral)
15. mytho + logy =
    (myth)
16. ophthalmo + logy =
    (eye)

Down

1. patho + logy =
   (disease)
3. astro + logy =
   (star)
4. neuro + logy =
   (nerve)
5. physio + logy =
   (natural science)
6. psycho + logy =
   (mind)
7. bio + logy =
   (life)
12. socio + logy =
    (society)

FIGURE 14.1   A crossword based on *logy.*

eponyms on cards, using a separate card for each one. If playing with derivatives, have children write a derivative on one card and its word of origin on another. If playing with acronyms, blended words, or eponyms, have children also write the original source of those words on separate cards. Explain to children that the game is played by placing the cards face down, and the players take turns picking up two cards at a time. If they pick up two cards connected in meaning, for example, *radar* on one card, and *radio detection and ranging* on another, they have a matching pair. If they have a match they keep the cards and take another turn. Tell the children that if they are not sure they should check on a class chart or in a dictionary. The player with the most cards at the end of the game is the winner.

- Have children refer to their spelling journals, word books, dictionaries, and class charts to make crossword puzzles for their classmates to complete (see Figure 14.1). Crosswords can help children develop meaning and visual strategies as they write the word and think about how the word looks. It may be necessary to teach children the basics of making crosswords by modeling how to construct one.

References

Beeching, C. L. 1988. *A Dictionary of Eponyms.* New York: Oxford University Press.

Bolton, F., and D. Snowball. 1993. *Teaching Spelling: A Practical Resource.* Portsmouth, NH: Heinemann.

Carroll, D. 1973. *The Dictionary of Foreign Terms in the English Language.* New York: Hawthorn Books.

Hall, T. 1979. *How Things Start.* Sydney: Collins.

Morris, W., and M. Morris. 1962. *Dictionary of Word and Phrase Origins.* New York: Harper & Row.

Partridge, E. 1983. *ORIGINS: A Short Etymological Dictionary of Modern English.* New York: Greenwich House.

Pickles, C., and L. Meynell. 1970. *The Beginning of Words—How English Grew.* London: Anthony Blond.

Roget's Thesaurus of Words and Phrases (many publishers).

Shipley, J. T. 1957. *Dictionary of Word Origins.* Iowa: Littlefield, Adams & Co.

Apostrophes for Possessives and Plurals

A n apostrophe is a mark of punctuation and if it is not placed in the correct position, or omitted when it should be used, or inserted when it should not be used, the word is misspelled. An apostrophe can be used to indicate that a letter has been omitted, as in contractions (see Chapter 9). It can also be used to indicate the possessive case (for example, "the dog's tail") and to indicate the plurals of letters and numbers (for example, "He finds it hard to write 3's"). Many children are aware that some words have an apostrophe but are confused about its function and where to put it. They may completely overuse apostrophes, placing them in any word that ends with an *s*, such as "Some oranges' were eaten." This usually occurs because they have not properly figured out the role of the apostrophe or because someone has simply given them facts about the apostrophe rather than involving them in an exploration that will enable them to discover and assimilate the facts themselves, which leads to true understanding.

Children often use apostrophes in their writing, so they should be given ample opportunity to properly explore their correct use. The incorrect use of apostrophes can affect the meaning of a piece of writing, making it very confusing for the reader. As suggested in Chapter 9, it is appropriate for most children to study the use of contractions as early as grade 2, but understanding the concept of possessive case is more complex. More experienced readers and writers in the older grades have more success with studies about the use of the apostrophe for purposes other than contractions. By observing your students' writing you will know whether to study the possessive case with your entire class of older children, or whether just a small group need further assistance.

Allow the study to continue long enough for all of the children to be able to explain the use and placement of apostrophes and to apply their knowledge in their writing. This usually takes several weeks, with a longer period of time spent daily when the exploration begins and, later, briefer sessions when individual students feel ready to share what they have learned. Other spelling focuses will be dealt with during the same periods; apostrophes will not be the only thing that children will be learning about at any given point. The type of study described in this chapter may be used with students at any age who are still having trouble with apostrophes to indicate possession; the only thing that would be different is the material they would read to find examples.

Evaluating Children's Understanding and Needs

Children are often confused about the use of apostrophes for possessive case and may have some vague idea that it is used when words end with an *s*. Examples of the types of errors that indicate that children need help with this aspect of spelling are the following:

- I went to my grandmothers house. (Apostrophe omitted.)
- We had several vacation's last year. (Apostrophe used when it shouldn't be.)
- All the boy's caps blew off at the same time. (Apostrophe in the wrong place.)
- Jennifers' finger was broken when she jammed it in the door. (Apostrophe in the wrong place.)
- The Brown's came to see us. (Apostrophe used when it shouldn't be.)

Even some children who usually use the apostrophe correctly may not be able to explain its purpose or be able to tell someone else when and how to use it.

By looking at various samples of children's writing and asking them to explain what they understand about apostrophes you will learn where they are confused and what they feel confident about. Use this knowledge as a starting point to focus the exploration in ways that will help your students.

Discovering the Generalizations About Possessives

Tell the children that you have noticed some confusion in their writing about when to use apostrophes and where to place them, so you are going to explore this subject together, using published authors' writing to find out how to use apostrophes correctly. You might show them some specific examples of their writing to help them see where they are confused.

If your children have been involved in explorations about other aspects of spelling they may be able to suggest how this study could take place and may even be able to work in pairs or small groups from the beginning. If they are not used to this way of learning you will need to give them more guidance. Begin by asking if anyone is able to provide explanations about how apostrophes are used and list their ideas on a chart. Throughout the study refer back to these ideas to compare the children's original statements with their current thoughts and to see if they wish to revise their earlier statements. At this early stage children may include some statements about contractions when explaining the use of apostrophes. If so, take this opportunity to clarify that they all understand this aspect of apostrophe use before going further with the exploration.

Select material containing examples of apostrophes used to indicate possession from familiar material, such as Big Books, overhead transparencies, or charts of songs or poems. As you reread the material together tell the children to watch for words that have apostrophes. As you find them, write the examples on a chart. You will need to write the entire sentence or enough of it to provide sufficient information about why the apostrophe is used; sometimes you may even need to include a prior sentence so that it is clear whether the noun is singular or plural. Such examples might be similar to the following:

> . . . here's an idea . . .
> . . . put yourself in the ant's place . . .
> . . . about the size of a person's thumb . . .
> Notice the ant's shape.
> They'd catch the smell . . .
> . . . someone's picnic lunch . . .
> . . . an ant's life . . .
> The bears all went in search of food. While they were gone the little girl wandered into the bears' den.
> . . . the leaves' colors . . .
> . . . the children's coats . . .
> . . . an octopus' body . . .

If you find only a few examples from one piece, you will need to add to the chart over several days until there are enough examples to begin a discussion about the purpose and placement of the apostrophe.

Tell the children that their job is to work out why an apostrophe is used by the writers and why it is placed where it is. They may first decide which examples are contractions, and if they already understand contractions you may delete contractions from the list. Encourage children to share their ideas and to comment on what the others say. After contractions, children usually notice that another purpose for an apostrophe has something to do with belonging to someone or something. This hypothesis can be checked using each of the examples.

Children will also notice that sometimes the apostrophe is placed before a final *s* and sometimes after it. The examples could be grouped accordingly:

Apostrophe before the final s

> . . . put yourself in the ant's place . . .
> . . . about the size of a person's thumb . . .

Notice the ant's shape.
... someone's picnic lunch ...
... an ant's life ...
... the children's coats ...

Apostrophe after the final s

... into the bears' den ...
... the leaves' colors ...
... an octopus' body ...

Ask children to watch for other examples during shared reading experiences and in their personal reading, and add these to the charts. Children should continue to share their thoughts about why the apostrophe is sometimes before and sometimes after the final *s*. Depending on the examples you have listed, children sometimes think that it is placed before the final *s* when the noun is singular, but then examples such as *children's* or an *octopus's* make them rethink their hypothesis. (Bear in mind that some of the material they read may have examples such as *an octopus'* because that is an alternative, correct way to form the possessive when the noun ends with the letter *s*.) Eventually the children should be able to explain the use of apostrophes for possessive case as listed below, but the explanation must be in their own words to be meaningful to them.

- Use an apostrophe and *s* at the end of the word to write the possessive case of a noun not ending in *s*, whether the noun is singular or plural, such as *dog/dog's, women/women's, children/children's, fish/fish's*.
- Use only an apostrophe at the end of the word to write the possessive case of a plural noun ending in *s*, such as *girls/girls', ladies/ladies', bears/ bears'*.
- Use only an apostrophe *or* an apostrophe and *s* to write the possessive case of a singular noun ending in *s*, such as *Charles/Charles'* or *Charles's, octopus/octopus'* or *octopus's, Denise Jones/Denise Jones'* or *Denise Jones's*.
- For the word *its*, as in *its tail*, an apostrophe is not used to indicate possession because the word is a possessive pronoun and apostrophes are not used in such pronouns (that is, *his, hers, theirs, its*). Children often explain why they shouldn't use an apostrophe in cases such as *its tail* because they realize that if they write *it's tail* their readers will assume they mean the contraction for *it is*. Make clear to the children that the purpose of all punctuation marks is to help the reader construct meaning, so it makes sense not to do something that would confuse the meaning.

When the children have had ample opportunity to verbalize their understanding about the use of apostrophes for possessives, and to listen to one another's explanations, ask them to write about what they know in their spelling notebooks. This will help you determine who is still confused. It also helps the children themselves to realize what they understand and what they still need to work at. Consider, for example, the following samples of children's writing.

Child 1

I know that you can use apostrophes when you are replacing a letter, like don't, you are replacing the letter "o". Apostrophes are also used to put before or after letters. I use apostrophes if it belongs to someone else like Danni's hair. You only use apostrophes if it belongs to another person or if it is more than one you put it after the word like the boys' bathroom.

Child 2

An apostrophe can be sometimes to replace a letter in a word. An apostrophe can make something say that it belongs to a noun or a proper noun in a sentence. An apostrophe is like a comma mark on the upper line. There are a lot of words with apostrophes like there's, it's bear's, we'll, he'll and more. An apostrophe cannot be used all the time. I would like to know more about apostrophes. Who invented apostrophes? When do we use an apostrophe? I don't think I know a lot about apostrophes. Well at least I know how to spell apostrophe.

From these writing samples the teacher can tell that the first child has a good idea about the use of apostrophes; the second child also understands a lot, but is not sure about everything and does not mention whether to put the apostrophe before or after an *s*. Considering how much some students overuse apostrophes, it is significant that the second child writes, "An apostrophe cannot be used all the time."

It is helpful for children to read each other's writing, first in pairs, to see if there is anything that the other has written that the partner also understands and could therefore add to his or her own explanation. The children can also have fruitful discussions about the areas of confusion. Encourage children to say what they are unsure of to see if any of the other children can help them with that particular topic. This will help you decide what areas need further investigation by the children as a class, in groups, or independently. Share written explanations with the class and talk about what makes an explanation understandable to others, such as grouping thoughts about the same issue together, perhaps in separate paragraphs, and providing examples.

The advantage of keeping the charts on display is that children can add to them as they find examples in their reading and can refer to them when they write. You may need to demonstrate during shared writing how the charts can be used as a resource. With many examples on the charts, the children can usually find one similar to what they are trying to write. Having many displayed examples helps them apply what they are learning. It is only when there are many such examples that the children can easily form hypotheses. Verbalizing and writing their explanations helps them organize their thoughts, realize what they know, and become aware of what they still have queries about. Eventually the children will understand enough not to need to refer to the charts for their own writing, and they will be able to write useful explanations in their spelling notebooks.

Discovering the Generalizations About Plurals of Letters and Numbers

During the exploration about apostrophes you or the children may find examples such as "there are two r's in her name" where the apostrophe neither replaces a letter nor indicates possession. In these instances the apostrophe is being used to indicate the plural of a letter or number. It may take some time before your class finds enough examples to form this hypothesis, so you may need to volunteer several examples of your own to help them. Make sure their search includes history books, where the children are more likely to find examples of decades and other dates. Have children reflect on what type of writing tends to use the apostrophe for this purpose, and ask them to add this information to their spelling notebooks.

Continuing Evaluation

The children's verbal and written explanations are a major indication of their understanding, and their writing is the best way for you to observe their ability to apply what they have learned. During shared writing you can also call on particular children to spell words where an apostrophe is required. If you call on children who previously were having trouble with apostrophes you will be able to assess their current understanding. In addition, children could be asked to return to previous pieces of their writing to specifically check for their use of apostrophes, and you could refer to examples of children's writing that you had noted previously contained mistakes to see how they would correct them. This will give the children the opportunity to evaluate their own growth. Also ask students to explain how they think their study of apostrophes will help them with their reading and writing.

Homework Ideas

Throughout this study children should be continually searching for examples of apostrophes in their reading, both in class and at home. Sometimes they may notice examples while reading and record them immediately and sometimes they may reread material to find examples. Show children how to use context to determine the purpose of the apostrophe so that they can group their examples and add them to appropriate classroom charts. Explain that you are encouraging them to read like writers, to notice what other writers do, and to learn from these writers.

Other homework tasks could include having the children write explanations in their spelling journals and share their journals with a partner the next day, or asking them to proofread their writing to check specifically for the correct use of apostrophes. At the conclusion of the study children could be asked to explain to their parents what they have learned and how this helps their writing.

Reference

Brenner, Barbara. 1997. *Thinking About Ants*. Greenvale, NY: Mondo.

Part Three

CHAPTER

16

Proofreading

n a publishing house editors work with writers on many aspects of their writing, including overall structure, style, and content. The purpose of the writing and the intended audience are important factors for writers and editors to consider as they meet to discuss possible changes. The editors also proofread for correct spelling, grammar, and punctuation, assuming that the writers have already done so. Sometimes writers and editors become so familiar with the writing that they do not notice errors, so another proofreader may be engaged to check the writing again before publication.

In a classroom the roles of teacher and student, and the responsibilities that accompany these roles, can closely resemble those of writers, editors, and proofreaders in a publishing house. The children are the writers, choosing their topics, deciding which works to publish, and learning the craft of writing, which includes learning how to revise and proofread. You, the teacher, guide the children's learning and usually also play the role of the editor and final proofreader. The writer's peers are the audience, who may also assist with ideas about revision and proofreading.

Proofreading is a spelling habit that all writers need to develop because the writing process involves so many things to think about that it is easy to make spelling mistakes while writing. Proofreading involves identifying words that are or may be misspelled and then attempting to correct the words, using resources to help if necessary. Children need to learn how to proofread independently, even though you will continue to support them just as an editor would, because it is a skill they will use all through their lives.

Proofreading also helps children choose personal words that would be useful to learn. The words they are not sure about in their writing provide an ideal group to choose from, their decisions being based on whether children think they will use these words in their future writing. (More information about ways to learn words is provided in the next two chapters.)

Demonstrating

As early as grade 1 some children may have reached the stage where they could benefit from your introducing the skills of revision and proofreading without inhibiting their writing. Demonstrations of proofreading are of great benefit at all grade levels because the discussion about spelling that takes place extends the children's repertoire of strategies for checking writing and for correcting misspellings.

Proofreading is not easy, and a writer may not even know that a certain word is misspelled. For these reasons, peer proofreading in addition to demonstrations can help. If the work is going to be published, you may need to be the final proofreader.

Use samples of children's writing to demonstrate that proofreading may be easier if a piece of paper is used to cover most of the writing, allowing the reader to see only one line of writing at a time. Proofreading means looking at each word to check that it is spelled correctly, but readers normally read chunks of text for meaning and do not necessarily notice errors. Select a piece of writing and check with the writer to make sure he or she agrees that the class can review it together to see what they can all learn about spelling. If possible, make an overhead transparency of the writing so that the entire class can easily see it. For younger writers, you may prefer to have them take turns writing on a large chart; this way the writing can easily be viewed without your having to make an overhead. Ask the writer to read the piece; then ask him or her to proofread it while the other children watch carefully but do not interrupt. The class should be gathered closely together to build a sense of community and a sharing of knowledge. Remember that the purpose of the demonstration is for the children to learn how to apply the process to their own writing.

Talk about how proofreading need not be so laborious if some of it is done while writing, or if the writer highlights or underlines words he or she is not sure about as the writing is done, rather than leaving it all for later. You could demonstrate these ideas during shared writing with the class or small groups. Statements such as "Don't worry about your spelling until the end—just get your ideas down first" may mislead some children into thinking that writers never think about their spelling until all of the writing has been done.

Working with Individuals

During independent writing you may confer with children about many aspects of their work, including spelling. Encourage them to check that their writing makes sense and to proofread their own writing before you meet with them. If you notice errors in their writing that the children have not picked up you could help them in several ways, depending on the needs of each writer and how much you want to focus on at any one time. Here are some techniques for pointing out errors:

- Indicate a line that contains a spelling error and ask the writer to find it and then try to correct it.
- Underline misspelled words that you think the writer should know and ask the writer to correct them.
- Show the writer how to spell a limited number of words that are misspelled if you think they would be useful words for the writer to learn.

Remember, if you do all of the children's proofreading for them they will not learn how to do it themselves. It's also useful for you to find out which words a child is able to detect as incorrect and to see what strategies he or she uses to try to correct such errors.

"Try It Out" or "Have a Go" Sheets

As part of the proofreading process you may want to introduce children to a tool that writers use for trying unknown words. Usually when we are writing on paper and are not sure how to spell a word we try it two or more different ways to decide what looks right. If we are still not sure we check with another person or a written resource. We may do this as part of the writing or we may grab another piece of paper on which to write our attempts. Children can learn to use this writing strategy. Give them a sheet of paper headed "Try It Out" or "Have a Go" and set up in columns to encourage them to try a word more than one way. (This does not mean, of course, that they should use such a sheet for every word they want to write.) There should be no rules about how many times the word should be tried. For example:

First Try	*Second Try*	*Third Try*	*Correct*
Yakees	Yankeys	Yankees	Yankees
picher	pitcher		pitcher
icecreem	icecream		ice cream
thay			they
staydiem	stadiem	stadeim	stadium
peanutts			peanuts
boll	bale	ball	ball

Filled-out "Try It Out" sheets can be a very useful source for children to return to in selecting personal words to learn. In the above example the child decided to learn the words *Yankees* and *stadium* because he frequently wrote about going to baseball games; the word *they* because it is a high-frequency word; and his teacher suggested he should learn the word *ball* because it contained a spelling pattern that would help him with many other words and because he used this word frequently in his writing.

Some teachers include a copy of this sheet in the workbooks they use for all curriculum areas or provide a number of copies stapled together or spiral bound into a booklet that is always available. In this way children realize the usefulness of the "Try It Out" sheet for all kinds of writing. It's also worthwhile to have a large-scale model of one next to the easel used for the class's shared writing so that you can demonstrate when and how to use the sheet. A word may be tried either during writing or during proofreading, after the writing is completed. Just make sure that the form is a useful tool for children as they write, not a hindrance. When kept over a period of time these sheets can be an informative record of children's spelling development and can be used during parent conferences to indicate changes and growth.

Spell-Check Computer Programs

When children use a computer to write it would indicate carelessness if they did not use the spell-check function. You should discuss the role of the computer with your students so that they understand that when they use the spell-checker they should think about whether each misspelling they find was caused by a keyboarding error or whether the computer is highlighting a word they did not know how to spell correctly. If it is a word they did not know it may be a good one to choose for personal learning. If so, they should immediately copy it into their spelling journal or wherever they list words to learn. It's a good idea for children to take their spelling journal to the computer whenever they are using the computer for writing.

You should also focus on the fact that the computer can only really help with spelling if the writer's words are spelled as closely as possible to the conventional spelling. For this reason, children must do their best when writing, and if the computer doesn't help them during the spell-check stage they may need to think more about the possible ways the problem word could be spelled. Because of this, and because the computer continually presents models of correct spelling while children are using a spell-checker, a computer can be helpful even for the child who is struggling with spelling.

Another point to make is that a computer spell-checker cannot do everything. For example, it cannot know if the correct homophone has been used. Thus, the writer must read for meaning in order to make sure that the intended words are in the final draft. Some writers find this easier to do by checking a hard copy rather than looking at the computer screen.

Resources for Checking Spelling

When writers think a word is misspelled or if they are not sure how to spell a word they use many resources to help them. These include dictionaries, word books, word lists, other people, fiction and nonfiction books, charts, environmental print, maps, atlases, and mechanical devices that help with spelling. One of the indicators of a good speller is the willingness to find out the correct spelling and the ability to choose the most useful resource to suit the word being checked. For example, it's easier to use a map or an atlas, rather than a dictionary, to find the spelling of a place name.

It's important to have a range of these resources, suited to your children's reading development, available in every classroom. You should model their use during shared writing, and children need to learn how to use these resources efficiently. This includes knowing how to select the most appropriate resource, understanding how to locate words through alphabetical order, being aware of the purpose of head words in resources such as dictionaries, and knowing the types of words that are likely to be found in the appendices of dictionaries.

Different dictionaries suit different purposes related to word usage, including pronunciation, grammar, and spelling. Some dictionaries and word books list many words in the same word family under an entry. This can help children see that knowing how to spell a base word can help with the spelling of many other words. Other dictionaries give information about the origin of a word. This, too, can help children understand why words are spelled the way they are and how words based on the same meaning or root will have the same or similar spelling. When selecting resources for the classroom it's wise to include a variety of them, including paperbacks that are easy to handle and cheap to replace, because it's also important that resources be up to date.

Children should also be encouraged to select a dictionary and/or word book that suits their personal needs to have at home. You could help parents by suggesting a range to choose from.

High-Frequency Words

he most common high-frequency words make up about fifty percent of written language. Because of this it is important that children learn to recognize these words in their reading and learn to spell them for their writing as soon as possible, even though they should be encouraged to attempt unknown words when they write. Good writers continually add to the number of words they can spell automatically, without thinking, and the words they use most often are the ones they should learn first.

Some Useful Lists

As your class builds lists of high-frequency words, consider the lists that follow. Your own class lists may contain other words because of your children's interests; you may also want to add the first name of each child in the class to the list.

High-Frequency Words in Kindergarten

Children in kindergarten may begin to recognize and use some high-frequency words conventionally in their writing if they have many opportunities for shared reading and shared or interactive writing. Encourage children to notice words that occur frequently, such as:

a	come	is	my	up
am	go	it	see	we
an	here	like	the	
and	I	look	this	
at	in	me	to	

The Most Common High-Frequency Words

You will find many lists of high-frequency words; the words that appear most often in such lists are:

a	about	after	all	am
an	and	are	as	at
back	be	because	been	big
but	by	came	can	come
could	day	did	do	down
first	for	from	get	go
going	got	had	has	have
he	her	here	him	his
I	if	in	into	is
it	just	like	little	look
made	make	me	more	my
no	not	now	of	off
on	one	only	or	our
out	over	said	saw	see
she	so	some	that	the
their	them	then	there	they
this	those	to	two	up
very	was	we	well	went
were	what	when	where	which
who	why	will	with	would
you	your			

Other Common Words

In addition to the words listed above, many children use the following words frequently in their writing (there may also be others that are commonly used because of your children's interests and cultures):

boy	brother	bug	can't	car
cat	children	dad	dear	didn't
dog	don't	family	father	friend
fun	girl	give	good	house
how	jump	know	love	many
mom	mother	name	nice	night

old	once	people	pet	play
pretty	rain	ran	read	ride
run	school	sister	small	sunny
teacher	thank	thing	those	time
too	trip	truck	us	want
won't	write			

When to Learn High-Frequency Words

Grades K–2

If young children have many experiences with shared reading and shared or interactive writing they will probably be able to spell some words conventionally. They also will recognize some words in shared and independent reading, particularly if you have been helping them develop a correspondence of sound with print during these experiences. This ability to recognize and spell some words may develop during the kindergarten year; it certainly should occur during first grade. When children show such awareness they are ready to learn high-frequency words. Before you focus on teaching them how to spell some words, however, make sure that your students feel confident about attempting unknown words. This may be after a few months of reading and writing experiences. When their personal writing shows that they are beginning to spell some words conventionally, they are ready to learn other words.

Appropriate strategies for learning high-frequency words are described below; from kindergarten through grade 2 the list of words children know will grow. If they are given the opportunity to read and write in kindergarten and they have many opportunities to do this in grade 1, most children may know the 100 most common high-frequency words by the end of grade 1.

Grade 2 and Beyond

In grade 2 and beyond, you should check at the beginning of the year to determine whether your students know how to spell the high-frequency words, then apply the strategies described below to any words that are not known. The suggestions also suit the years in which ESL children are in transition to English, and the procedures can be applied to learning high-frequency words in other languages as well.

One of the expectations you should establish with the children is that once these words are known they should be spelled correctly in all the writing the children do. In one classroom where high-frequency words were listed on a word wall, a child told his parents that he didn't need to learn those words because they were on display. When she heard this, his teacher realized that this child had misunderstood the purpose of the whole exercise.

Invented Spelling vs. Permanent Misspelling

Although it is important for writers to continue to attempt words whether the spelling is known or not, be very observant of children who no longer experiment with the spelling of a word and consistently spell it the same incorrect way. You will need to make a careful decision about whether to intervene or not. A child may write *went* as *wt* for a period of time because of the stage of spelling development he or she happens to be in, but if a child is beyond the phonetic stage of spelling and consistently spells *went* as *whent* or *they* as *thay* you probably need to step in, particularly if it is high-frequency words that are being misspelled. It is very hard to break the habit of misspelling a word if the writer has repeatedly misspelled it the same way for a long time. Point out that you have noticed it is a word the writer often uses, so the conventional spelling should be learned. Add it to the class or individual list of words to learn, and talk about useful strategies for learning it. More experienced writers of English who are in the habit of misspelling a word need to work at changing their automatic spelling to the correct one. The suggestions in this chapter will help them do this.

Awareness of Children's First Language

If children's first language is not English they may make consistent errors with some high-frequency words because they are applying what they know from their first language. For example, Spanish-speaking children may write *my* as *may* or *we* as *wi* because they are using the Spanish spelling for the sounds in the English words. Errors can also occur when their first language does not have the some sounds that they hear in English words. For example, Spanish-speaking children may write *this, they,* and *there* as *dis, dey,* and *der*. It is helpful to be aware of what may be causing children's confusion and help them by showing them how the words are different in English.

Introducing High-Frequency Words

If children are going to learn words, they need to be constantly aware that the purpose of doing so is to improve their writing and reading rather than to pass a spelling test. One way to demonstrate this is to suggest words to learn based on your observations of children's writing: "I notice that many of you are using the word *they* in your writing, so this would be a useful word to learn." Also, although you may have a list of high-frequency words, their usefulness becomes more significant if the children are asked to find them. During shared reading or writing, ask children to watch out for the words that seem to be used most frequently. Draw their attention to such words by highlighting them as you reread familiar material. Individual children may also share their discoveries as a result of their personal reading and writing and the teacher can also add to the list.

Begin to make a list of high-frequency words on a special chart with the heading "Words We Often Use as Readers and Writers," and talk about why it would be useful for all the children to learn to read and write them. Even the use of such a heading rather than calling the list simply the "word wall" helps children understand the significance of the words listed.

Learning High-Frequency Words in the Younger Grades

Find a suitable location in the classroom for an alphabetical word wall, preferably at children's eye level and where they can have easy access to the words that will be placed on the list.

You may begin listing words alphabetically, perhaps starting with children's names written under the appropriate letter. Or you may want to start with a random list if you plan to introduce the concept of placing words in alphabetical order later. If you begin listing words randomly, when the words become difficult to locate quickly suggest that they be organized in some way to speed up the process of finding them. If children have been exposed to picture dictionaries or other dictionaries they may suggest alphabetical order without your needing to steer them in this direction; or you may show them this arrangement. A Big Book version of a picture dictionary, such as *My Picture Dictionary* (Green and Snowball 1994) can be helpful here. Make sure that the picture dictionary you select correctly lists words in alphabetical order in columns; many of those available provide incorrect models of how a dictionary is used.

As children suggest high-frequency words write each one on a card. Some teachers like to cut the card into the shape of the word to allow children to use the shape as a cue to recognizing the word. Others like to write words in different colors, using one color for the words used in most writing and another color for words related to a specific topic that the class is currently studying. Another possibility is to use a special color or to otherwise highlight words that can be used as a base for writing many other words by changing the first letter(s), such as *an* (*can, fan, man, pan, ran, span, tan, than*). Make sure that you write the words large enough for the class to read easily.

If possible, attach the words to the word wall with a pin or with Velcro tape, or in any other way that makes the words movable. A set of large pocket charts hanging together is very suitable. Usually only one word per day should be added to the word wall so that children have ample time to discuss strategies for learning it. High-frequency words that have the same spelling pattern, however, such as *could, would, should,* may be added on the same day because it makes sense to connect such similar high-frequency words to each other. (Such words may have been initially listed on a chart of, for example, *ould* words before each is placed in its correct alphabetical location on the word wall.)

Make sure that the word wall is at a height suitable for the children to easily see the words, and for them to actually take a word card and have it beside them when they need to copy it or check it in their writing. However, because the main purpose for selecting these words is to help the children learn how to automatically write them, if a child frequently needs to refer to the word wall for a particular word, help that child learn that word.

Strategies for Learning the Words

As each word is added to the word wall discuss strategies to help children remember its spelling, noting the part(s) that the children may need to think most about or the part that surprises them. Here are some examples of such strategies for specific words:

- For *said:* We need to remember it has an *ai* spelling pattern in the middle, just like the word *rain.* (Try to link it with another *ai* word that children may already be familiar with.) *Said* is part of the family *say, saying, said,* so that's why it is spelled with an *a* even though we pronounce it with an /e/ sound.
- For *could:* We don't hear the *l,* and it's the same spelling for *would* and *should.*
- For *little:* It has *le* at the end.
- For *going:* It's the word *go,* with *ing* added.
- For *they:* We can see the word *the* at the beginning.
- For *big:* It's just like it sounds.
- For *two:* It's spelled with the same beginning as *twin* and *twice,* because these words are all to do with two things.
- For *who, when, where, why:* They are all question words, and all begin with *wh.*
- For *where:* The word *here* is in the word.
- For *there:* The word *here* is in the word.
- For *once:* It begins with *o* even though we hear a /w/ sound; it's like the word *one.*

Encourage children to share ideas about the ways they remember words, such as the child who explained that she remembered the *o* in *people* because she thought of the *o* as a face. Another child pointed out that the ending was *le,* just like in the word *little.*

The Importance of Modeling Spelling Strategies

By continually referring to different strategies for learning words you are modeling the range of strategies that good spellers use, giving children a language for talking about spelling strategies, and building a repertoire of strategies they can use for writing or learning personal words. It's important that children develop an understanding of the structure of English words so that they don't get the mistaken impression that spelling is just a matter of learning words by rote. If the children's first language is not English it is particularly useful for them to understand the differences between writing other languages and writing English. For example, if their first language is Spanish, they may only think of using the strategy of listening for the sounds in words.

The "Look, Say, Name, Cover, Write, Check" Strategy   One strategy for remembering any word is to try to picture all of it (or parts of it if it's a long word), and then write it from your mind. Teach the children how to do this, using the following steps:

1. *Look* at the word, perhaps noticing words within the word, looking at the parts of the word, or underlining known parts.
2. *Say* the word.
3. *Name* the letters of the word.
4. *Cover* the word and picture it in your mind.
5. *Write* the word from the picture in your mind.
6. *Check* to see that you have all of the letters in the word, and in the correct order.

Do this several times, as quickly as possible, until the children automatically write the word correctly. Some children may need help understanding that when they look at the word they need to be able to picture the way the word is written in their mind. Ask them to close their eyes to see if they can picture the word and if not, to try looking at the word again to get this picture. As each new word is added to the word wall have the children try the entire process after you have discussed the other strategies for remembering the word because the other strategies may give some help to picturing the word.

Play a game by regularly choosing one or two words from the word wall and asking the class to write them quickly, then having a partner check them. Also provide small erasable boards or chalkboards for children to practice writing the words as they are added to the word wall. These could be set up at a table with the word of the day written on cards for children to use the "look, say, name, cover, write, check" strategy. Children should write the word and erase it many times until they think they know how to spell it automatically.

The "look, say, name, cover, write, check" strategy is particularly useful when children are copying a word from any resource. Rather than copying it letter by letter, which does not allow them to get an image of the word and so results in their probably not remembering it even five minutes later, teach children how to look, say, name, cover, write, and check. Poor spellers in particular usually copy words letter by letter rather than getting a picture of the word or parts of the word. You may also want to use sand, shaving cream, or a textured carpet piece for some children to write the word with their finger if this seems helpful. But it's very wasteful of time to engage all the children in activities such as pasting little pieces of paper over a tracing of the word.

Capital Letters   Some children do not recognize high-frequency words in their reading when the words occur at the beginning of sentences. This is most likely to occur when the capital letter looks different from the lowercase letter, such as *A* and *a*. As much as possible try to write the high-frequency words with an initial capital as well as in lowercase, and when a word is added to the word wall show how it looks when written with an initial capital. Pairs of word cards for each word, one with an initial capital letter and the other in lowercase, could be used for word matching games.

Activities with High-Frequency Words

Although the children should be learning the words as they are added to the list, it is important to keep all the high-frequency words on the word wall so that you can refer to them for other word activities, such as when the class is searching for words with a particular sound or a particular letter or spelling pattern. The goal is to have as many children as possible learn each word as it is added to the word wall, but it is helpful to have some children be able to refer to these words repeatedly and in many contexts. Here are suggestions of ways to refer to high-frequency words.

Locating High-Frequency Words in Sentences   During shared reading of Big Books and class writing ask children to locate the word and read it. A word frame or highlight tape may be used to help children focus on the word.

Constructing Sentences   As each of the words is selected ask children to suggest sentences with the word. Write the sentences on sentence strips and have children read them as they point to each word, and cut the sentences into individual words for children to read and reconstruct sentences from. Use highlight tape for the word wall words, and leave sentences on display in a pocket chart for children to work with independently or in pairs.

Writing the Words   During interactive writing ask individual children to write any of the words that have already been added to the word wall. Some children may want to check the spelling of the word by referring to the word wall.

Constructing the Words   Create a word center where children can use magnetic letters to construct high-frequency words. Write a sign such as:

Can you make these words?
and   come   said   were   my

Making New Words   When appropriate, use high-frequency words as a basis for making new words by changing the beginning, middle, and/or final letters, such as:

big: pig, dig, fig, rig, wig
big: bug, beg, bog, bag
big: bib, bid, bin, bit

Show children how to do this, using magnetic letters if possible, and then encourage them to do the task independently. Provide children with small erasable boards or chalkboards and ask them to try new words. Talk about how knowing one word can help them read and write other words and that they could use this knowledge for their own reading and writing. Demonstrate this during shared reading and shared or interactive writing. For example, when reading a piece that contains rhyming words with the same spelling pattern, show the children how to use knowledge of the first rhyming word to work out the next one. For example:

Jack and Jill
went up the hill

You could say, pointing to the first rhyming word, "If we know this word is *Jill,* what will this word be?" pointing to *hill* and if necessary using magnetic letters or a whiteboard to show how the first word changes to make the new word. Or when writing something where a known word helps with a new word, such as:

The fairy said she would [pay] the girl with gold.

you could say, "We already know how to write the word *day.* How can that help us write the word *pay?*" Again, if necessary use magnetic letters or an erasable board to help with the demonstration.

Some books are ideal for demonstrating this strategy, such as *Zoo-looking* by Mem Fox, where reading the word *back* in the story can help the children to read words such as *black, smack, whack,* and *quack* on subsequent pages.

When listening to individual children read or observing them as they write, show them how to use this strategy when suitable, if you notice that they are not doing so on their own. In reading they would use this strategy in conjunction with others, to make sure the word makes sense and sounds right.

Many of the high-frequency words are easy to use in making new words just by changing the beginning letter(s). Whenever a high-frequency word is added to the word wall make a list of the children's suggestions for other words they could make from that word. These lists may be kept on charts that may be made easily available, perhaps by clipping them onto clothes hangers. Children may return to these lists to add or to locate words, but the most important aspect of this analogy work is that children are developing a sense of how words are related and how knowing one word can help them figure out other words.

High-frequency words that are most suitable for changing the beginning letter(s) to form new words are the following:

about (out)	big	dog	look	saw
all	bug	get (pet)	made	school
am	by (my)	go (no, so)	make	then (when)
an (than, can, ran)	came (name)	him	more	there (where)
and	come (some)	his (is)	nice	thing
as (has)	could (should, would)	in	night	trip
at (cat)	dad (had)	it	not	truck
back	day (play)	jump	now	up
be (he, me, she, we)	did	just	old	well
been	do (to, two, who)	like	rain	went
			run	will

As you build lists of words with the same spelling pattern the children may suggest words with the same sound but that do not have the same spelling pattern. Accept these suggestions, but write them in a different column and discuss how English words may sound the same but be spelled differently. For example:

do	shoe	boo	Sue	you
to		coo		
two		moo		
who		too		
		zoo		

Also encourage children to think about how to add simple endings to words, such as *s* and *ing,* and how this can also help them as readers and writers. Kindergarten children can usually add *s* to words, but they may not understand how to add other suffixes until grade 1 or 2. By grade 2 encourage the children to think of building compound words or adding prefixes such as *re* and *un* when possible. For example, a list of words that could be built from the word *play* would include *say, way, may, day, clay, bay, gay, hay, lay, pay, ray, tray* and *playing, played, player, plays, playdough, playground, playmate, replay, replays, replayed, replaying.* At this stage it's not necessary to teach generalizations about adding *ing* to words, although you may want to point out that sometimes the last letter is doubled *(run/running)* and sometimes the *e* is dropped *(come/coming).*

When constructing new words from the word wall words, you need not add the new words to the word wall unless the children decide that one of these words is also a word they use a lot. The word lists should be displayed so that children can refer to them as needed.

Word Searches Using the Word Wall   To draw children's attention to the features of high-frequency words play word search games. Have them do such activities as the following:

- Find a word with the same spelling pattern as *day.*
- Write another word with the same spelling pattern as *come.*
- Find three words that have the smaller word *an* in them.
- Find two words that begin with *wh.*
- Find a word with a double letter.

You may want to ask individual children to select the words or you may ask the class or a group to write the answers.

Building New Words   Demonstrate how known words can be used to construct other words by using words from the word wall. For example, show how the word *brown* can be constructed using the onset *br* from *brother* and the rime *own* from *down.* You could refer to these as the first part of *brother* and the last part of *down.* Encourage children to try to construct words this way.

Word Sorts   If you have a duplicate set of the word wall words on cards, have individuals, pairs, or small groups sort the words into like groups according to features the children notice in the words—for example, words with double let-ters, words that contain the same letter, long words, short words, words with the same sound, words with the same spelling pattern, words that have little words in them, and words that end the same.

Guess My Word   Another activity that encourages children to notice the fea-tures of words may be done with the class, or in small groups where one of the children may be the leader. Mentally select a word and then provide clues about the word until children work out what it must be. For example: "It's a word on the word wall. It has four letters. It begins with *pl*. It ends with the same spelling pattern as *day*." As you give each clue the children can write what they think the word is or locate the word on the word wall.

Learning High-Frequency Words in the Older Grades

At any grade level you will find that there are words that all of the children are using frequently. Choosing common words to learn is still appropriate for older grades, and an alphabetical word wall is still a suitable place to display them.

The Most Common Words

If children in grades K–2 have been using the ideas presented earlier to help them select and learn the most common words, in grades 3 and beyond it should only be necessary for you to check that the children know these words at the be-ginning of the year, either by looking at samples of the children's writing or by asking the children to spell a group of the words each day for several days. If you find that they do not know some of the words, point out that these are the first words that the class should learn, and use the strategies previously outlined to help them do so. You may also want to select some of the activities suggested to reinforce the learning of these words. Children in older grades who are learning English as a new language may need to learn all or most of the high-frequency words at this time.

Other Frequently Used Words

Once they know the most common high-frequency words, ask children to sug-gest other words that they think they use often and need some help to learn. They are apt to suggest words such as *really, special, through,* and *because*. Record the words on an alphabetical word wall and share strategies for learning them, such as:

- For *really:* The base word is *real;* just add the suffix *ly.*
- For *special:* Tell them that although we hear a /sh/ sound it's spelled *ci* (or you could say that the ending is *cial*). If children know Spanish they can think about how the word for *special* is pronounced in that language and how that will help them to remember the spelling in English.
- For *through:* The spelling pattern is *ough,* like *though, rough, cough, enough.*
- For *because:* The spelling pattern is *ause.* Another word like this is *pause.* Also, *use* is at the end of the word.

Suggest that children practice any of these words that they do not know by using the "look, say, name, cover, write, check" strategy, and discuss how knowing these words can help with the spelling of other words, such as:

> *real: really, realize, realizing, realized, realizes, realization, reality*
> *special: specially, specialize, specializing, specialized, specializes,*
> *specialization, specialty, specialties, especially*
> *through: throughout*
> *because: cause, causing, caused, causes*

Topic or Theme Words

When you and your students are studying a specific topic or curriculum area, you may often encounter the same words in a given topic or curriculum area, such as *hundreds, same,* and *different* in mathematics. You may keep a separate chart of these words for children to refer to or you may add them to the word wall. You could write them on different-color cards from the other high-frequency words to make them easier to locate. When appropriate, have children add an illustration to the card. Talk about strategies children can use to remember how these words are spelled. For example, here are some observations about words related to the study of dinosaurs:

- *Dinosaur, brontosaurus, Tyrannosaurus Rex:* All of these words have *saur* in them because *saur* means lizard.
- *Gnaw:* the *g* at the beginning is not pronounced.
- *Earth:* the word *ear* is in this word.

Ask children to watch out for frequently used topic words, or point out the ones you notice they do not know how to spell, and deal with them in the same way as suggested for other high-frequency words. Students in the older grades should not be thinking just about spelling patterns and memory aids; they should also use their knowledge of base words and prefixes and suffixes, and should find out the derivation of the word.

For example, here are some observations regarding words commonly encountered in mathematics:

- *Probability:* The base word is *probable* (which ends with the word *able*); think about the way it sounds (prob/a/bil/i/ty); other words in that word family are *probably* and *improbable.*
- *Probabilities:* Start with *probability* and then remember the generalization to change the *y* to an *i* and add *es.*
- *Multiplication:* The base word is *multiply;* think about the way it sounds (mul/ti/pli/ca/tion); the /shun/ sound at the end is *tion* just as in such words as *fraction, attention, section;* other words in the family are *multiplies, multiplying, multiplied.*

The following words may be discussed in science when the class is studying electricity:

- *Electricity:* The base word is *electric;* other words in the family are *electrical, electrically, electrify, electrified, electrician, electric shock, electrode,* electronic, *electronically, electron.*
- *Current:* Remember that it is not spelled curr<u>ant</u> because an *ant* would eat the curr*ant.*
- *Batteries:* The base word is *battery;* change the *y* to an *i* and add *es.*
- *Watt:* This electrical measurement is spelled *watt* after the name of the scientist who worked with energy and power.

This type of discussion about how to learn different words serves as a model the children can use in learning personal words on their own. It also helps them understand the organization of English spelling, and may also be a springboard for further spelling studies, such as generalizations for adding prefixes and suffixes (discussed in detail in Chapter 13). It is helpful to have dictionaries in the classroom that provide information about the derivation of words and that list word families, or to have a word book that shows word families, such as *A Writer's Word Book* (Snowball 1996).

When the topic or theme words are no longer being used you could remove the cards and make them into a topic word book by gluing them into a blank notebook or by writing them on the pages of a notebook, using a new page for each letter of the alphabet. Or you could punch a hole in the cards and place each topic set on a ring. These resources can be placed in the reference section of the classroom library or in the writing center so that children may add to them and use them as references for future writing and word search activities.

In middle school and high school these suggestions can also be used by subject teachers, who will expect children to learn the words being used in the particular subject areas. A lot of this work will be incidental and need not take a lot of time, but it's beneficial for students to observe all teachers working with words in a similar manner.

Continuing Evaluation

You and your students should be aware of the correct spelling of high-frequency words in their writing as an assessment of whether the words have been learned; but because children will be learning new words each week they probably would like more immediate feedback about their learning. Although the following routine is not really necessary if children are all learning the same words, it is a good opportunity to teach children to work with a partner, which will be necessary when they all have different personal words to learn.

Have children work in pairs, taking turns saying each of the weekly words, then having the partner write them. When they have each had a turn at this each child checks his or her own spelling. If a word is incorrect the child might ask the class for some help with ways to learn it. It is better to call this activity *feedback* rather than a *test* and for the children to correct the words themselves so that they can see that the real purpose for learning words is to improve their writing and that they need to accept responsibility for their learning and for checking their own progress. Also, if you treat the activity as a test and give a mark based on the number of correct words, the children are likely to get the idea that the reason for spelling words correctly is to pass a test rather than to help others read their writing more easily.

If you teach in a school where parents expect their children to learn words each week, you may want to establish some sort of routine, such as the following:

1. Add a word to the word wall each day of the week, discussing strategies for spelling each word and giving children time to practice it.

2. Each day the children can add the word to their spelling journal, which can be just a blank notebook, with children starting a new page for each week; or at the end of the week you can provide each child with a list of the words.

3. The children can continue to practice the new words at home over the weekend or during the following week. They can also try to write other words that the weekly words would help them to spell. Children can try each other out in pairs at the end of the week. Be sure that parents are made aware of the strategies you are encouraging the children to use to learn the words.

When children are ready they can also learn personal words, as described in Chapter 18.

If you are teaching in a school where grades have to be given for spelling you may be accustomed to basing the grades on scores the children have obtained from their learning. However, a test of how children spell a list of words is not necessarily a true indicator of their spelling proficiency; you must also look at each child's writing and probably observe the children as they write to determine what strategies they use in attempting unfamiliar words and what other strategies and habits they have adopted that good spellers use.

When looking at the results of spelling tests you will see that some children are able to memorize some words, but use very inappropriate spelling strategies for words they cannot remember; yet they may score higher than other children who have a better grasp of ways to try unfamiliar words. For example, child A below consistently scores higher than child B. Here are the words each child misspelled:

Child A	*Child B*
ceoaud (could)	cood (could)
caedl (candle)	candel (candle)
ferh (fresh)	freshe (fresh)
	sircus (circus)

It's obvious that child A needs more help with spelling, so using the score from the weekly spelling tests as an assessment tool can actually mislead the teacher, the child, and the parents about the child's level of spelling proficiency. Unless the teacher analyzes the misspellings to note the strategies each child is using or not using, the test alone will not give him or her an idea of the child's spelling strengths and needs and will not result in a fair report of each child's progress.

Refer to Appendix A for checklists of strategies and habits that you need to look for in the children's writing, and see Chapter 3 and Appendix A for further ideas about evaluating spelling.

Word Walls for Alphabetical Order

Some time perhaps during grade 1 and certainly during grade 2 and beyond children will be ready to learn about alphabetical order, especially if they can see a useful purpose for it. When children need to locate a word quickly on a word wall, point out how much more difficult it is to find a word when the list is long. Ask if anyone can suggest a way to list the words to make it easier to find a specific word. If necessary, show the children how to look at the second letter of the words to reorganize the words that begin with the same letter. When there are several words that begin with the same first and second (and perhaps even third) letters, such as *the, they, their, there, this, them, that,* ask children to suggest what to do. If necessary, show them how to look at the third and fourth letters to order the words.

Compare this method of ordering with how picture dictionaries and other sorts of dictionaries are organized and discuss how this helps to find words faster. Demonstrate with a big version of a picture dictionary (make sure it is written correctly in columns in alphabetical order). Allow time for children to practice this task, and encourage them to practice in pairs, with one child suggesting a word the other has learned and the other trying to find it in a dictionary as quickly as possible.

As each new word is added to the word wall have the children decide how to place it in alphabetical order, with their moving other words to slot the new one into the correct location.

When children are using dictionaries that have head words, extend their knowledge about quickly locating words by helping them discover the purpose of these head words. Ask children to look at several pages of the dictionary to see if they can figure out why the words are at the top of the page and how they can help people to use the dictionary better. As children work out the answer to this question ask them to explain what they are thinking. Gradually more and more children will understand the function of head words and will be able to help others who need more explicit explanation.

☞ *Homework Ideas*

If you want to provide spelling homework be sure that the activities children are given to do actually help with spelling. Writing words several times will not help because children often write a list of words one letter per line in a vertical column, without thinking about the features of each word or picturing it in their mind, which they do with the "look, say, name, cover, write, check" strategy.

Having children write words in alphabetical order will not help them with the spelling of words. If you want the children to learn alphabetical order for quick use of dictionaries and other alphabetical resources, give them some specific tasks with such references and use the word wall for demonstrations.

Having children write words in a sentence allows you to check if children know the meaning of the words, but this should not be necessary if the words are chosen from material the children are reading and from the writing they are involved in. Only when the word being learned is a homophone, homonym, or homograph is it useful to have them write the word in a sentence.

As described previously, thinking about ways to remember a word, using the "look, say, name, cover, write, check" strategy, and thinking about other words that are spelled the same way or other words that can be built from the base word are much more useful ways to learn the spelling of a word.

Depending on the experience of the writers and the types of spelling explorations your class has been involved in, the following activities are also worthwhile because they help children think about the ways words are constructed and the probability of certain letter sequences in English words. Demonstrate each of the activities to your class and use them frequently as quick incidental games. Build a class list of suggestions for homework according to what you think your children can do independently; be sure to consider these carefully, as many of the activities require a lot of knowledge about words. Refer to Appendix C for possible homework lists for younger and older grades, but make sure that homework expectations are based on strategies and activities that you have demonstrated in class. Also encourage children to choose activities that they think will really help them.

- List words with the same spelling pattern, such as *can (fan, man, pan, ran, tan, van)* or *said (pain, rain, again, train, plain, gain, main, stain, chain, paid, laid, maid, wait, rail, sail)*. If possible, children should check to make sure that what they have come up with are really words by looking them up in a dictionary or by asking someone.
- Find words within a word. Have children try to find smaller words within a larger one, such as words from *they (the, hey, he)* or *teacher (teach, each, her, ache, tea, he)*.
- Make compound words. Have children use base words to build compounds—for example, *some: somewhere, someone, something, somehow, sometimes.*
- Add a letter to make a new word. Children can try adding a letter somewhere to make a new word, using such words as *and (hand), like (likes), the (they),* and *her (hear)*.
- Delete a letter to make a new word. Have children try deleting a letter somewhere to make a new word, using such words as *where (here), once (one),* and *and (an)*.
- Change a letter to make a new word. Children can try changing any letter to make a new word, such as *her* to *hen, and* to *aid,* and *he* to *me.*
- Make a word chain by changing one letter at a time. Children can change a letter to make a new word and then continue doing so to create as many words as possible—for example, start with *dear* and progress to *hear, head, dead, deed, need, seed, sees, bees, been, beep, keep, kelp, help, held, hold, cold, cord, core, pore, sore, some, come, came, same,* . . . This activity could be played in pairs, where the children take turns changing a letter.
- Build new words from base words—for example, *read, reading, reader, reads, reread, rereading, rereads.*

If the students keep spelling journals the activities can be done or kept in their journals, and you can collect them periodically to review what the children are doing and to assist where necessary. If you give the children a homework sheet each week the children should keep them in a folder or a ring binder as a record of their ongoing growth in spelling. These collected assignments could be useful at parent interviews.

Informing Parents

It is wise to let parents know that even though it is important that children continue to try to spell any words they wish to use in their writing they will also gradually learn words that are used most frequently. As the children help to select words to learn each week provide a list of these for parents and ask the children to talk with their parents about the strategies they are using to learn the words. Explain why children's learning these strategies is better than their learning words by rote, and that you are choosing only a few words at a time to give children the chance to really learn them. Encourage parents to help their children think of strategies for learning words.

When writing at home it is natural for children to ask their parents how to spell many words. If the parents are aware of the high-frequency words their children have learned they can expect their children to spell these words independently.

References

Fox, M. 1995. *Zoo-looking*. Greenvale, NY: Mondo.

Green, R., and D. Snowball. 1994. *My Picture Dictionary*. Greenvale, NY: Mondo.

Snowball, D. 1996. *A Writer's Word Book*. Greenvale, NY: Mondo.

Personal Words to Learn

part from the high-frequency words you want them to learn, children should be aware of other words they use in their own writing and select some to learn if they cannot already spell them conventionally. Developing writers learn how to spell more and more words that just "come off the pencil" without their needing to think about how to spell them.

If the class is involved in selecting and learning words that they all use frequently this group learning provides many opportunities for you to demonstrate successful strategies for learning words (as described in Chapter 17). Once children have been exposed to sufficient modeling of these strategies and have had independent practice with them, they can apply the strategies to the learning of words they choose on their own. If the class has not had these demonstrations, you should work with the children on some commonly selected words before having the children learn their own words.

You can help students choose which words to learn by observing their writing and making comments such as, "I notice this is a word you write often; it would be a good one for you to learn." Don't choose more than a child can cope with, and think about which words will be most beneficial for his or her future writing. You may point out the parts of the word children already know how to spell, suggest another word they know that may help them work out the spelling of this word, or write the word for them or suggest a resource where they could find the word themselves. If they copy the word from somewhere you will need to check that it's been copied correctly before it is learned.

Children may also select words to learn from material they are reading, from class lists developed during explorations of sounds, spelling patterns, prefixes and suffixes, and so on. Whenever children are selecting personal words to learn they should be sure that they know the meaning of the words and are sure they will use the word in their own writing or can realize some particular benefit in learning it. They also need to realize that it would be a waste of time to choose words they already know.

Selecting Words from Personal Writing

If children know how to proofread (as described in Chapter 16) they can use this task to pinpoint words that would be worth learning. You may need to teach them how to proofread and how to select useful words to learn. This is easily done by selecting samples of children's writing for the class or a group to look at together to see what they can learn about proofreading and learning words. Point out that the purpose of the demonstration is for the children to learn the process—which involves proofreading; trying misspelled words again or finding out how to spell them; selecting words to learn; deciding on the best strategies to learn the word, focusing on the part that was spelled wrongly; and listing other related words—and once they have learned it, to apply the process to their own writing.

The following examples show how the process was demonstrated in some classrooms. You do not need to do this with each child individually; just choose some samples of children's writing to show the class what to do. The demonstration also provides opportunities to discuss the many strategies used for spelling. In each example, the class knew that the focus would be on spelling; at other times pieces of writing may be used in a study of other aspects of writing, such as content, structure, revision, grammar, or punctuation.

The first example is from a grade 6 student's math journal. In this class, students used the journal to write reflections on their math learning. With Danny's permission, the teacher made an overhead of a piece of his writing and told the class they would look at it to see how they could learn more about spelling and how they could use the same process with their own writing. Danny first read his writing aloud and then proofread it, circling the words he thought were not spelled correctly and inserting words such as *Braille* and *patterns* so that the writing piece made sense.

In today's math lesson we started out with Braile. We looked for patterns and tryed to find the missing characters. Soon, lesson went in to how many possibilitys of chacaters.

What I really understood and liked about this lesson was finding and to bring numbers to different powers. The whole piont of this lesson was to look for patterns to find brail characters and the second part was to bring numbers to higher powers.

Danny then used a blank transparency and attempted to spell the circled words correctly. This inspired a great deal of discussion. For example, for the spellings *Braile* and *brail* the talk went as follows:

Danny: I really know how to spell that, but I was just being careless.

Teacher: What's something we have all learned from that?

Other child: When you now how to spell a word it's easier to write it correctly than to have to come back later to fix it up.

Danny went back to *tryed* and wrote it two ways, *tryed* and *tried*.

Danny: I think *tried* looks better.

Teacher: Does anyone know why it is definitely spelled *tried?*

Danny: Because it's one of those words where you change the *y* to an *i* before adding *ed*.

Teacher: Does anyone know of any other words like that?

The children suggested several other words—*carry/carried, marry/married, cry/cried, bury/buried, multiply/multiplied, hurry/hurried*—and the teacher listed them.

Teacher: So this is a generalization that will help us to spell lots of words when we are writing.

For *possibilitys,* Danny had this to say:

Danny: That should be *possibilities*. It's just like the other word where we change a *y* to an *i*.

Teacher: So let's look at the base word and see what happens when we make it plural. [*She wrote possibility.*]

Other child: The *y* is changed to an *i* before you add *es*.

Teacher: Can we think of any other words like that?

The children suggested several other words—*strawberry/strawberries, baby/babies, party/parties, city/cities, butterfly/butterflies*—and the teacher wrote them down for the class to see.

Teacher: Here's a similar rule that can help us spell lots of words. Watch out for other words like this in your reading and writing.

Danny then turned to *chacaters*.

Danny: I spelled it properly the first time I wrote it and then I got careless.

Teacher: When we look at the ways you have written it your sloppy handwriting makes it hard to tell what letters you have there. That's something for you to work at because then you will probably realize that the word doesn't look right. If you look at the word *lesson* at the end of the fourth line you can see what I mean. You may have spelled it correctly but because of the way you write some letters it's hard to tell.

Danny: Yeah, I know how to spell that word.

Teacher: Which words that you misspelled would you select to learn and why?

Danny: I'll choose *possibilities* and *tried* because I use them a lot in my math writing.

Teacher: What strategies will you use to learn each of those words?

Danny: I can do lots of "look, say, name, cover, write, check" with them and I'll remember about changing the *y* to an *i*.

Teacher: And remember that it's just as important in your math journal as it is in other types of writing to think about doing your best in spelling.

In this instance it could have been just as suitable for Danny not to choose specific words to learn from the writing, but to engage in an exploration to find out more about the generalization of changing a *y* to an *i* before adding a suffix and how this can be applied to many suffixes. If there are several children who do not know this generalization you could work with the group or the class to explore it, as described in Chapter 13.

Our next example begins with a story written by Judy, a grade 2 student.

The cat and the mouse

One day a cat was trying to catch a smert little mouse. That cat always trys to catch that fast little smert mouse. The cat planed a millon times to catch the mouse but it never worked. So the cat gave up. His brothers and sister,s camplaned that the mouse had to get [out] of the house but he did,nt lisen.

The teacher made a transparency and explained that this piece would be used to see what the class could learn about spelling. Judy read the piece, circling words she thought were not spelled correctly, and inserted the word *out* so that the sentence made sense. She then tried the circled words again on a blank transparency, and the following discussion took place.

Teacher: I can see that Judy knows a lot about spelling. She knows how to spell high-frequency words, she is willing to try words she doesn't know how to spell, she knows a lot of common spelling patterns like *ay* and that some words end with an *e,* she is able to proofread to notice many of her spelling mistakes, and she knows that some words have an apostrophe but isn't sure about where to put it. Let's try the words you thought were wrong.

Judy turned to *smert,* wrote *smart,* and said that looked better.

Teacher: So a good strategy we could all use is to try a word again and see which one looks right. What would be a way to remember the part of the word you were confused about?

Judy: I can see *art* in *smart.*

Other child: I can also see *mart* in *smart.*

Teacher: So looking for smaller words in the word can help us to remember what words look like. What other words can we think of that have an *ar* spelling pattern?

Class suggestions, written on the overhead, included *chart, Mars, far, star, car, bar, tar, park, guitar, tarp.*

Judy moved on to *million* and wrote *millin.*

Judy: That still doesn't look right, but I'm not sure what else it could be.

Teacher: How could we find out?

Judy: Ask someone who's good at math.

Other child: It's *million.*

Third child: I can see *lion* at the end of *million.*

Fourth child: I thought it might be *millyn* because I can hear a /y/ sound.

Teacher: Yes, one strategy is to listen for the sounds in words, but that won't always help. But we can also check with a resource to help. What other number words do you think might be spelled the same way?

Judy: Billion.

Other child: Trillion.

Teacher: So these would be good words to remember together.

Next, Judy rewrote *camplaned* as *complaned.*

Teacher: You have nearly everything right, and *plane* is a possible way to spell that part of the word. Do you know another way to try that?

Judy: No.

The teacher wrote *complained* for the class to see.

Teacher: Do we know any other words with the spelling pattern *ain?*

The children suggested *train, rain, main, Spain, grain.*

Next Judy looked at *did,nt.*

Teacher: What is *didn't* a contraction of?

Judy wrote *did not.*

Teacher: What letter is replaced by the apostrophe in *didn't?*

Judy: The letter *o.*

The teacher put a line through the letter *o* and wrote *didn't* directly under *did not.*

Teacher: The best strategy for all of you when you are writing contractions is to think of what letter is being replaced by the apostrophe. I notice that many of you are confused about these types of words so we will study more about them next week. Start watching out for them in your reading.

When Judy got to *lisen,* she had this to say:

Judy: I know this part is wrong [*pointing to the part where the letter* t *was missing*], but I'm not sure what it should be.

Teacher: Do you know enough about the word to try to find it in a dictionary?

Judy then found the correct spelling in a dictionary. A discussion then took place about the fact that not every letter in a word is always heard. The teacher showed them other examples: *glisten, whistle, rustle.*

Then, after Judy had reviewed her entire piece, the teacher asked for some final thoughts.

Teacher: Which of these words do you think you should learn?

Judy: Smart, million, and *didn't* because I use them often.

Teacher: What strategies could you use to learn each of those words?

Judy: For *smart* I'll remember the word *art* in it, for *million* the word *lion* is at the end, and for *didn't* I need to remember that the apostrophe is higher up and it's instead of the letter *o.*

Teacher: And you can do "look, say, name, cover, write, check" for all of them until you can write each word very quickly, and then see if you can write any other words like those words.

The teacher then asked if anyone else could help with the proofreading of Judy's piece and in this way the other two misspelled words, *trys* and *sister,s,* were identified and corrected. This led to a discussion about the value of peer editing when material is to be published, because writers do not always notice their own mistakes, especially when they are trying unknown words. The session finished with a discussion about the things the class had learned about proofreading, trying words, and ways to learn words, and how they could use these strategies with their own writing.

Our third example is a piece of writing by Susie, who is in grade 3. It is a retelling of a story she had read.

Wuns apon a time an old woman lived in a vinager bottel. She was not hapy in the bottel and wished she cold live in a prity house with a gardn. A farry came by and sed she cood have her wish. So the old woman woke up in a house with a gardn. Then she was still unhapy and wonted to live in a castel. The ferry seid she cood. So she woke up in a castel with lots of servants. But she was still unhapy and wonted to live in a manshen with lots of rooms. So the ferry made her wish happen. In the end she was in her vinager bottel agen.

An overhead transparency was made of the writing. Then Susie read the piece and proofread it, noticing some of the misspelled words.

The teacher asked the class to comment on all of the things that Susie was good at in relation to spelling; this resulted in observations that she knew how to spell a lot of high-frequency words, she was willing to try words she did not know, she knew she should try a word a couple of different ways if she was not sure about it, she was very good at sounding out words, but she needed to use other strategies too. The teacher also pointed out that almost 80 percent of Susie's words were spelled correctly, which was very important for this child to hear, as she had a very poor impression of her own spelling ability, and this was reinforced by criticism from her parents.

The following discussion took place about the words she circled during proofreading. First, about *apon:*

Susie: It doesn't look right at the beginning.

Susie wrote *upon.*

Susie: That looks better.

Teacher: That's a very important strategy you have used—to think about which part doesn't look right, to try it again, and think what it looks like. I would like you to work at that more often. What could help you to remember that word?

Susie: I can see the words *up* and *on.*

About *sed* and *seid:*

Susie: I know it has an *s* and a *d* but I don't know what's in the middle.

The teacher wrote the word *said,* underlining the *ai.*

Susie: Ai—how interesting!

Teacher: So it's the *ai* spelling pattern that we need to remember about this word, like in the word *rain.* Let's look at this.

The teacher wrote

say, saying, said
pay, paying, paid
lay, laying, laid

and asked the children to notice how *said* is spelled the same way as *paid* and *laid* even though it is pronounced differently. He suggested that this may help them remember the spelling of *said.*

When Susie got to *cold* and *cood,* she was stumped.

Susie: I don't know how to spell this one.

Teacher: You know a lot about the letters in that word. Who can help?

Other child: Could.

Teacher: So we need to look at the spelling pattern again. This time it's *ould.* What other words have the same spelling pattern?

The children suggested *should* and *would* and the teacher suggested *shoulder,* pointing out that we can even hear the 1 in this word.

About *vinager,* the discussion proceeded as follows:

Teacher: Where could you find this word?

Susie: In the book.

Teacher: Sometimes the best strategy, especially for words you don't use often, is to think of the best place to find it. And you're right, a dictionary is not always the best resource to use, especially if you know a book where you will find the word.

When Susie got to *unhapy,* she wrote *unhappy.*

Teacher: That's right. Trying it again has helped you, and you could check in a dictionary or word book this time. Let's all think of other words that we can build from the word *happy.*

The children suggested *happier, happiest, unhappiest,* and *happy birthday;* the teacher suggested *happily.*

Teacher: Once you figure out how to spell a word it's worth thinking about other words in the same word family that would help you spell, and if you look up a word in a dictionary or word book take the time to have a look at other similar words that are listed. Good spellers don't just learn words; they also think about the other words those base words can help you spell.

The teacher then turned to Susie.

Teacher: Which of the words you circled do you think you should learn and why?

Susie: All of them except *vinegar,* because I would use them a lot in my stories.

Teacher: And I would like us to have a look at one more word today because I think you will also use it often. It's the word *once.*

The teacher wrote *once.*

Teacher: What do you notice about the beginning of that word, and can you think of a number that starts the same?

Susie: It's an *o,* not a *w.* Like *one.*

Teacher: So the main thing you need to work at is to think about what words look like because you are already good at phonetic strategies where you listen for the sounds in words. This is a strategy we all need to use more often. Keep that piece of writing, and I will meet with you during writing time next week to work with some other words.

The teacher also explained that when writers proofread their own writing they may not know that some of the words are not spelled correctly, so a peer editor or another editor, such as the teacher, could then help. If the writing is going to be published, this editing assistance will probably be necessary. If it's not going to be published, further correction is not necessary, unless the writer wants to return to the same writing on future occasions to choose more words to learn.

Working through this process with the whole class leads to rich discussions about spelling strategies. Regardless of whose writing is used there is always something to learn, and every child's contribution is valued. Obviously the same thing could be done with small groups or with individuals, depending on the children's needs and the time you have to help children learn to proofread and select words to learn.

A System for Learning and Checking

Develop a system that will make it easy for you and your students to record the words each child is going to learn. You may want to use word cards in a pocket in children's writing folders or in an envelope glued onto the inside cover of their journals or writer's notebooks. If you have plenty of blank cards, children's individual words can be written on those and placed in the pocket or envelope as required. Each child may also regularly record words to learn in a spelling journal or a blank exercise book, starting a new double-page spread each week so as to allow space for the activities related to learning the words. You may even begin this process in grade 1 by providing each child with a word book that has blank pages at the back where you can write a word that you have noticed the child should practice.

You may also want some type of routine for children to learn the words and for someone to check them. Establish a system where children regularly choose some words to learn on a particular day and then check with a partner on a particular day. Here is one way to organize this activity.

Day 1   Children select words to learn. They should only select words they don't already know and will personally find useful for their writing. These may include words that the class has decided everyone should know, perhaps from various curriculum areas being studied at the time. Others may be from the word wall, from a theme list, from the students' reading, from class lists developed during explorations about words, from "Try It Out" or "Have a Go" sheets, or from their own writing in various curriculum areas, including words that you think should be learned. The children should select only the number of words that they could really manage to learn. Have class discussions about how many this might be and how it may not be the same number each week or the same number for each child. The class may decide to select a few words that they think would be worthwhile for the whole class to learn and an additional few personal words. Use some system to check that each child's words are spelled correctly. Perhaps the children could leave their journals available so that you or another adult can quickly glance at their lists. In some school communities parents can check the words the first night the list is taken home for learning. Some teachers find it helpful to allow children to have time at school to work in small groups, telling each other the words they have chosen and sharing ideas about ways to learn them.

Days 2, 3, and 4   Children then learn the words at school or at home. Demonstrate how to do this, helping children think about the best strategy for each word and perhaps making a note of what it is, and using the "look, say, name, cover, write, check" strategy several times until each word can be written quickly and accurately. Activities such as writing the words in alphabetical order, writing them in sentences, and writing them five times each will *not* help children learn words permanently; more suitable ideas are suggested in the previous chapter. Children should also try to think of other words they might know based on the words they have learned; these may be words with the same spelling pattern or with prefixes and suffixes added. The work you have been doing as a class will influence children's ability to think about words in this way. Children may write all of this word work in their spelling journal, as a record of what they are doing (see Figures 18.1 and 18.2).

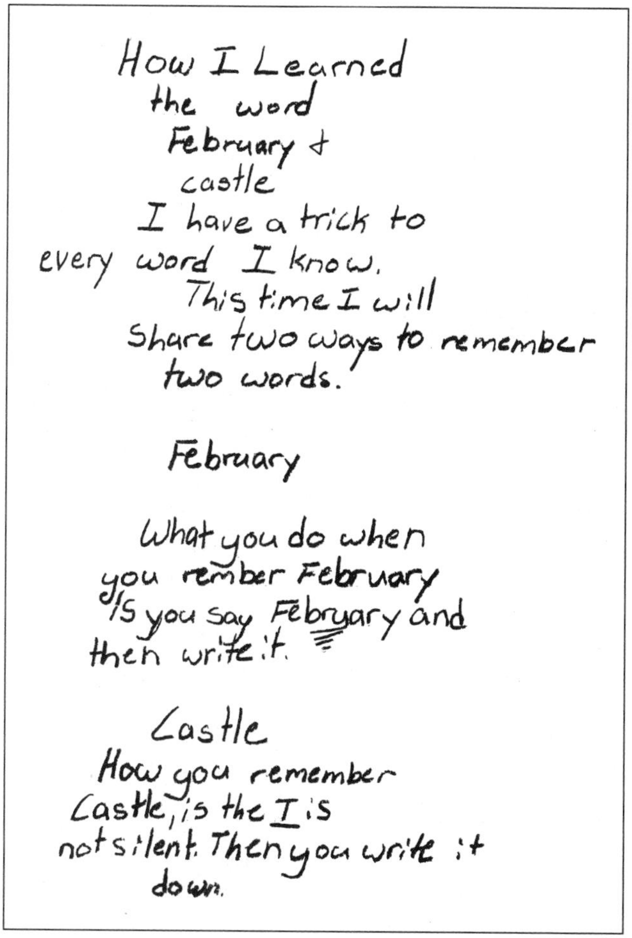

> How I Learned
> the word
> February +
> castle
> I have a trick to
> every word I know.
> This time I will
> Share two ways to remember
> two words.
>
> February
>
> What you do when
> you rember February
> is you say Febryary and
> then write it.
>
> Castle
> How you remember
> Castle, is the I is
> not silent. Then you write it
> down.

FIGURE 18.1 A child's notes on learning specific words.

Day 5 On the fifth day, children work in pairs to check each other's words. Child 1 reads child 2's words and child 2 writes them. Child 2 then checks to see if the words are spelled correctly and if not, which part is wrong. Then the child writes the word(s) correctly. The children then change roles. A variation on this is to have each child try to recall their own words and write them, because if they have really learned the words they will probably remember what they are.

Ask children to share with the class any good strategies they found to help them learn particular words, or invite them to ask for ideas about words they have trouble remembering. Also ask them to talk about how this is helping them as writers and readers.

A sample homework form to help children learn personal words is provided in Appendix D.

> instrumentally — it has instrumental in it. Just remember to add ly.

FIGURE 18.2 A grade 5 child's notes on learning a specific word.

Getting Started with Demonstration

You must demonstrate the whole process of proofreading, selecting the most useful words to learn from suitable sources, deciding how many to learn, thinking about strategies for learning each word, and then listing other related words for several weeks before expecting the children to do this independently. Choose a different child's piece of writing each week to be the focus for the demonstration. You will find that rich discussion about spelling can be generated from any piece of writing. If a child's piece has many misspellings use only part of it for the demonstration so as not to overwhelm the writer.

After several demonstrations you may wish to ask a few children who are most ready for learning individual words to accept the responsibility of taking on this task independently with their own personal writing. Introduce more children to the process as they are ready. Perhaps they could do it at school for the first few weeks and eventually do most of the work as homework.

To check on how the children are doing, collect a few spelling journals each week. Looking at several weeks of work at one time will give you a better indication of the types of words children are selecting and how they are learning them. Don't be overly concerned over whether each child is spelling every one of his or her personal words correctly in future writing, because this will be very difficult for you to monitor; but do have high expectations about their spelling of high-frequency words that you have chosen together and about children's taking on responsibility to do their best all of the time. What you should look for is an increase in the number of words being spelled in the conventional way and the building of a range of strategies for trying unknown words.

You may prefer that children select words every two weeks; and some children may find it more beneficial to learn words and get feedback every couple of days. Select a routine that both suits you and meets your students' needs.

Personal Word Books

When children have learned personal words they may want to record them in a book organized alphabetically. Younger children often like to do this, probably because it is concrete evidence of what they have learned. Such a book can provide a record for parents of one aspect of their children's spelling, and it can be treated as a list of the words you expect children to spell correctly when writing or to correct independently when proofreading. You should ask children to keep such a book only if it serves a useful purpose.

🎡 Continuing Evaluation

Above all, you should remember that spelling is not just about learning words; it is learning the strategies used by competent spellers that is the major goal. Analyzing children's spelling mistakes is more revealing than the score on a spelling test. Looking at their writing or a perfectly spelled list of words may not provide the total picture. Some writers only use words they know how to spell or are very good at memorizing words for a spelling test but have little idea about the range of strategies to use to attempt new words in a way that will allow them to be correct or close approximations.

Your students' learning of words can be used as part of a spelling assessment, but you also need to consider such factors as the child's ability to proofread, to choose appropriate words to learn, to use a variety of strategies to learn the words, and whether the spelling of these words improves in subsequent writing. By collecting a few of the children's spelling journals and some samples of their writing each week you will be able to observe what has been occurring with their spelling over a period of time and decide who may need more help with the process of learning words. This approach is more manageable than trying to look at every child's work every week, and it will also give you more information to guide your teaching decisions. You can also look at this picture of a child's spelling during writing time in any curriculum area. Establish realistic goals for yourself about how many children you can meet with each week, bearing in mind that having in-depth conferences during which you and the child discuss current strengths and future goals for the child to work at is the most effective approach to ensure the child's learning. During these conferences you may wish to deal with other aspects of writing along with spelling, or you may make it clear that a particular conference will focus just on spelling.

If you are teaching in a school where the limitations of spelling tests have not been addressed and you are expected to give a grade in spelling based on a mark from weekly spelling tests, use the scores from the children's "tests" with their partners. This will at least meet the administrative requirement of recording a score, but for real teaching purposes you must look more closely at the child's work.

Homework and Parents

Once children have established a routine for choosing words to learn and know how to learn them, the entire process can be done as homework. The same activities that we suggested for high-frequency words in Chapter 17 can be used for children's individual words. You will want to check on the words the children have chosen to make sure they are spelled correctly and to observe how they are coping with the task by observing them during partner feedback time. If you feel that some children are not choosing appropriate words, are choosing too few or too many, or are not working as well as you would expect on their own, give them more guidance and direction.

Inform parents about why certain words are being learned and why their children will have individual words to learn as well as some class selections. Even seven-year-olds can easily explain why it is a waste of time for writers to learn words they already know how to spell or to learn words that they will not use in their writing, so this should not be difficult to explain to adults. Usually parents just want to know why you are doing something differently from the way it was done in their own school days. Explain that it is much easier to give the same list of words to every child, whether they are useful or not, and to give one test to everyone, but you are trying to do a better job than that. Point out that published lists of words to learn may contain words the children do not know the meaning of, words they can already spell, or words the children will not use in their writing. Also get the children involved in informing the community about spelling. The more children understand about why they are doing the spelling work you are assigning them, the more they will be able to help their parents understand the value of what you are doing.

You may want to give parents a copy of Appendix B to help them better understand your approach to the teaching of spelling.

Part Four

CHAPTER

19

Sample Schedules for a School Spelling Program

The plans shown here are examples only. Our intention is to provide a sense of what a balanced spelling program might look like at each year level of elementary and middle school.

Generally, plans for a ten-day period are given for each grade level. However, for the kindergarten year we provide three plans, to reflect the focus of teaching in the beginning, middle, and late stages of the year, because of the degree of variation in teaching emphases required as kindergarten children's knowledge of the English spoken and written language develops. The other grade levels' emphases do not change as much in the course of the year. In addition, grades 5 to 8 have a combined plan, because the spelling focuses remain the same.

The plans in this chapter expand upon the general outline for each grade given in Chapter 3. For example, in that chapter we suggested that sound explorations (see phonic strategy) in grade 1 would account for approximately 25 percent of the time in the overall plan; the ten-day outline we provide here allocates this same proportion of time for work with sounds. In addition to the outline in the plans children would also be selecting personal words to learn and time may be set aside for checking these on a regular basis.

As mentioned in Chapter 3, when planning your daily literacy experiences, allow more time for reading and writing than spelling. Although you will devote more time to spelling on some days than on others, on average, across the entire curriculum, you should not need to spend more than ten to fifteen minutes a day specifically on spelling.

During reading and writing experiences the following aspects of spelling may be planned for:

KINDERGARTEN	A possible five-day planner for early in the year			
Day 1	Day 2	Day 3	Day 4	Day 5
Letter names Play I Spy using children's initials. Search for words containing a focus letter. List words.	*Phonological awareness* Syllables: Tap syllables in words. *Letter names* Read alphabet book. Search for words with focus letter. List words.	*Letter names* Play I Spy. Search for words with focus letter. List words. *Phonological awareness* Tap syllables in I Spy words.	*Letter names* Read alphabet book. Group listed words according to position of focus letter. Form generalizations.	*Letter names* Read alphabet book. Group words according to sounds letter represents, if appropriate. Write generalizations in class journal. *Phonological awareness* Tapping syllables in words.

During reading and writing experiences the following aspects of spelling may be planned for:

KINDERGARTEN	A possible five-day planner for the middle of the year			
Day 1	Day 2	Day 3	Day 4	Day 5
Letter names Play Hopscotch using alphabet tiles. Search for words containing a focus letter. List words and underline focus letter.	*Letter names* Read alphabet book. Search for words with focus letter. List words and group according to position of letter. Form generalizations.	*Phonological awareness* Blending (e.g., "I am thinking of a fruit. I am an /a/-/p/-/ll/"). *High-frequency words* Search for high-frequency words. Have class learn a high-frequency word; add to word wall. Show how knowing to spell learned word helps spell others.	*Letter names* Read alphabet book (continued from Day 2). Group words according to sounds focus letter represents. Revise and record generalizations. *Phonological awareness* Blending.	*High-frequency words/ onsets and rimes* Revise high-frequency word list. Learn a high-frequency word and add to word wall. Select a high-frequency word for onset/rime activity.

During reading and writing experiences the following aspects of spelling may be planned for:

KINDERGARTEN	A possible ten-day planner for late in the year			
Day 1	**Day 2**	**Day 3**	**Day 4**	**Day 5**
Letter names Read alphabet book. Read entries for a focus letter in a picture dictionary. Search for words with focus letter in all positions. List words.	*Letter names* Continue searching for words with focus letter; list words. Group words according to position of letter. Begin forming generalizations. *Phonological awareness* Syllable deletion task.	*Word families* Develop word family lists (e.g., *play/plays*). *Letter names* Read alphabet book. Group words according to sound focus letter represents. Review and write generalizations in class journal.	*Letter names* Read alphabet book. *High-frequency words/ onsets and rimes* Search for high-frequency words; add to class list. Have class learn a high-frequency word; add to word wall. Use high-frequency word for onset and rime activity.	*Letter names* Search for words containing a focus letter in all positions. List words. *High-frequency words* Have class learn a high-frequency word; add to word wall. Show how knowing to spell learned word helps spell others.
Day 6	**Day 7**	**Day 8**	**Day 9**	**Day 10**
Letter names Read alphabet book. Continue searching for words with focus letter; add to class list. Group words according to position of letter or sound focus letter represents. Begin forming generalizations.	*Letter names* Read alphabet book. Revise and write generalizations. *Phonological awareness* Syllable or phoneme deletion tasks.	*Letter names* Read alphabet book. *Word families* List words in word family (e.g., *run/runs*). *Evaluation/revision* Word sort according to common letters, common rimes, word families, high-frequency words, etc.	*Letter names* Read alphabet book. *High-frequency words/ onsets and rimes* Search for high-frequency words; add to class list. Have class learn a high-frequency word; add to word wall. Use high-frequency word for onset and rime activity.	*Phonological awareness* Syllable or phoneme deletion tasks. *Letter names* Read alphabet book. Search for words with focus letter in all positions. List words (to be continued).

During reading and writing experiences the following aspects of spelling may be planned for:

GRADE 1	A possible ten-day planner			
Day 1	Day 2	Day 3	Day 4	Day 5
Sounds Listen for a focus sound. List words.	*Sounds* Continue searching for words with sound. Group words according to letters/spelling patterns that represent sound. Form generalizations.	*Letter names* Play I Spy.	*Sounds* (Cont. from Day 2.) Review generalizations.	*High-frequency words/ changing letters* Have class learn a word; add to word wall.
High-frequency words Search for and list high-frequency words.	*Phonological awareness* Alliteration.	*High-frequency words/ onsets and rimes* Have class learn a high-frequency word; add to word wall.	*High-frequency words/ changing letters* Search for and list high-frequency words.	Change letters in high-frequency words to form new words (e.g., *man–men–met–get*).
Have class learn a high-frequency word; add to word wall.	*High-frequency words* Have class learn a high-frequency word; add to word wall.	Use a high-frequency word for onset/rime activity.	Have class learn a high-frequency word.	*Phonological awareness* Sound segmentation in high-frequency words (e.g., in *man,* /m/ is first sound, /a/ second, /n/ third).
		Word families List words in word family (e.g., *fig/figs*).	Change letters in high-frequency words to form new words (e.g., *do–go–no–so–to*). List words.	

During reading and writing experiences the following aspects of spelling may be planned for:

GRADE 1	A possible ten-day planner (continued)			
Day 6	**Day 7**	**Day 8**	**Day 9**	**Day 10**
High-frequency words	*High-frequency words/ word families*	*Letter names*	*High-frequency words/ word families*	*Sounds*
Have class learn a high-frequency word; add to word wall.	Have class learn a high-frequency word; add to word wall.	Read alphabet book.	Have class learn a high-frequency word; add to word wall.	Listen for a focus sound; list words.
Show how knowing to spell learned word helps spell others.	Use high-frequency words to develop word families.	*High-frequency words*	Use high-frequency words to develop word families.	Identify letters and spelling patterns that represent the focus sound.
Onsets and rimes	*Phonological awareness*	Have class learn a high-frequency word; add to word wall.	*Onsets and rimes*	(To be continued.)
Select high-frequency word for onset/rime activity.	Sound segmentation: identify sounds heard (e.g., *back*: /b/ is first sound, /a/ second, /k/ third).	Show how knowing to spell learned word helps spell others.	Select high-frequency word for onset/rime activity.	*High-frequency words*
List words.		*Phonological awareness*	List words.	Have class learn a high-frequency word; add to word wall.
		Sound blending: using high-frequency words (e.g., "This word means 'not bad.' It is *g-oo-d*. What is it?").		Show how knowing to spell learned word helps spell others.

During reading and writing experiences the following aspects of spelling may be planned for:

GRADE 2	A possible ten-day planner			
Day 1	**Day 2**	**Day 3**	**Day 4**	**Day 5**
Spelling patterns Search for and list words with a focus spelling pattern in all positions. Identify sound that spelling pattern represents. Begin forming generalizations.	*Spelling patterns* Continue searching for words with spelling pattern. List words. Identify sound that spelling pattern represents, and group words accordingly. Revise generalizations.	*Spelling patterns* Review generalizations and write in class journal. *High-frequency words* Search for topic-related high-frequency words; add to word list.	*High-frequency words/word family* Have class learn a topic-related high-frequency word; add to word wall. Select a high-frequency word to build word family.	*Sounds* Listen for a focus sound in all positions in words. List words. Identify letters/spelling patterns representing sound. Search for other words with sound.
High-frequency words Have class learn a topic-related high-frequency word; add to word wall. Show how knowing to spell learned word helps spell others.	*High-frequency words/ word family* Have class learn a topic-related high-frequency word; add to word wall. Select a high-frequency word for word family activity.	*High-frequency words* Have class learn a word; add to word wall. Show how knowing to spell learned word helps spell others.	*Compound words* Search for compound words. List words. Identify smaller words in compound words. Begin forming generalizations.	*High-frequency words* Search for topic-related high-frequency words; add to list. Have class learn a word; add to word wall. Show how knowing to spell learned word helps spell others.

During reading and writing experiences the following aspects of spelling may be planned for:

GRADE 2	A possible ten-day planner (continued)			
Day 6	Day 7	Day 8	Day 9	Day 10
Sounds Continue searching for words with focus sound. List words. Underline letters/spelling patterns that represent focus sound; group words accordingly. Form generalizations. *High-frequency words* Have class learn a topic-related high-frequency word; add to word wall. Show how knowing to spell learned word helps spell others.	*High-frequency words* Have class learn a topic-related high-frequency word; add to word wall. *Compound words* (Cont. from Day 4.) Continue searching for compound words. List words: identify words within compound words. Group words; form generalizations. *Compound words/word family* Use a compound word to build word family (e.g., *lighthouse, houseboat, boathouse*).	*Sounds* Listen for a focus sound in all positions in words. List words. Underline letters/spelling patterns representing sounds. *High-frequency words* Search for and list topic-related high-frequency words. Have class learn a high-frequency word; add to word wall. Show how knowing to spell learned word helps spell others.	*Sounds* Continue searching for words with focus sound; list words. Underline letters/spelling patterns representing focus sound and group words accordingly. Form generalizations. *High-frequency words* Have class learn a topic-related high-frequency word; add to word wall. Show how knowing to spell learned word helps spell others.	*Spelling patterns* Search for words containing a focus spelling pattern. List words. Underline spelling pattern and identify sound that spelling pattern represents. Begin forming generalizations. (To be continued.) *High-frequency words* Have class learn a topic-related high-frequency word; add to word wall. Show how knowing to spell learned word helps spell others.

During reading and writing experiences the following aspects of spelling may be planned for:

GRADE 3	A possible ten-day planner			
Day 1	**Day 2**	**Day 3**	**Day 4**	**Day 5**
Spelling patterns Search for and list words with a focus spelling pattern in all positions. Identify sound that spelling pattern represents. Begin forming generalizations.	*Spelling patterns* Continue searching for words containing spelling pattern. List words. Identify sound that spelling pattern represents and group words accordingly. Revise generalizations.	*Homophones* Search for a homophone set. List homophones in surrounding clauses and sentences. Begin forming generalizations.	*High-frequency words/word family* Have class learn a topic-related high-frequency word; add to word wall. Select a high-frequency word to build word family.	*Homophones* Continue searching for homophone set. List homophones in surrounding clauses and sentences. Revise generalizations.
High-frequency words Have class learn a topic-related high-frequency word; add to word wall. Show how knowing to spell learned word helps spell others.	*High-frequency words/word family* Have class learn a topic-related high-frequency word; add to word wall. Select a high-frequency word to build word family.	*High-frequency words* Have class search for topic-related high-frequency words; add to list. Have class learn a word; add to word wall. Show how knowing to spell learned word helps spell others.		*High-frequency words* Search for topic-related high-frequency words; add to list. Have class learn a word; add to word wall. Show how knowing to spell learned word helps spell others.

During reading and writing experiences the following aspects of spelling may be planned for:

GRADE 3	A possible ten-day planner (continued)			
Day 6	Day 7	Day 8	Day 9	Day 10
Homophones (Cont. from Day 5.) Continue searching for homophone set. List homophones in surrounding clauses and sentences. Revise generalizations. *High-frequency words* Have class learn a topic-related high-frequency word; add to alphabet word wall. Show how knowing to spell learned word helps spell others.	*High-frequency words* Have class learn a topic-related high-frequency word; add to word wall.	*Homophones* (Cont. from Day 6.) Continue searching for homophone set. List homophones in context. Revise and record generalizations. *High-frequency words* Search for and list topic-related high-frequency words. Have class learn a high-frequency word; add to word wall. Show how knowing to spell learned word helps spell others.	*Homophones* (Cont. from Day 8.) Continue searching for homophone set. List homophones in surrounding clauses and sentences. Revise and record generalizations. *High-frequency words* Have class learn a topic-related high-frequency word; add to word wall. Show how knowing to spell learned word helps spell others.	*Spelling patterns* Search for and list words with a focus spelling pattern in all positions. Identify sound that spelling pattern represents. Begin forming generalizations. (To be continued.) *High-frequency words* Have class learn a topic-related high-frequency word; add to word wall. Show how knowing to spell learned word helps spell others.

During reading and writing experiences the following aspects of spelling may be planned for:

GRADE 4	A possible ten-day planner			
Day 1	Day 2	Day 3	Day 4	Day 5
Suffixes	*High-frequency words*	*Suffixes*	*Spelling patterns*	*Spelling patterns*
Search for words containing a suffix.	Have class learn a topic-related high-frequency word; add to word wall.	Continue searching for and listing words with suffix.	Search for and list words containing a spelling pattern in all positions.	Continue searching for and listing words containing spelling pattern.
List words with base word.	Show how knowing to spell learned word helps spell others.	Group words according to changes made to base word.	Identify sound that spelling pattern represents.	Identify sound that spelling pattern represents; group words accordingly.
Begin forming generalizations.		Record generalizations.	Begin forming generalizations.	Revise and record generalizations.
High-frequency words	*Suffixes*	*High-frequency words*	*High-frequency words*	*High-frequency words*
Search for topic-related high-frequency words.	Continue searching for and listing words with suffix.	Have class learn a topic-related high-frequency word; add to word wall.	Have class learn a topic-related high-frequency word; add to word wall.	Have class learn a topic-related high-frequency word; add to word wall.
Learn one; add to alphabet word wall.	Group words according to changes made to base word.	Show how knowing to spell learned word helps spell others.	Show how knowing to spell learned word helps spell others.	Show how knowing to spell learned word helps spell others.
Show how knowing to spell learned word helps spell others.	Revise and record generalizations.			

During reading and writing experiences the following aspects of spelling may be planned for:

GRADE 4	A possible ten-day planner (continued)			
Day 6	**Day 7**	**Day 8**	**Day 9**	**Day 10**
Suffixes (Cont. from Day 3.) Continue to search for and list words containing a suffix. Group words according to changes made to base word. Continue recording and forming generalizations. *High-frequency words* Search for topic-related high-frequency words. Learn one; add to alphabet word wall. Show how knowing to spell learned word helps spell others.	*Suffixes* Continue grouping Revise and record generalizations. *High-frequency words/ word family* Have class learn a topic-related high-frequency word; add to word wall. Select a high-frequency word to build word family.	*Word family* Build word families. *High-frequency words* Search for and list topic-related high-frequency words. Have class learn a word; add to word wall. Show how knowing to spell learned word helps spell others.	*High-frequency words/word family* Have class learn a topic-related high-frequency word; add to word wall. Select a high-frequency word to build word family. *Sounds* Search for and list words containing a focus sound in all positions. Underline letters or spelling patterns that represent sound. Begin forming generalizations.	*Sounds* Continue searching for words with sound. List words. Underline letter or spelling pattern representing sound; group words accordingly. Revise and record generalizations. *High-frequency words* Have class learn a topic-related high-frequency word; add to word wall. Show how knowing to spell learned word helps spell others.

During reading and writing experiences the following aspects of spelling may be planned for:

GRADES 5–8	A possible ten-day planner			
Day 1	Day 2	Day 3	Day 4	Day 5
Prefixes Search for words containing a prefix. List words. Begin forming generalizations. *High-frequency words* Search for topic-related high-frequency words. Learn one; add to alphabet word wall. Show how knowing to spell learned word helps spell others.	*Prefixes* Continue searching for prefix. List words. Revise and record generalizations. *High-frequency words/word family* Have class learn a topic-related high-frequency word; add to word wall. Select a high-frequency word to build word family.	*Word family* Select words to build word families. *High-frequency words* Search for topic-related high-frequency words. Add these to high-frequency word list. Have class learn a word; add to word wall. Show how knowing to spell learned word helps spell others.	*High-frequency words/word family* Have class learn a topic-related high-frequency word; add to word wall. Select a high-frequency word to build word family. *Derivations* Search for words containing a root. List words. Begin forming generalizations.	*Derivations* Continue searching for derivations. List words. Revise and record generalizations. *High-frequency words* Have class learn a topic-related high-frequency word; add to word wall. Show how knowing to spell learned word helps spell others.

During reading and writing experiences the following aspects of spelling may be planned for:

GRADES 5–8	A possible ten-day planner (continued)				
	Day 6	Day 7	Day 8	Day 9	Day 10
	Suffixes Search for words containing a suffix. List words. Begin forming generalizations. *High-frequency words* Have class search for topic-related high-frequency words. Learn one; add to alphabet word wall. Show how knowing to spell learned word helps spell others.	*High-frequency words* Have class learn a topic-related high-frequency word; add to word wall. Show how knowing to spell learned word helps spell others. *Suffixes* Continue searching for words with suffix. List words. Group words according to changes made to base word. Revise generalizations.	*Suffixes* Continue searching for and listing words with suffix. Group words according to changes made to base word. Revise and record generalizations. *High-frequency words* Have class learn a topic-related high-frequency word; add to word wall. Show how knowing to spell learned word helps spell others.	*Spelling patterns* Search for words containing a focus spelling pattern in all positions. List words. Identify sound that spelling pattern represents. Begin forming generalizations. *High-frequency words* Have class learn a topic-related high-frequency word; add to word wall. Show how knowing to spell learned word helps spell others.	*Spelling patterns* Continue searching for words containing spelling pattern. List words. Identify sound that spelling pattern represents; group words accordingly. Revise and record generalizations. *High-frequency words* Have class learn a topic-related high-frequency word; add to word wall. Show how knowing to spell learned word helps spell others.

Appendix A
Student Checklists

The following checklists are intended to help children realize that good spellers are not necessarily people who know how to spell everything. Try to develop similar checklists using your own students' ideas and wording. They may not be able to do all of the things listed, but the checklists will make them aware of what they can do and what they may strive to achieve.

Checklist for Beginning Writers

Am I a good speller?

- I write a lot.
- I read a lot.
- I try unknown words.
- I try to write the sounds I hear in a word.
- I think about what the word looks like.
- I think of other words I know to help me write new words.
- I use class word lists, books, and dictionaries to find words.
- I try my best when I write.
- I check my writing.
- I know how to spell some words I use often.
- I am learning how to spell some other words I use in my writing.
- I ask for help when I can't work out how to spell a word by myself.
- I am interested in words.

Checklist for Experienced Writers

Am I a good speller?

- I write a lot.
- I read a lot.

- I attempt unknown words, trying to get them as close as possible to the correct spelling.
- I can use many strategies to try new words:
  - I listen for the sounds I hear in a word and know there is more than one way to represent a sound.
  - I think about what the word looks like, knowing the common spelling patterns.
  - I think about the spelling of the base word and then add a prefix or suffix to it.
  - I know about the generalizations for ways to add suffixes like *ed* and *ing*.
  - I know the generalizations for forming plurals.
  - I can use knowledge about the derivation of a word.
- I think of other words I know to help me write new words.
- I use class word lists, books, and dictionaries to find words.
- I try my best when I write, and I proofread my writing to correct errors.
- I use a variety of resources to check my spelling.
- I know that someone else needs to check my writing before it is published.
- I know how to spell the most frequently used words.
- I am learning how to spell some other words I use in my writing, and I know how to choose the best words to learn.
- I have a range of strategies to help me learn new words.
- When I learn a new word I think of other words it will help me spell.
- I know how to use apostrophes for contractions and possessive case.
- I am interested in words.

Appendix B
Questions Parents Ask

Why are children taught to spell in a different way from when we went to school?

Teachers and parents noticed that children could write words correctly in a spelling test but not write the same words correctly in their writing. Teachers also noticed that when they would tell children rules about spelling some children became confused and were unable to apply these rules correctly. So teachers have been searching for better ways to teach spelling because the techniques of the past did not work for some children.

By encouraging children to write as soon as they are ready to communicate with written marks, we have learned a lot about the way children learn about written language and how similar it is to how they learn to speak. Children become competent speakers by formulating rules about how the language works and testing out their hypotheses. Similarly, children acquire mastery over written language by formulating rules about the way written language works and testing out their hypotheses. As they become more experienced users of written language through many reading and writing experiences, children's written approximations more closely resemble, and ultimately become, the conventional spelling. This happens more readily if they know how to use a range of strategies to work out how various words are spelled.

Spelling is no longer considered to involve just memorizing words, without a sense of why they should be learned. Spelling nowadays is viewed as a problem-solving task, where the writer uses many strategies to solve the problem. These strategies include listening for sounds in words, using common spelling patterns, using knowledge of the meaning relationships between words, and knowing how to apply common rules, or generalizations, about how to construct words. Children are also encouraged to develop good spelling habits, such as trying unknown words and using many resources to check their spelling.

Should children learn a list of words each week?

Spelling is used in writing, so the words children learn must be useful for them in their personal writing. There is no point in children's learning words they will never use or words they already know. So although educators believe it is still useful for children to learn how to spell specific words, it's not really helpful for all the children in a class to learn the same words, and it's much better if the children learn how to choose most of these words themselves.

Children need to be taught how to proofread their writing and how to choose words they do not know how to spell and words they think they would find useful for future writing. Teachers and parents can guide them to make wise choices, because children do not always realize they are misspelling some words they use often. It's important that they not choose too many words each week. There is no one particular number per week they should learn; the right number of words is the number they can learn well.

One of the best ways to learn a word is to use the "look, say, name, cover, write, check" strategy:

1. *Look* at the word and get a picture of it in your head.
2. *Say* the word.
3. *Name* the letters in the word.
4. *Cover* the word.
5. *Write* the word as quickly as possible.
6. *Check* whether the word is correct.

Children should do this several times per word until they can write the word automatically the correct way.

It's also useful for children to think of words that these new words can help them to spell. For example, knowing how to spell *day* will help them spell *may, say, play, ray, bay, clay, lay, pay, way,* and so on. Children with more experience with language may also realize that knowing *day* will help them spell *Monday, Tuesday, Wednesday, daytime,* and so on. Learning how to build words from just a few words is a much more powerful technique than just learning a list of words by rote.

How do children learn how to spell?

Children learn to spell from their reading, where they continually see words spelled conventionally. They also learn to spell while writing, as they use various strategies in attempting to spell unfamiliar words. Children are taught to listen for sounds in words and how to represent these sounds using different letters. When they have seen a word many times in their reading they will begin to recognize when a word looks right or not. As they become more experienced readers and writers they will also think about the meaning relationships between words. For example, knowing how to spell *soft* will help them spell *soften,* even though they can't hear the *t.*

Children are also taught to spell through activities planned by the teacher, based on his or her observations of the children's needs. Sometimes these activities are so thoroughly woven into other reading and writing activities that they seem incidental, but many times the teacher will focus specifically on spelling activities for a period of time.

What makes someone a good speller?

A good speller is not necessarily someone who spells all words correctly. In fact, no one probably knows how to spell all words correctly. A child who writes with no spelling mistakes may just be a safe speller who is not willing to try unfamiliar words.

Good spellers take risks and attempt new words. Good spellers are also interested in words and try to do their best, always being aware that their writing needs to be easily read by others. Good spellers also use different strategies to try words, and they use resources such as books, word lists, dictionaries, and word books to check their spelling. Beginning writers will not be able to do all of these things, but they should feel that their writing is as valued as that of someone who knows how to spell many words the conventional way.

If a child misspells a word many times, will he or she continue to spell it incorrectly?

Children should be encouraged to try unfamiliar words and to experiment with the spellings of words. They may go through a long period of this kind of experimentation as they form hypotheses about spelling. But at the same time they need to read a lot so that they get continuous feedback about what a word looks like, and they need to have peers read their writing so that they have an authentic purpose for learning about spelling.

There is also a right time to point out that a frequently used word is being misspelled and so is a good one to learn. Teachers need to know when and how to do this so that their spelling guidance does not impede the children's writing. Suitable intervention can be different for each child. Skillful teachers and parents are able to encourage risk taking in children without letting them develop bad habits that are hard to change. It's usually better to say something like "If you are not sure how to spell a word try it anyway, but do your best" than simply "Don't worry about your spelling."

Should a child use a dictionary to find out how to spell a word?

Good spellers use all kinds of resources to check spelling, but it's helpful if they try the word first so that they have some idea of its spelling. Children should try a word first, think about which part may not be right, try it again, and then check their ideas in a dictionary or some other resource. It's hard to find a word in a dictionary if you don't have at least some idea of how it is spelled.

Children should also be encouraged to think about the best place to find a word, such as in a book where they know they've seen the word, in signs in the environment, in an atlas or on a map if it's a place name, by asking a person they think will know the word, and so on. If they frequently ask how to spell a word, they should be encouraged to try the word first.

Why don't teachers correct children's spelling mistakes?

Rather than having the teacher correct children's spelling, it's much better if children learn to take responsibility for proofreading their own writing because this is an important aspect of being an author. Children are writing so much more these days in the classroom that it's impossible for teachers and parents to check everything they do. Teachers encourage children to always do their best, but they know that children will not know how to spell every word they want to use, and risk taking is important.

Teachers and parents can work together to help children after they have proofread their work. If the work is going to be published, teachers and parents can play the role of editor and help children with words they do not know. This may be done by typing the work or, if the child wants to rewrite the piece, by writing the correct form of words above the child's writing.

It's worth being mindful of the total writing process: in the first draft the writer may concentrate more on getting ideas down and may not notice spelling mistakes. Parents could ask their children if the writing is a first or final draft and help the children accordingly. Also, focus on what children have done well rather than only noticing their spelling mistakes. Otherwise children may want to write less in the future or they may become safe spellers rather than good spellers. Remember, too, that not all writing needs to be polished, because not all writing in everyday life is perfect.

Should spelling rules be taught?

Rather than telling children the rules, children will learn better if they are guided through explorations that will help them discover generalizations that apply to the spelling of many words. For example, by listing many words that end with the suffix *ed*, children can be guided to notice what happens when this suffix is added to different base words, such as *hope/hoped, hop/hopped, carry/carried*, and *land/landed*.

It is even more helpful if the teacher links the explorations to the types of misunderstandings children display in their own writing, and if the children are encouraged to describe the generalizations in their own words.

The generalizations children learn should cover a range of spelling topics, including ways to form plurals, ways to add prefixes and suffixes to words, and some phonic generalizations.

Should children be taught phonics?

One of the strategies writers use is listening for sounds in words. Children will be encouraged to use this strategy and to learn how each sound in the English language may be represented by different letters or spelling patterns. Children can return to the books they are reading to find examples of words with each of the sounds, discover how these sounds are represented, and think about how this knowledge can help them as writers. This does not require the use of published workbooks, which may have inaccuracies or may have exercises with words that children do not know the meaning of.

How can parents help their children with spelling?

Parents should encourage their children to write for a variety of purposes—shopping lists, letters, messages, reminders, diaries, stories, and so on. The children's writing should be enjoyed and appreciated by their parents both for its content and for the attempts at spelling it contains, whether unfamiliar words are spelled correctly or not.

Children should be given many opportunities to read and be read to. The material should be varied so that they will have many models of different kinds of words and will often see high-frequency words.

Parents need to set an example by writing themselves, demonstrating how they attempt unfamiliar words or try words they are not sure of, how they proofread, how they use resources to check their spelling, and how spelling is not the only thing that matters in their writing.

Parents and children need to enjoy reading and writing, rather than seeing it as a chore that has to be done. Raising the level of anxiety will not make reading and writing more enjoyable.

Parents and children need to enjoy playing with language through word games, songs, nonsense rhymes, and poetry.

If spelling homework is given, parents and children could do some of it together. Parents could ask their children how they are learning spelling in school rather than assuming that spelling should be taught the same way it was when they were students. At the same time, they could share ideas they learned that have always been helpful. Above all, parents should appreciate doing one's best in writing.

Appendix C
Class Words

The following activities are one possible way that spelling homework may be dealt with.

For Younger Grades

These are the words our class decided to learn this week:

If you do not know how to spell the words use these activities to help you learn them:

1. *Look* at the word so that you have a picture of it in your head.
   Say the word.
   Name the letters in the word.
   Cover the word.
   Write the word.
   Check the word, letter by letter.
   Do this many times with each word until you think you know it and can write it very quickly.
2. For each of the words above, try these activities:
   • Write any smaller words you can see in the word.
   • Write something that surprised you about the word and something that will help you remember how to spell it.
   • Write any other words that have the same spelling pattern. Check a resource to make sure you are right.
   • Can you add a letter to any of your words to make a new word?
   • Can you make a compound word with any of your words?

For Older Grades

These are the words our class decided to learn this week:

If you do not know how to spell the words use these activities to help you learn them:

1. *Look* at the word so that you have a picture of it in your head.
   Say the word.
   Name the letters in the word.
   Cover the word.
   Write the word.
   Check the word, letter by letter.
   Do this many times with each word until you think you know it and can write it very quickly, even automatically.

2. For each of the words above, try these activities:
   - Write any smaller words you can see in the word.
   - Write something that surprised you about the word and something that will help you remember how to spell it.
   - Write any other words that have the same spelling pattern. Check a resource to make sure you are right.
   - Can you add a letter to make a new word?
   - Can you delete a letter to make a new word?
   - Can you change a letter to make a new word? Can you make a chain of words by changing one letter at a time?
   - Can you make a compound word with any of your words?
   - Can you change any words to plurals?
   - Can you add any prefixes or suffixes to any of your words to create other words?

Appendix D
Personal Words

How you wrote your words	Correct spelling	What surprised you about each word? Write something that will help you remember the spelling.

Look at the correct spelling of each word. For each word try this many times until you are sure you can write the word correctly without even thinking about it:

Look at the word so that you have a picture of it in your head.
Say the word.
Name the letters in the word.
Cover the word.
Write the word.
Check the word, letter by letter.

Use each of your words to help you spell other words that are similar in some way.

Index

Also of Interest

Spelling Inquiry
How One Elementary School Caught the Mnemonic Plague

Kelly Chandler and the Mapleton Teacher-Research Group

Teachers who are seeking a more effective approach to teaching spelling to K–5 students will appreciate this accessible and lively narrative describing how classroom teachers turned to teacher research to develop a genuinely student-centered and inquiry-based spelling instruction program. Using a unique collaborative process, Kelly Chandler and the Mapleton Teacher-Research Group discuss how to foster inquiry-based learning about spelling in their classrooms and also provide a detailed look at the workings of their schoolwide teacher-research group.

Whether you are interested in spelling instruction or teacher research, *Spelling Inquiry* will help you pose personally compelling questions and develop a workable plan for answering them.

1-57110-303-1   176 pages/paperback